CAUSEWAY
COASTAL ROUTE

SETH LINDER

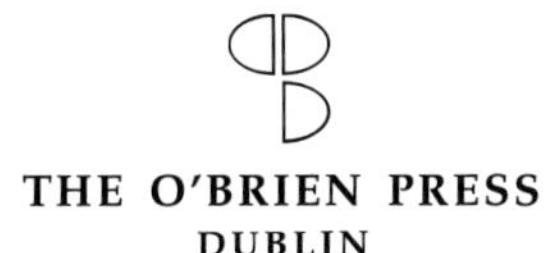

THE O'BRIEN PRESS
DUBLIN

ABOUT THE AUTHOR

A Londoner by birth, Seth Linder has lived in Northern Ireland for over 20 years. One of Ireland's leading tourism writers, he has worked as a journalist, author and scriptwriter on numerous projects exploring heritage, history and culture, including that of the Causeway Coastal Route.

Seth's most recent book is *Ireland's Greening of the World*, published by O'Brien Press, a celebration of 10 years of greening the world's most iconic buildings each St Patrick's Day. Other recent books include *Belfast Walks* (O'Brien Press), which takes readers on self-guided trails through the city's fascinating heritage and beautiful natural world.

Seth is the coauthor of *Ripper Diary: The Inside Story*, published by Sutton Publishing.

ACKNOWLEDGEMENTS

I wish to thank Tourism Northern Ireland and its commissioned photographers, in particular Brian Morrison Photography (brianmorrison.co.uk), for use of many of the images in this book and for their help with research; and Tourism Ireland and its commissioned photographers, including Beth Ellis, Tony Pleavin and Stefan Schnebelt, for use of their images.

I would also like to thank the following for their photos: Andy McInroy (Murlough Bay, p. 76; Fair Head, p. 78; Rathlin coast, p. 85; Rathlin caves, p. 86; East Lighthouse, Rathlin Island, p. 87; Dunseverick Castle, pp. 98–9; Giant's Causeway, pp. 100–1, 103, back cover; Lacada Point, p. 112); Patrick Lennon (St Aidan's Church, p. 124); Sean Paul McKillop (hurling match, p. 48); Chris Hill/Tourism Ireland (Giant's Causeway, these pages; SS Nomadic and Titanic Belfast, pp. 8-9; HMS Caroline, pp. 10–11; Glory of the Glens, pp. 44–5); Art Ward (the Aquarium, p. 27); the Morelli family (Morelli tea rooms, p. 113) and Carsten Krieger (Elephant Rock, p. 33 and Giant's Causeway, p. 102). Image of Whitehead Railway Museum (p. 24) courtesy of Mid and East Antrim Borough Council.

I am grateful to the following for their help in the research and writing of this book: Liz Weir, Ciaran Mullholland, Patrick Lennon, Brian Connolly, Lynette Conlon, The Londonderry Arms and the Morelli family.

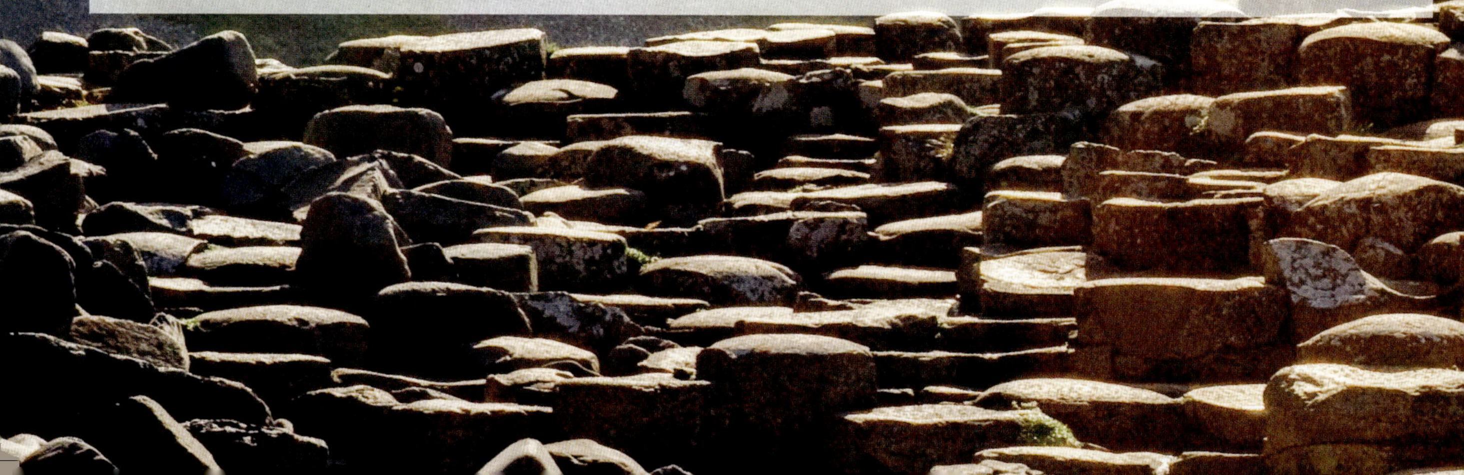

CONTENTS

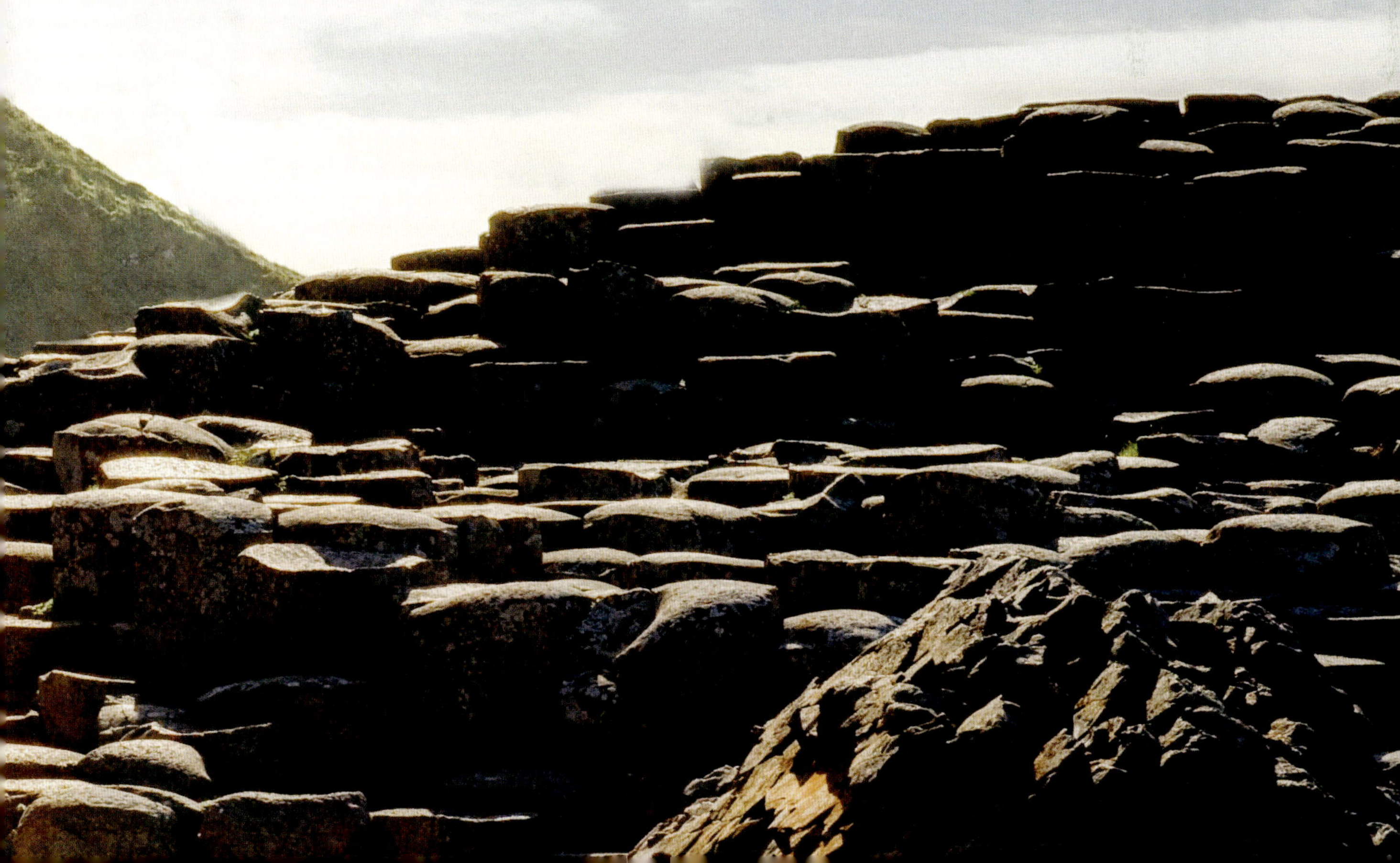

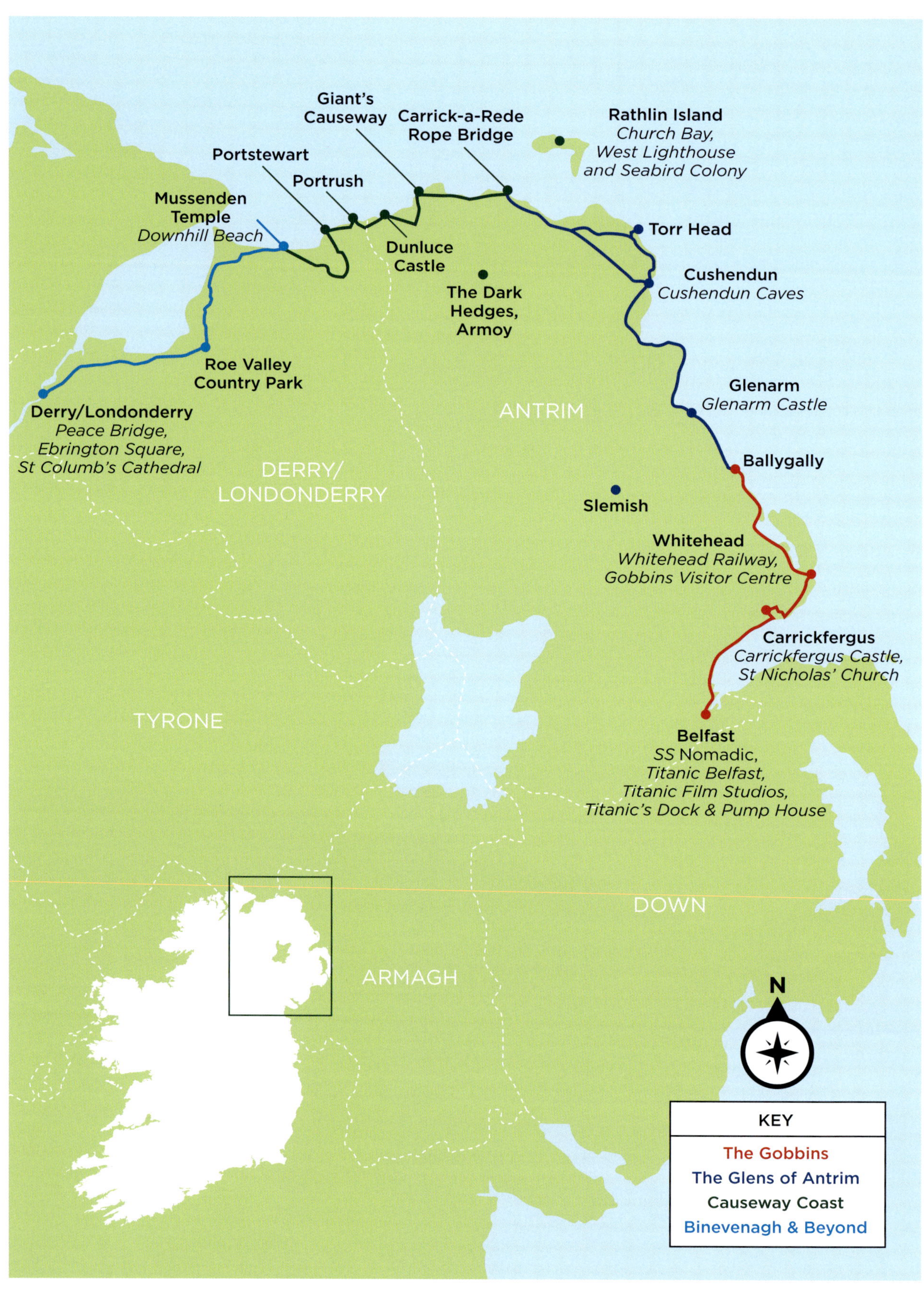

Giant's Causeway
Carrick-a-Rede Rope Bridge
Rathlin Island
Church Bay, West Lighthouse and Seabird Colony
Portstewart
Portrush
Mussenden Temple
Downhill Beach
Torr Head
Dunluce Castle
Cushendun
Cushendun Caves
The Dark Hedges, Armoy
Roe Valley Country Park
Glenarm
Glenarm Castle
ANTRIM
Derry/Londonderry
Peace Bridge, Ebrington Square, St Columb's Cathedral
Ballygally
DERRY/LONDONDERRY
Slemish
Whitehead
Whitehead Railway, Gobbins Visitor Centre
Carrickfergus
Carrickfergus Castle, St Nicholas' Church
TYRONE
Belfast
SS Nomadic, Titanic Belfast, Titanic Film Studios, Titanic's Dock & Pump House
DOWN
ARMAGH
N
KEY
The Gobbins
The Glens of Antrim
Causeway Coast
Binevenagh & Beyond

INTRODUCTION

Imagine this. Brooding castles perched on the edge of towering cliffs; a coastline forged by volcanic activity millions of years ago, with atmospheric caves and basalt stacks rising from the sea. A remarkably beautiful and unspoilt landscape marked by centuries of conflict between warring medieval clans, not to mention spectacular mountains, dense forests, endless sandy beaches and plunging waterfalls. Is it any wonder that HBO chose Northern Ireland's Causeway Coast as the location for so many of its outdoor scenes in *Game of Thrones*?

Everywhere we go on this route, we follow in the footsteps of the houses of the Seven Kingdoms – Stark, Lannister, Targaryen, Tyrell and the rest – just as we trace the story of the great clans of Ulster who struggled for power here over the centuries, from their cliff-top castles to the beautiful estates where their descendants live today: the McQuillans, O'Cahans and, above all, the MacDonnells, whose stories offer a mirror to *Game of Thrones*.

On your journey you will encounter the birth of *Titanic*, Ireland's most impressive medieval castle, a world-famous walk built into the cliffs, a nostalgic steam-train museum, the world's oldest licensed distillery, a UNESCO World Heritage site, pretty Victorian harbours, towns steeped in history, picturesque fishing villages and some of the most breathtaking scenery the island of Ireland has to offer.

So, let us set off on our trek around the Causeway Coast, one of Europe's greatest road trips.

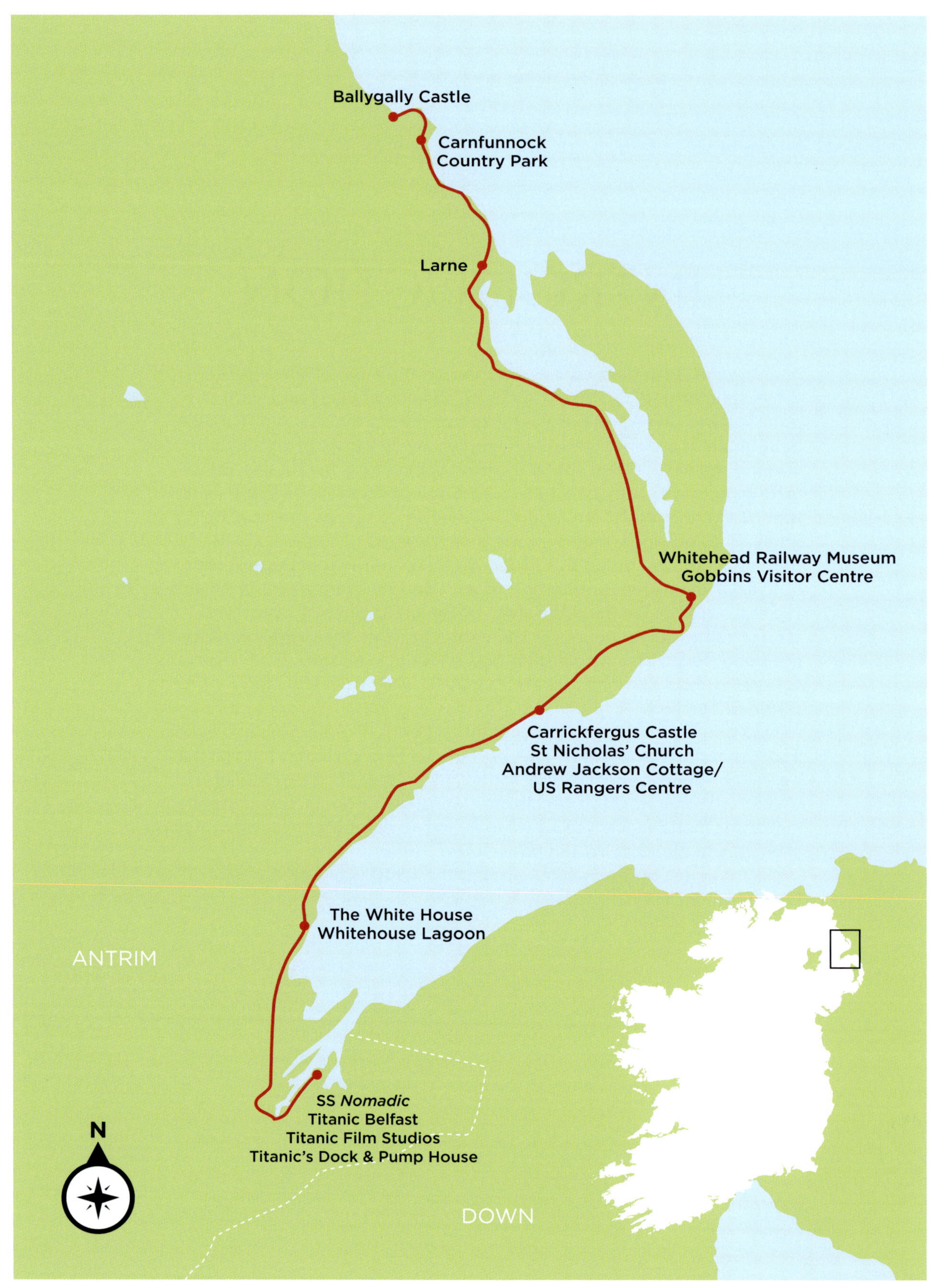

Ballygally Castle
Carnfunnock Country Park
Larne
Whitehead Railway Museum
Gobbins Visitor Centre
Carrickfergus Castle
St Nicholas' Church
Andrew Jackson Cottage/
US Rangers Centre
The White House
Whitehouse Lagoon
ANTRIM
SS Nomadic
Titanic Belfast
Titanic Film Studios
Titanic's Dock & Pump House
DOWN
N

BELFAST LOUGH TO BALLYGALLY

We begin at Queen's Island, the source of the *Titanic* legend and home of Harland & Wolff, the firm that built so many innovative ships. The world's largest *Titanic* attraction, Titanic Belfast, and SS *Nomadic*, the tender that took passengers to *Titanic* in Cherbourg, await you here.

The first leg of this epic journey takes us around Belfast Lough: to Whitehouse Lagoon, the official start of the Causeway Coastal Route, then through the historic town of Carrickfergus, with its magnificent castle, to Whitehead and a nostalgic steam train museum. Near here is one of Northern Ireland's leading visitor attractions, The Gobbins: a unique path blasted into the cliffs.

Then we head for the ancient port of Larne and the beginning of the famous Coastal Road. At Ballygally, we stop at the 17th-century Ballygally Castle and get our first glimpse of *Game of Thrones* territory.

Check thegobbinscliffpath.com before planning your route to make sure the path is open to the public. The visitor centre and cafe remain open, even when the path is closed for repairs.

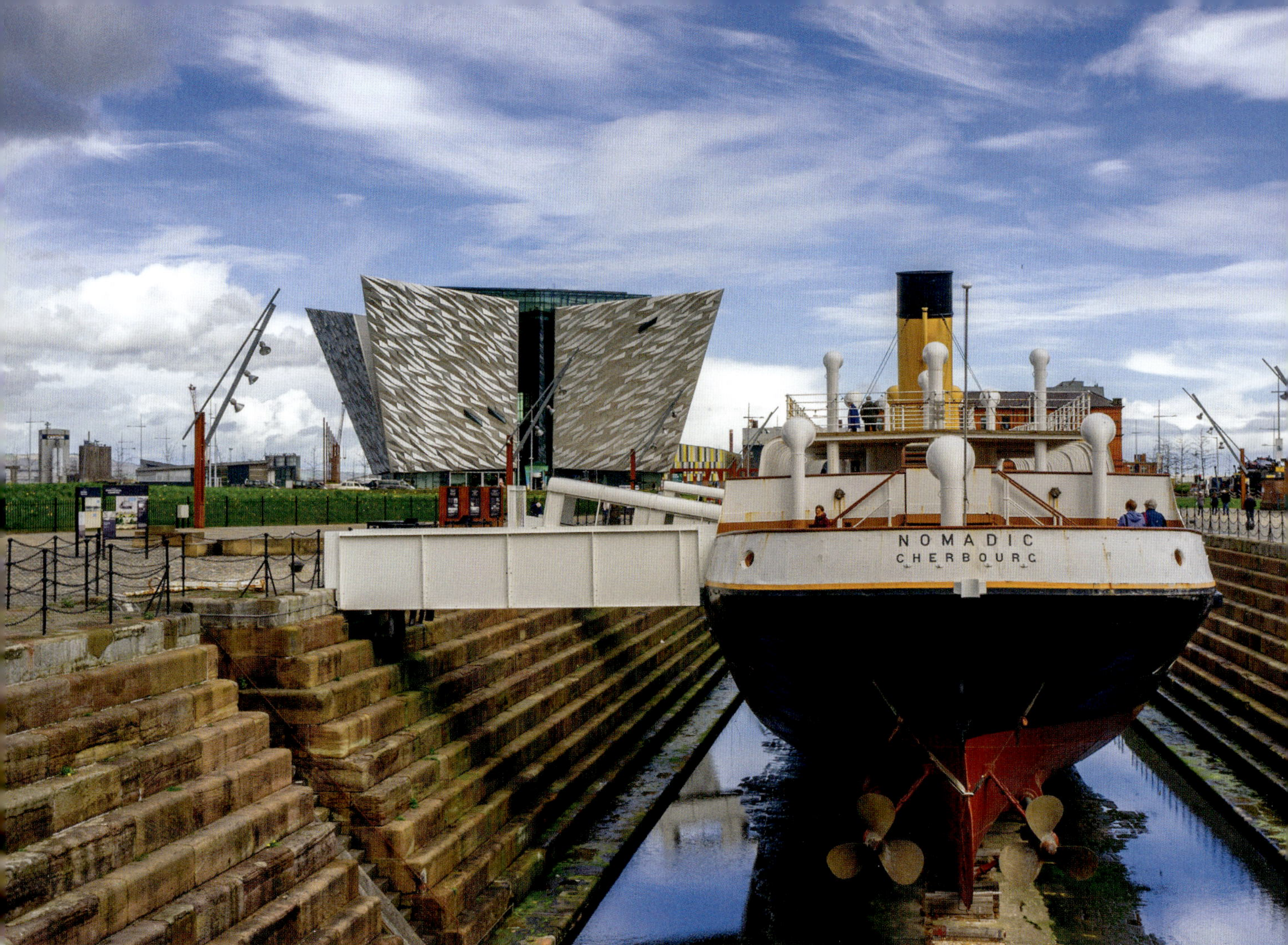

SS *NOMADIC*, BEFORE TITANIC BELFAST

START OF THE ROUTE

QUEEN'S ISLAND AND THE *TITANIC* CONNECTION

The Causeway Coastal Route officially begins (or ends) at the Whitehouse Lagoon, just around the lough from Belfast. But why miss an opportunity to explore the city that, along with the Causeway Coast itself, was awarded Best Region to Visit (in the world!) by Lonely Planet in 2018?

So we're going to start one of the world's epic road journeys at the place where the world's most famous ship was built, and the studio where the mega-hit TV series *Game of Thrones*, which features in numerous locations along the route, was filmed – Queen's Island, or Titanic Quarter as it is now known.

Built in the mid-1800s with leftover material from the deepening of the main channel into Belfast Harbour, it was here that Harland & Wolff (H&W) developed into one of the world's greatest shipbuilders.

Fast forward to 1989, when H&W began to specialise in marine engineering and renewable energies and focused its activities on the northern end of Queen's Island. No longer was there any need for the drawing offices, dry docks or, indeed, more than a fraction of the space the company had inhabited when Queen's Island was a city within a city, employing over 30,000 people at its peak. Today the area is being developed for education, business and tourism purposes, and reminders of its illustrious past are everywhere.

Go down Queen's Road, its central

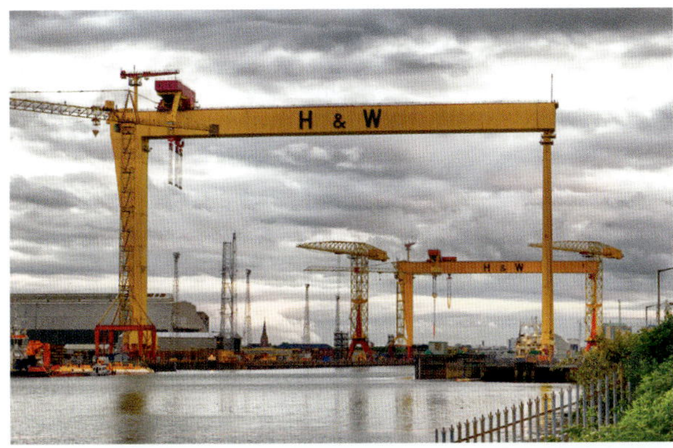

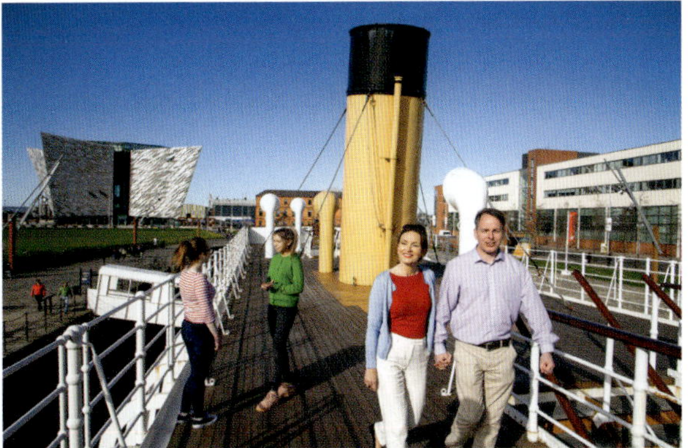

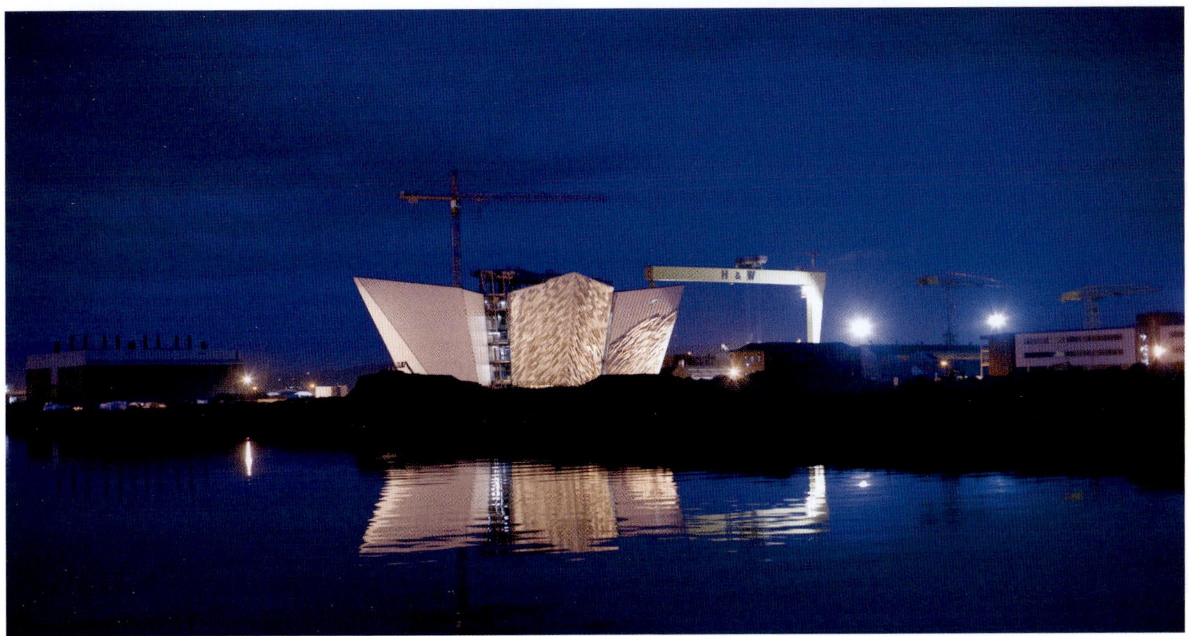

TOP: H&W CRANES AND SS *NOMADIC*. ABOVE: TITANIC BELFAST

thoroughfare, past the SSE Arena, stopping first at SS *Nomadic*. '*Titanic*'s little sister' is the last surviving White Star liner. Also built by H&W, it once took first-class passengers to *Titanic* when the latter was docked in Cherbourg Harbour. It sits in the 1860s Hamilton Graving Dock.

From *Nomadic* it's a short walk to the magnificent Titanic Belfast, voted the world's leading tourist attraction at the 2016 World Travel Awards, which tells the story not only of *Titanic* but of Belfast's late Victorian and Edwardian heyday too. A tour of the six-storey building includes a ride through the old H&W shipyard and a chance to see a recreation of *Titanic*'s famous staircase. Just across from

here is the former H&W headquarters where *Titanic* was designed, now converted into a luxury hotel, where the old drawing office is now a spectacular bar and dining area.

In the space between are two original slipways; one used for *Titanic*, the other for her sister *Olympic* (there was a third in the series – *Britannic*). Around them illuminated blue lines reveal the breadth of the two ships, their height demonstrated by tall poles.

Look beyond and you will see the Lagan, at its broadest here, flowing into the harbour. That would have been *Titanic*'s route as she sailed out that fateful April day in 1912 while thousands of people thronged the harbour. It's one we will loosely follow ourselves for a while.

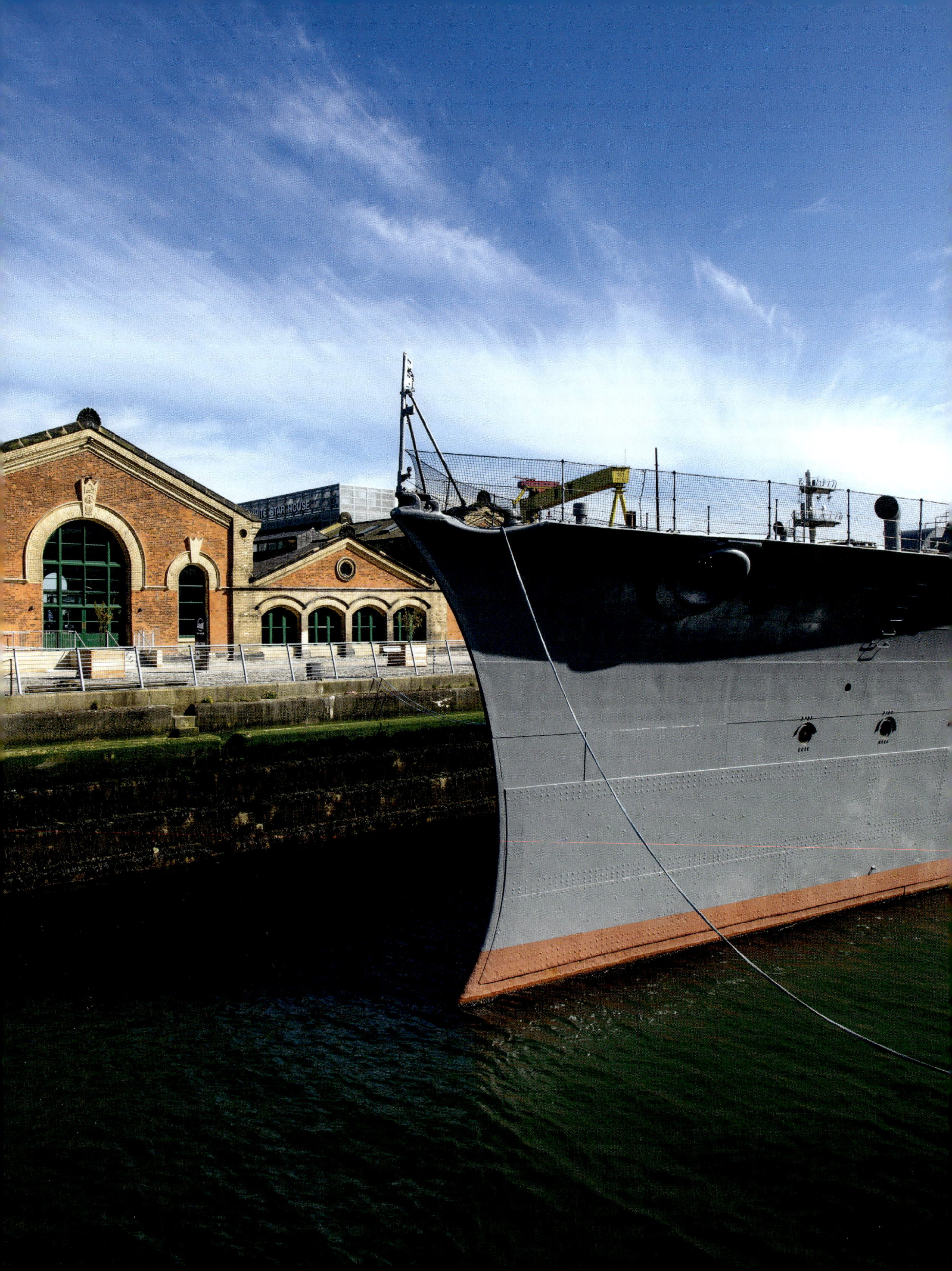

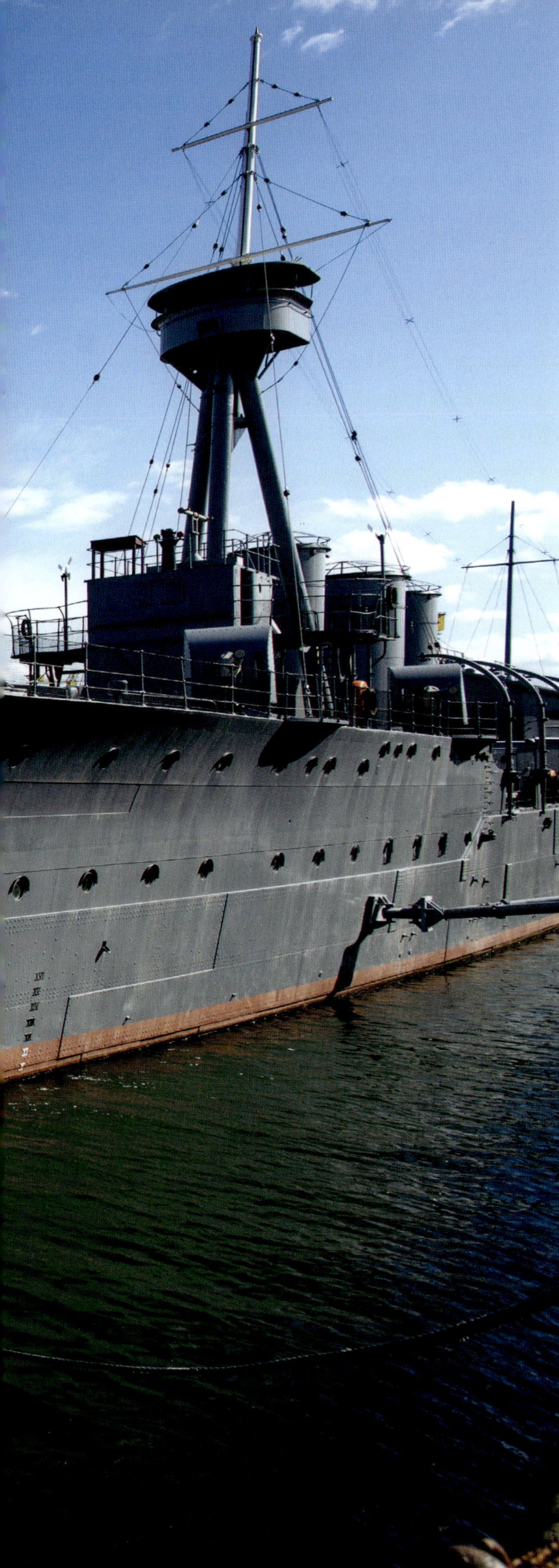

GAME OF THRONES, WHERE IT ALL BEGAN

There may have been a few who questioned Northern Ireland Screen's funding support for HBO's *Game of Thrones* at the outset, but it has turned out to be one of the shrewdest moves a national film agency has ever made. In return the makers of the world-famous series have largely based its production in Northern Ireland, thus ensuring legions of tourists would visit the countless filming locations, many of them around or near the Causeway Coastal Route.

Running down to the water at what used to be Victoria Wharf is the Titanic Film Studios, based in the old H&W paint hall. As well as *Game of Thrones*, numerous films and TV series have been shot here. On this road trip we will be stopping at locations where *Game of Thrones* was filmed, but this is where it all began.

HISTORIC DOCKS

Not far along Queen's Road is the turning towards the old Alexandra Graving Dock, now occupied by HMS *Caroline*, the only surviving ship from the Battle of Jutland in 1916 and recently restored as a visitor attraction. You can enjoy a stirring film about her battle days, and the cabins have been recreated as if the crew were still on board.

Take the cobblestoned path on the right-hand side of *Caroline*, and you'll soon come to *Titanic*'s Dock and Pump-House. The dry dock here was built especially for *Titanic* and her sister ships, *Olympic* and *Britannic*. Next to it is the pump-house, which pumped water into the vast dock. Discover its history at the audiovisual exhibition here. There's a pleasant and airy café to relax in as well.

HARLAND & WOLFF TODAY

From the Titanic Dock (originally known as the Thompson Dry Dock), walk by White Star House and exit left into Queen's Road. Pass the series of buildings to your left, and warehouses across the road, until you reach the final location of H&W, where marine engineering and ship repairs had replaced a century of ship building.

HMS *CAROLINE* IN THE ALEXANDRA GRAVING DOCK

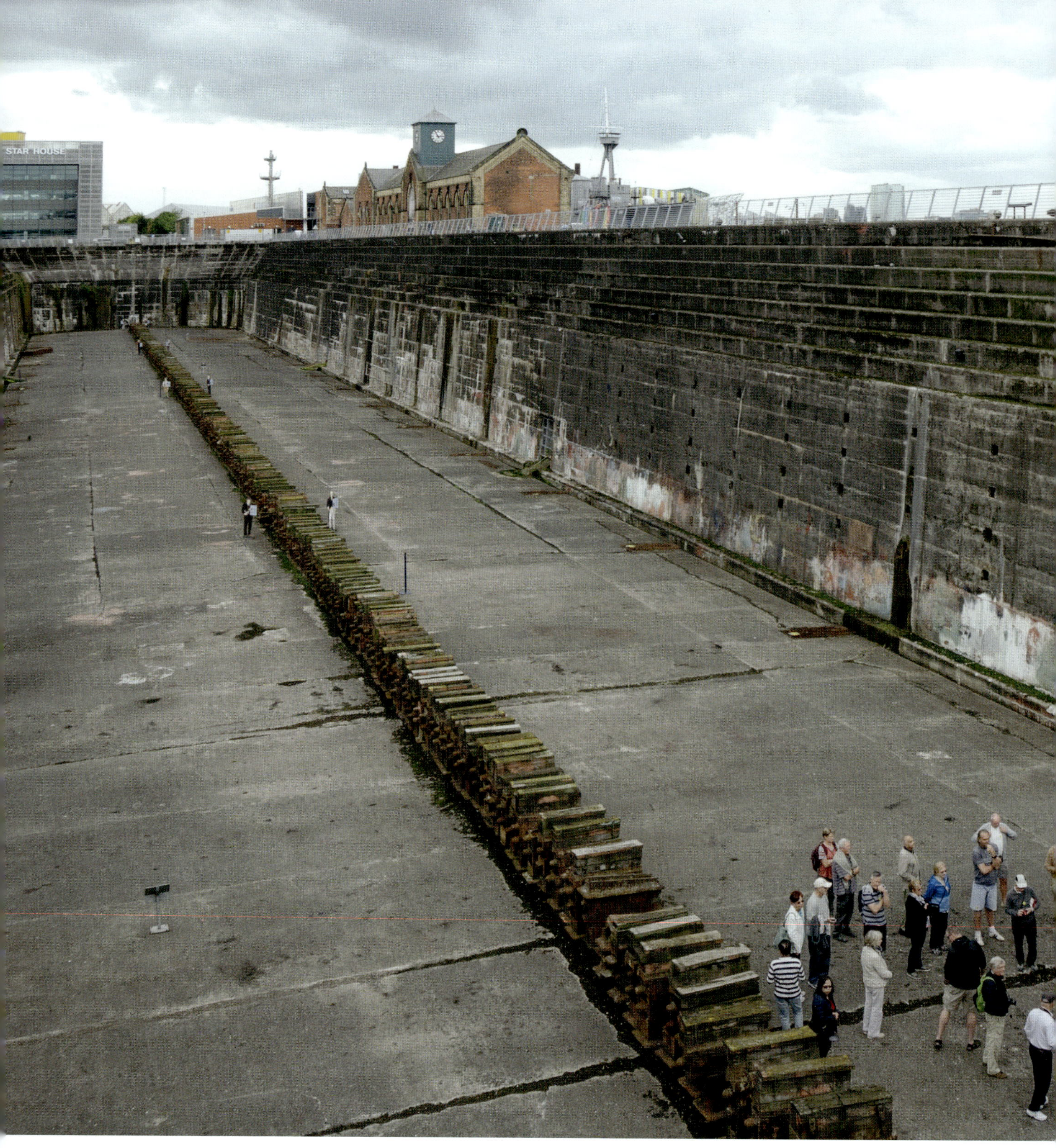

TITANIC (FORMERLY THOMPSON) DRY DOCK

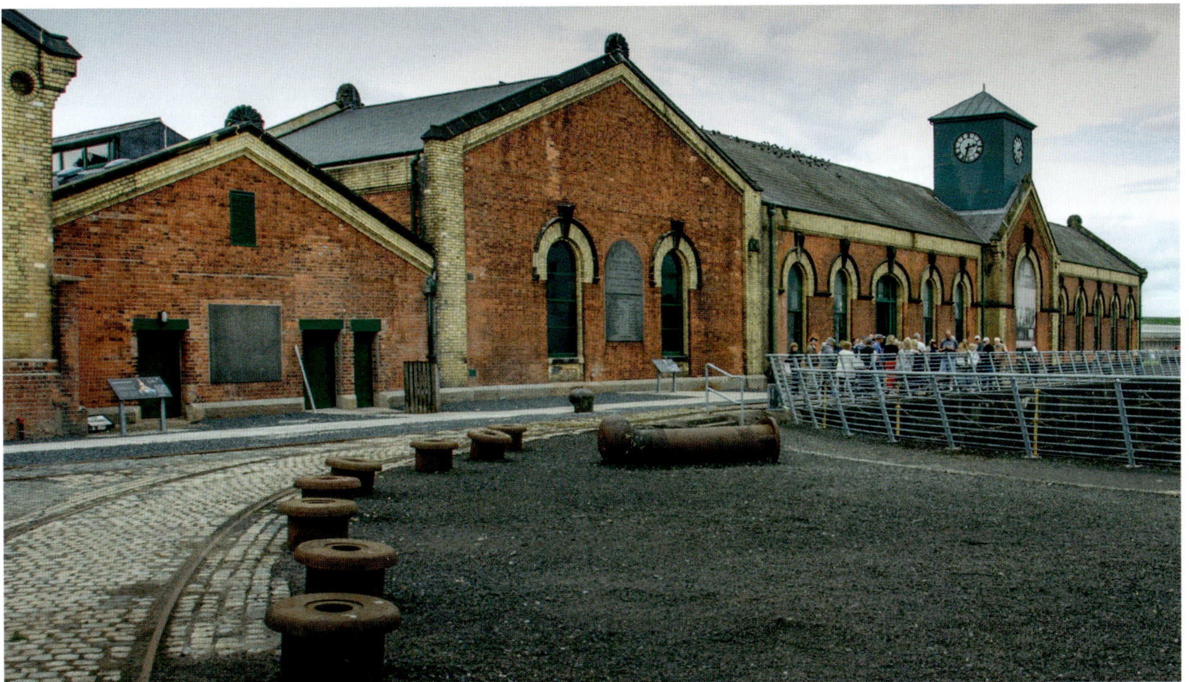

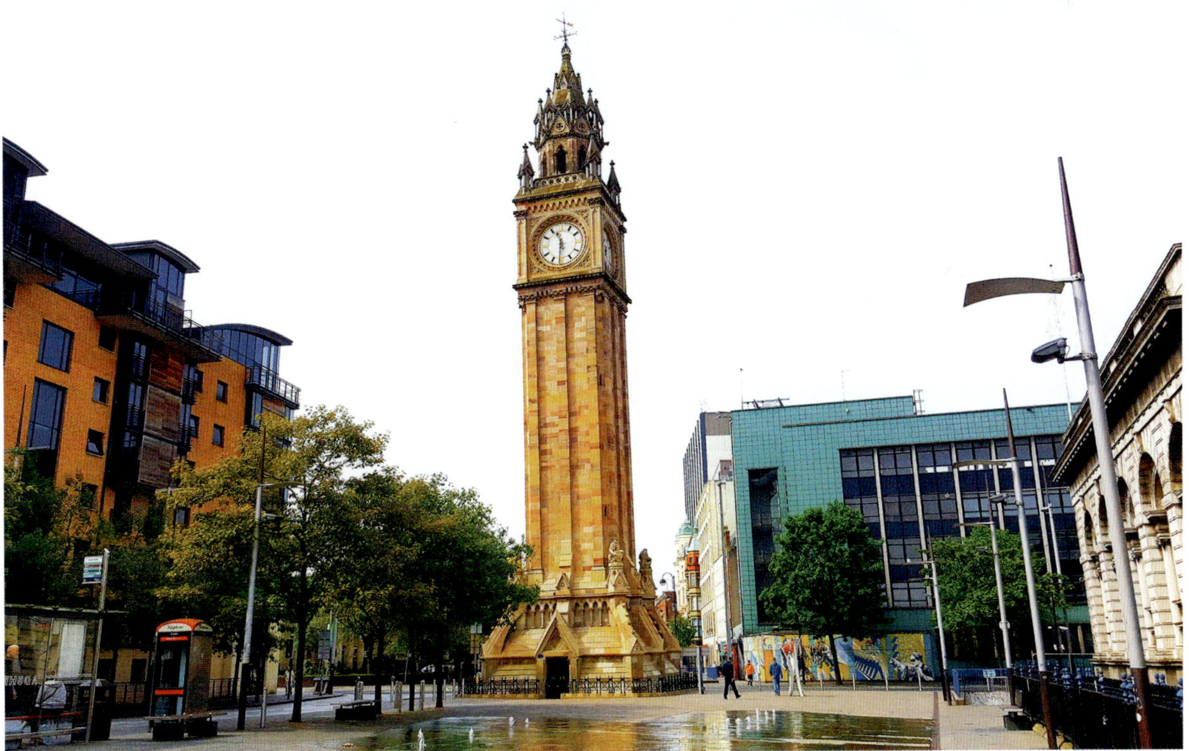

TOP: *TITANIC* PUMP-HOUSE. BOTTOM: ALBERT MEMORIAL TOWER

ALBERT MEMORIAL TOWER

En route to the Causeway Coastal Route you will see the Albert Memorial Tower, known as 'the Leaning Tower of Belfast' until a restoration in the 1990s corrected its list. It's sited near where Queen Victoria and Prince Albert alighted to an enthusiastic reception from the citizens of Belfast in 1849. In April 1912, people climbed to its top to cheer off *Titanic* on her maiden journey as over 100,000 lined the harbour.

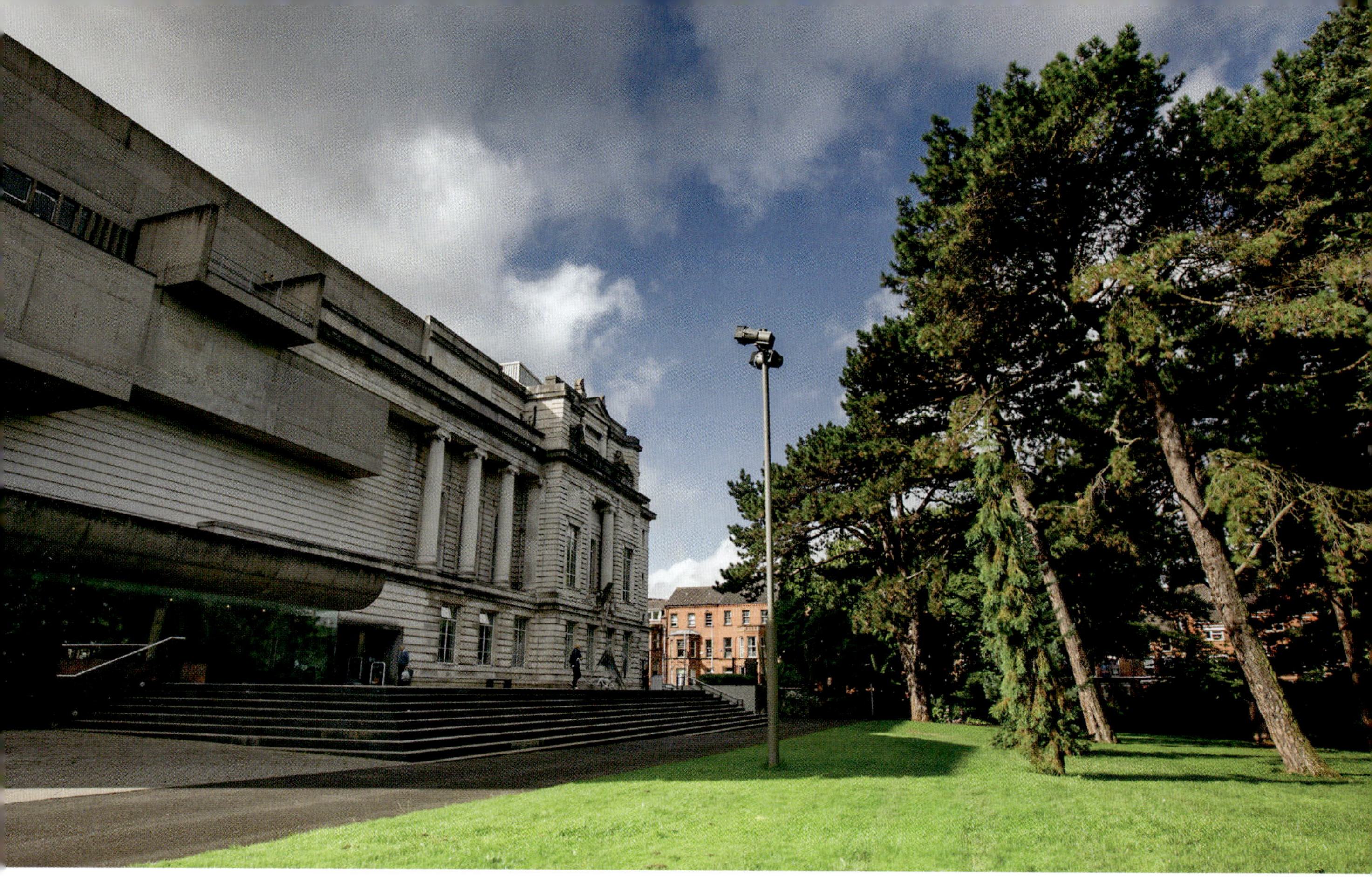

ULSTER MUSEUM

As well as being filmed at the studios in Titanic Quarter (and Linen Mill Studios in Banbridge), *Game of Thrones* has other Belfast connections. A magnificent tapestry depicting many of the scenes from the series, including key battles, has been woven from linen thread supplied by the last manufacturer of quality linen in Northern Ireland, Thomas Ferguson of Banbridge. Currently around 80 metres long, Northern Ireland's answer to the Bayeux Tapestry, which is owned by Tourism Ireland, is occasionally exhibited at the Ulster Museum, the city's main museum, in south Belfast.

In 2019, a special *Game of Thrones* trail – a series of colourful stained-glass windows depicting scenes from the series – was erected in Belfast, culminating at the Titanic Studios. Each window commemorates a major house from the show.

WHITEHOUSE LAGOON AND NORTHERN IRELAND'S OLDEST BUILDING

The official beginning of the Causeway Coastal Route, the Whitehouse Lagoon is an absorbing sight when the tide goes out and it becomes crowded with wading birds as they probe the mud in search of food. A short drive from here is Gideon's Green, named after Gideon Boonivert, a Huguenot soldier who wrote about the historic landing at the ancient quay near here of William III's army in 1690. At the car park you'll have a close-up view of the mud flats.

You'll find out more at the White House around the corner (only open 1pm–5pm Saturdays and Sundays). Dating back to at least 1569, the White House was the headquarters of General Frederick Schomberg, who was in charge of the Williamite forces during their battles with King James II on Irish soil. It is thought that William and Schomberg planned William's campaign in Ireland, which changed the course of Irish history, here. There's an interesting exhibition that relives that fateful period.

THE Dark Horse & Door №. 10

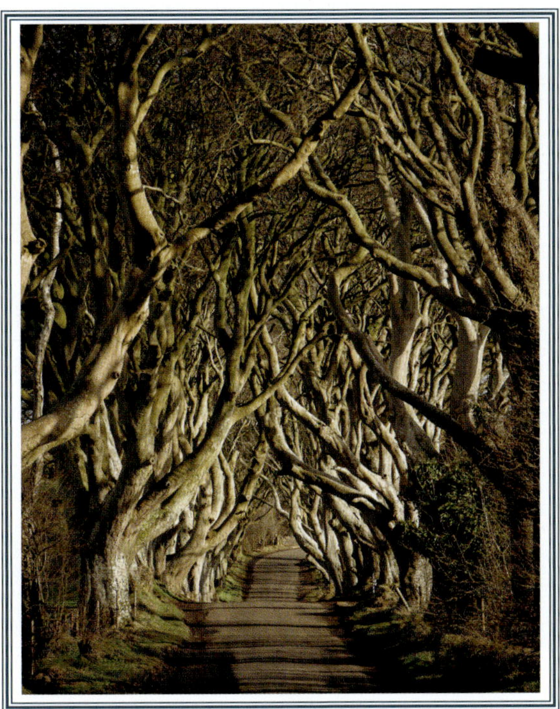

When high winds blew down some of the famous beech trees of the iconic Dark Hedges (which represents the Kingsroad in *Game of Thrones*) in Armoy, Co. Antrim, 10 special *Game of Thrones* themed doors commissioned by Tourism Ireland were carved from their wood and placed in hospitality outlets in areas with links to the series.

One of these can be found at the Dark Horse coffee bar in Belfast's cobblestoned Cathedral Quarter. The door sums up the state of play at the end of Season 6 and offers a subtle hint as to the possible parentage of Jon Snow.

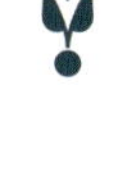
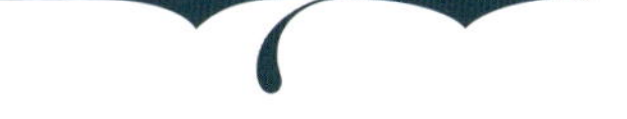

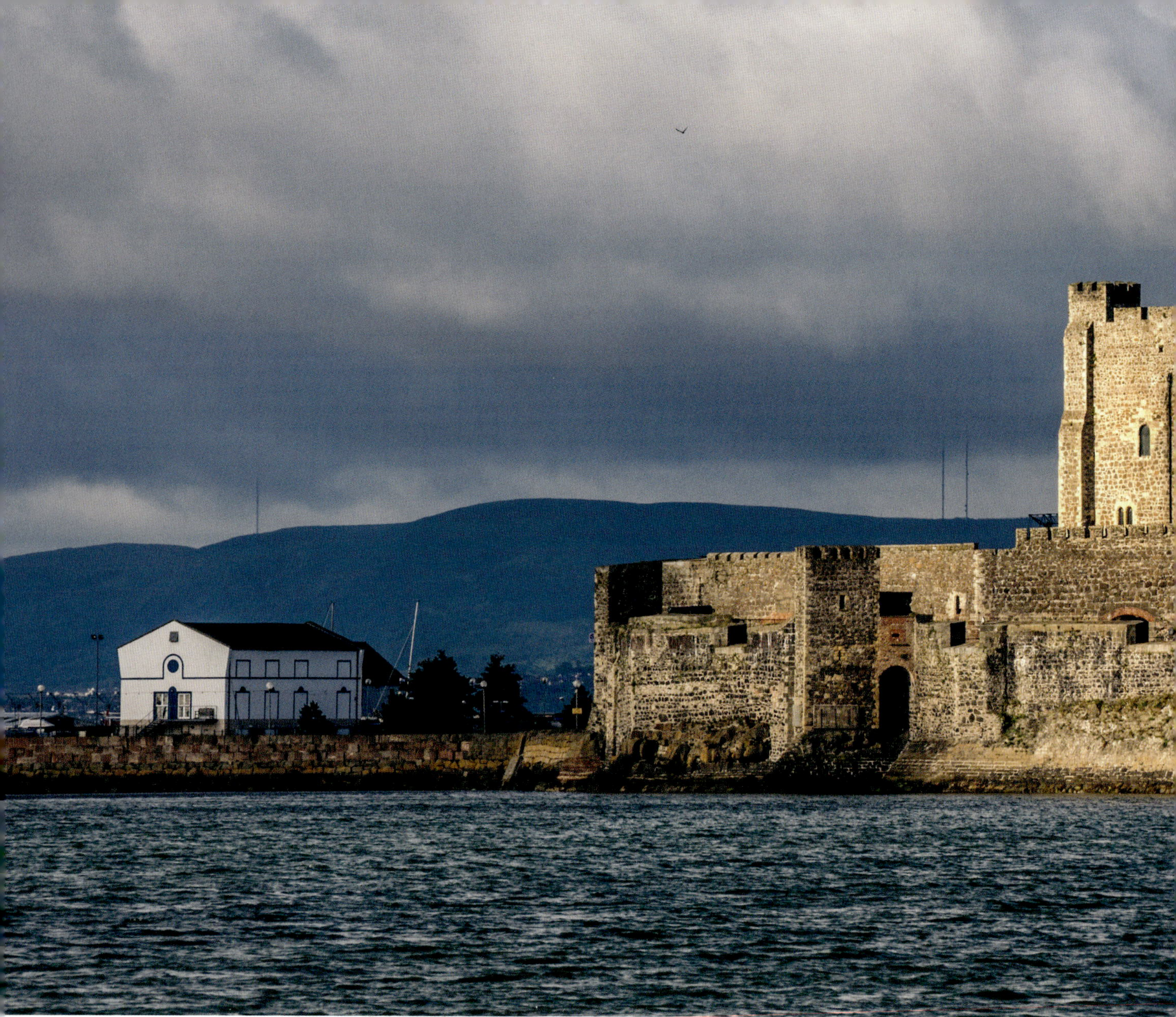

CARRICKFERGUS – A THOUSAND YEARS OF HISTORY IN A DAY!

Until the 1700s Carrickfergus was a more substantial and important town than Belfast, and its history goes back much further. Fortunately, much of it remains today, not least in two fascinating buildings, both originally built by the Anglo-Norman adventurer John de Courcy.

IRELAND'S FINEST MEDIEVAL CASTLE

Arriving here back in 1177 and needing a stronghold against the Ulster clans he was deposing, de Courcy built a castle on the shores of the lough. Under the Anglo-Normans and then the English Crown (it was besieged by Robert the Bruce's brother Edward as well as Scottish and Gaelic Irish armies, and even the French briefly captured both castle and church), Carrickfergus remained a vital strategic town for the next few centuries.

Given the pounding it has taken over the years, the castle – keep, walls, tower and chambers – is in remarkably good shape and well worth a tour.

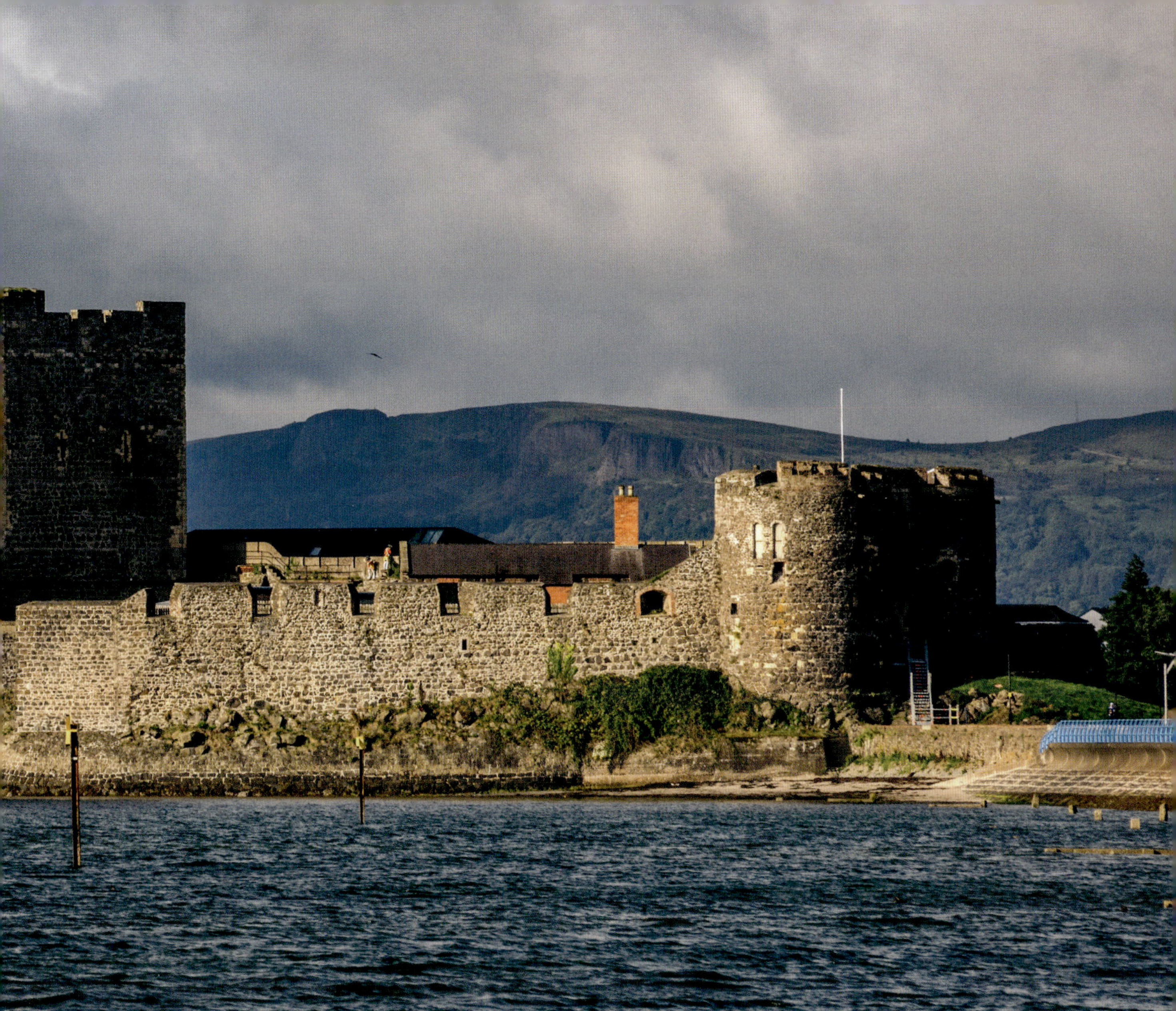

CARRICKFERGUS CASTLE

De Courcy conquered Ulster with a few knights and about 300 soldiers. His personal ambition, ignored by Richard the Lionheart, was ultimately punished by Richard's brother John, who had de Courcy forcibly replaced. The Norman influence grew and prospered here but was already waning when Scot Edward Bruce made his ultimately doomed bid for the Irish Crown in 1315, capturing the town but not the castle.

The next centuries saw the growing influence of Gaelic clans such as the MacDonnells of north Antrim (whom we will meet many times on this tour) and the Clandeboye O'Neills, who burned Carrickfergus to the ground in 1575. Two years later Sorley Boy, the fearsome head of the MacDonnell clan, captured both town and castle. This in turn was revenge for a terrible massacre on Rathlin Island (which we will visit later on) by Crown troops under the command of the Earl of Essex.

Carrickfergus was a vital base for Crown forces during the Nine Years War, the final revolt of the Gaelic chieftains. When this ended in defeat for the Irish in 1603, it heralded the large-scale plantation of English, Scottish and Welsh settlers which would have such a significant impact on Irish history. And no one did more to lay the ground for plantation than the brutal Sir Arthur Chichester, though, ironically, he had argued against the concept of large-scale plantation.

Chichester was made Governor of Carrickfergus in 1598 and would become Lord Deputy of Ireland seven years later. As the previous governor, his brother John, had been beheaded by the O'Neills, this was not good news for the clan. Chichester ordered the complete encirclement of the town by defensive walls (about half of which can be seen today – they are older than the walls of Derry), later destroying the countryside around with a 'scorched earth' policy designed to preclude any possibility of Gaelic rebellion. He restored St Nicholas' Church, which had also been built by John de Courcy.

Post-plantation Carrickfergus was a power base and defence for the Protestant population of this part of Ulster. It was here that King William landed on 14 June 1690 with a large fleet to confirm his capture of the English Crown by defeating the forces of James II on Irish soil.

By this time William's second in command, Schomberg, had already recaptured Carrickfergus Castle from James's forces following a savage siege that did serious damage to the castle. You can still see the gaps in the wall to the east of the North Gate caused by the mortar fire. Within weeks of landing here William had won the Battle of the Boyne. His ultimate victory solidified English rule and Protestant ascendancy.

ST NICHOLAS' CHURCH

Here too it seems that every invasion, change of power or tumultuous local event has left its imprint. In summer there are tours each Tuesday and Saturday but group tours can be arranged too if you ring ahead.

It was Sir Arthur Chichester in the early 1600s who transformed de Courcy's ruin into the beautiful church we see today. His presence is felt everywhere, not least in the unique marble and alabaster memorial to his family. His brother is also commemorated, head intact. This allegedly caused his beheader, on a visit to the church, to remark 'I am sure he was a head shorter last time I saw him.'

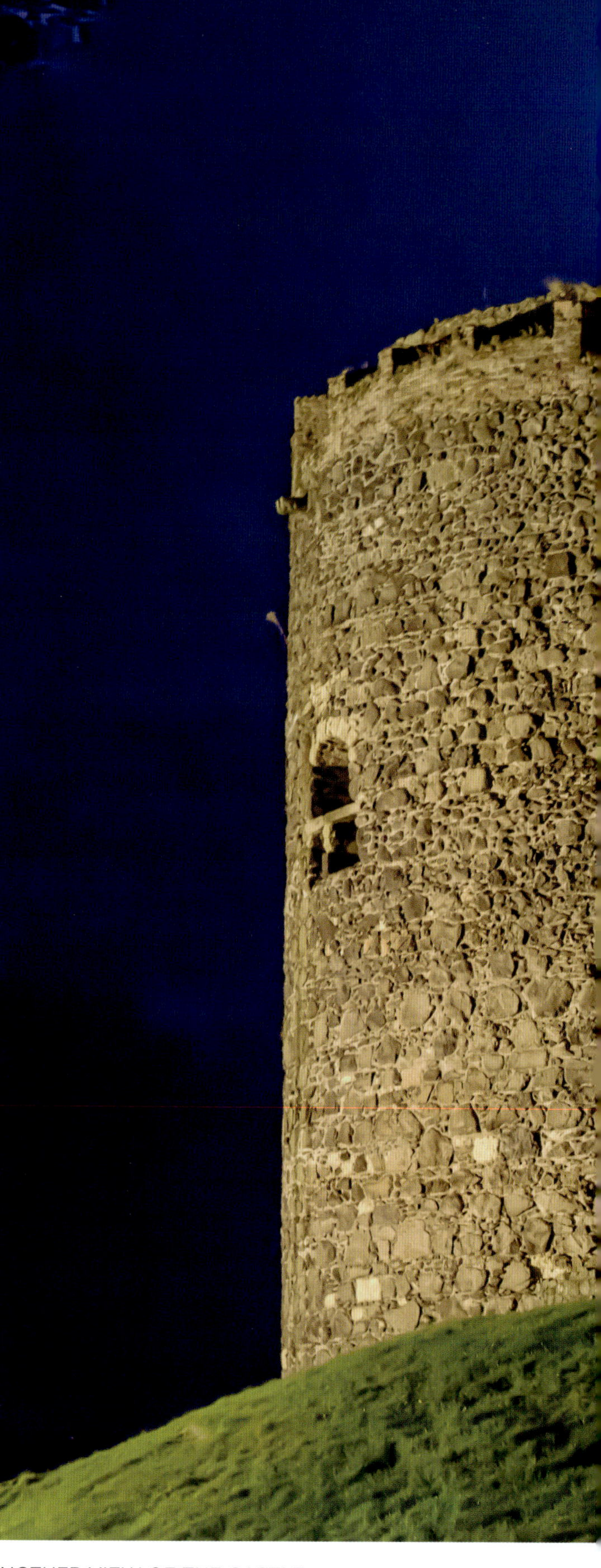

ANOTHER VIEW OF THE CASTLE

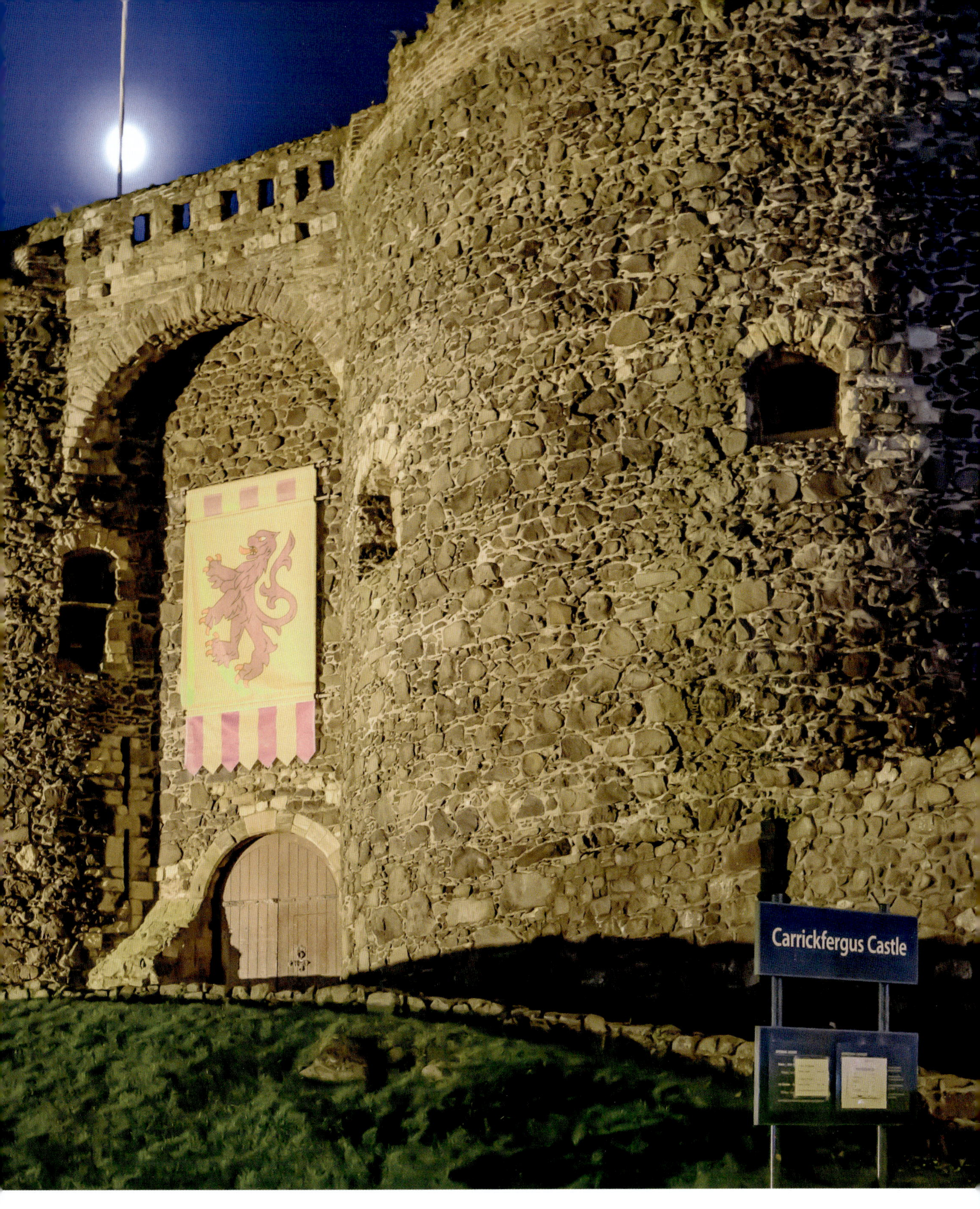
Carrickfergus Castle

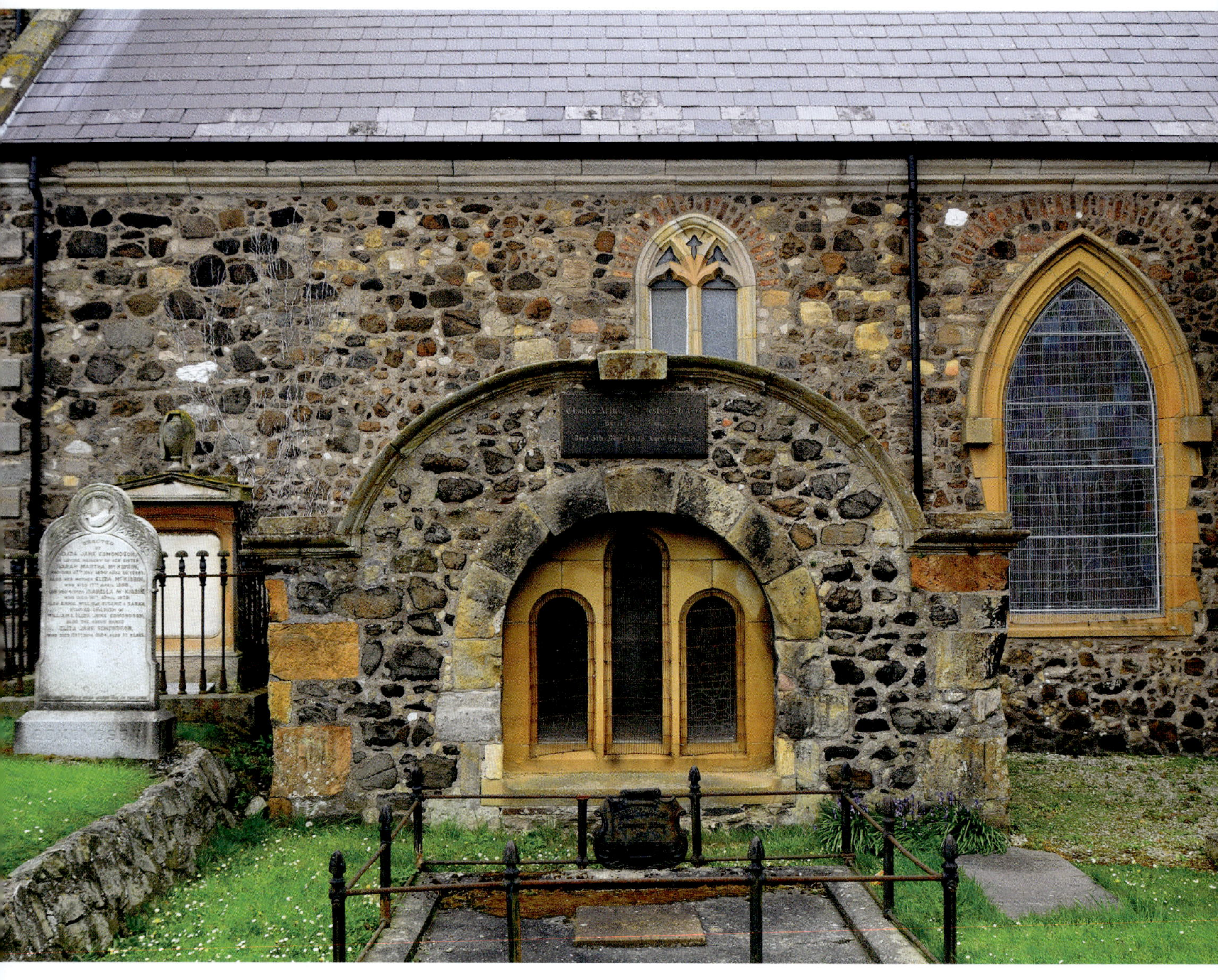

ST NICHOLAS' CHURCH

One of the most fascinating churches in Northern Ireland, St Nicholas' Church was founded by the Anglo Norman conqueror of Ulster, John de Courcy, in the 12th century. It has been at the centre of Carrickfergus life ever since. You can still see its original Norman pillars and memorials to the Chichester family, who oversaw its restoration in the early 17th century.

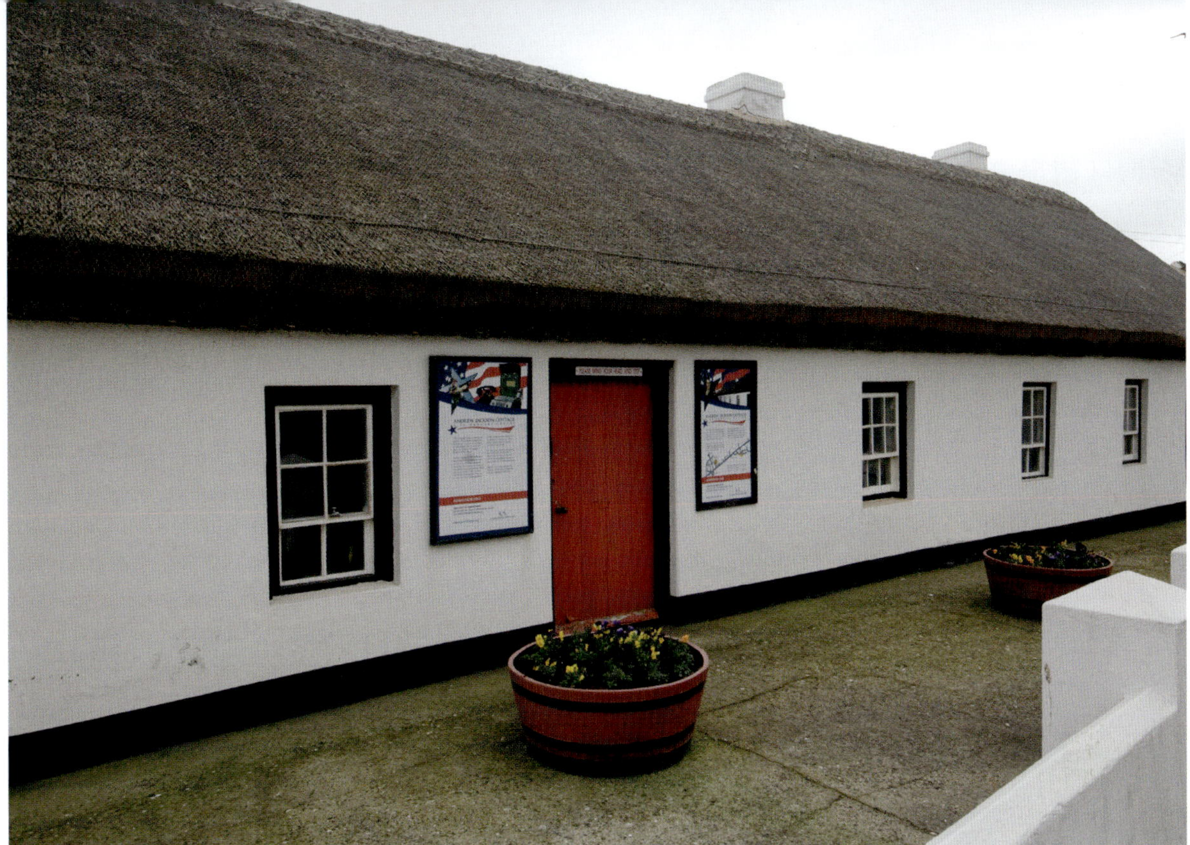

Encased in the present walls for hundreds of years, the original Norman pillars are now revealed again. In the baptistery nearby, once used as a coroner's court, you can see marks left by soldiers sharpening their swords. There's an ancient piscina used to ward off witches and a window where communion was given to those afflicted with leprosy. Most sat in the Freeman's Aisle for services, looking up at the Chichester family in the raised aisle opposite.

By the way, the very unusual crooked aisle symbolises that Christ's head fell to the right when he was crucified. Also look out for communion tables and chairs carved in ancient Irish bog oak, the staff of poet Louis MacNeice's father, Bishop John MacNeice, and a copy of the Book of Kells.

CARRICKFERGUS MUSEUM
Around the corner is the old courthouse and jail, now Carrickfergus Museum. The old town walls, well signposted, are in this direction too. Some famous trials took place at the courthouse, including that of the United Irishmen martyr Henry Orr ('Remember Orr!' was a rallying cry for the 1798 uprising) and the last witchcraft trial in Ireland, which will we soon return to on our journey.

Volunteers also run the Gasworks Flame, one of only three preserved gasworks in Britain and Ireland, not far from St Nicholas'. If you're interested in industrial heritage, this is paradise. If not, pass. Again, check ahead for opening hours, which are limited.

AN AMERICAN STORY
Just a mile out of Carrickfergus you will see a sign for the Andrew Jackson Cottage, a thatched 1750s farmhouse near the shore. It's been furnished to look like the modest cottage Andrew Jackson's parents emigrated to the US from in 1765. The original, which was nearby, was demolished in 1860.

The cottage hosts an exhibition about the seventh President of the United States of America, who was born just two years after his parents emigrated. In the cottage grounds is the US Rangers Centre, a museum dedicated to the men of the First Battalion of the US Rangers, first 'activated' in Carrickfergus in 1942 and the only elite American force ever formed outside the US. They went on to help turn the tide of war in Europe.

ABOVE: THE ANDREW JACKSON COTTAGE

WHITEHEAD

A smallish town, right on the coast, Whitehead has preserved enough of its Victorian character to make it a pleasant stop en route. It's also a must for steam-train lovers.

In Edward Road you will find the Bank House, where Sinead Brennan has established a cafe famed for delicious home-made cakes and scones and its deli of local and international foods and local crafts. Also in the historic building is an old-fashioned wool shop, which hosts workshops on the craft of knitting.

Around the corner is one of two main reasons visitors come to this area, Whitehead Railway Museum, HQ of the Railway Preservation Society of Ireland.

STEAM-TRAIN ROMANCE

Nearby Whitehead NIR Station is still running, with a train every half hour from Belfast. The railway, extended here in Victorian times, was a major reason for the opening up of this beautiful area for tourism, and for our other main stop here, The Gobbins.

The Railway Preservation Society of Ireland was founded over 50 years ago in what had been the Whitehead excursion station. Special trains used to arrive here, unloading visitors to be taken by horses and jaunting cars to The Gobbins, which at that time was more popular than the Giant's Causeway.

It's best to book a guided tour beforehand, which will take you out to the platform where you can inspect old railway carriages and pull the levers of an old-fashioned signal box like a traditional signalman.

After that you'll be taken to the exhibition in the original Stables, which was built to house the horses and carriages used to ferry visitors to and from The Gobbins. Next you go into the massive sheds hosting the old steam engines (most of them working) and vintage carriages (including a number of heritage wooden carriages and items of rolling stock, in one of which Irish presidents travelled, and another of which was used to convey the Queen). It's a must for Thomas the Tank Engine fans as well as their grandparents,

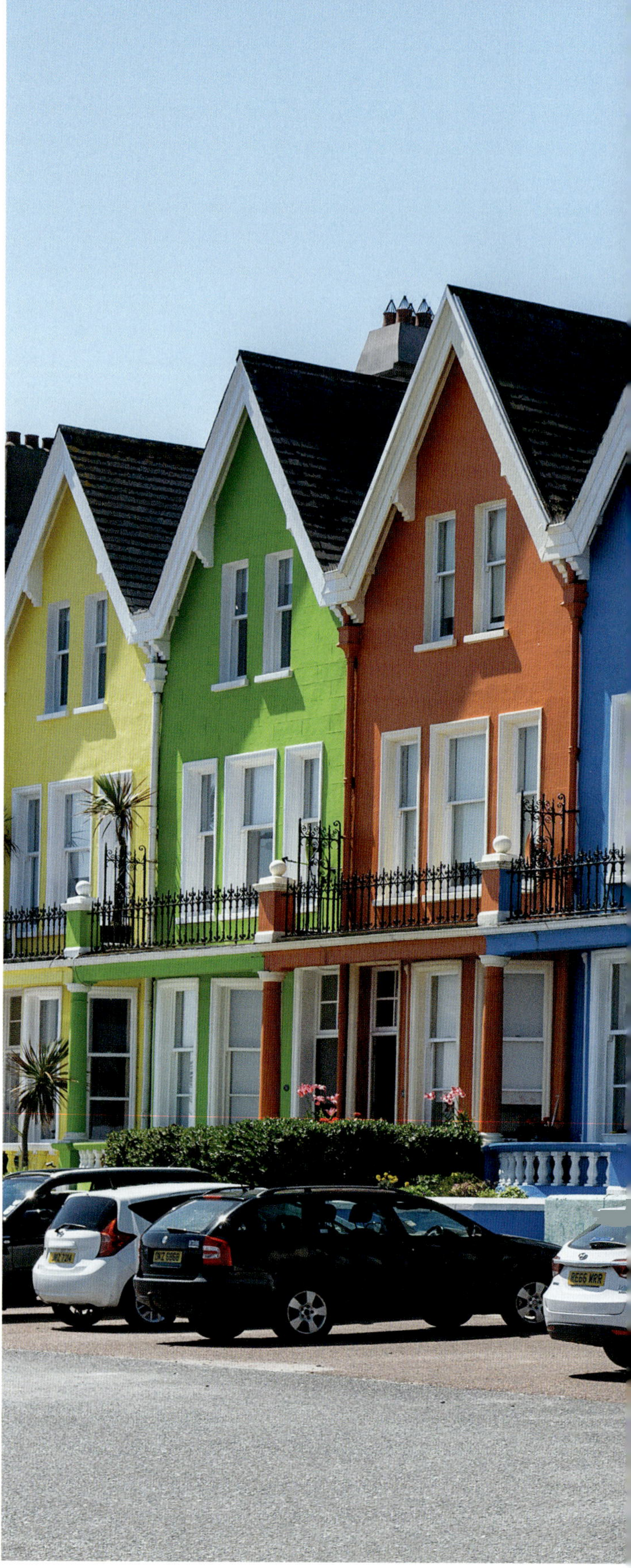

COLOURFUL WHITEHEAD

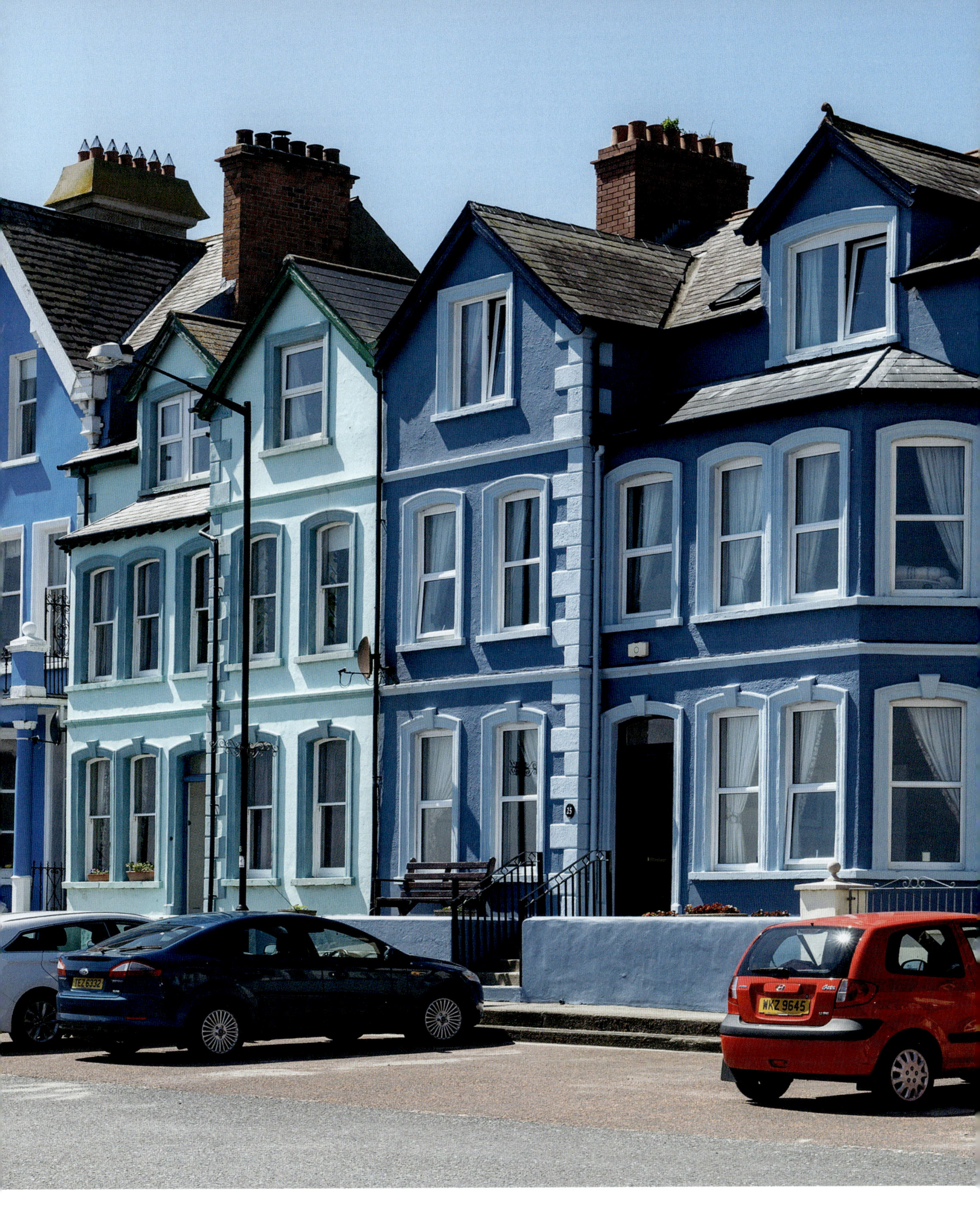

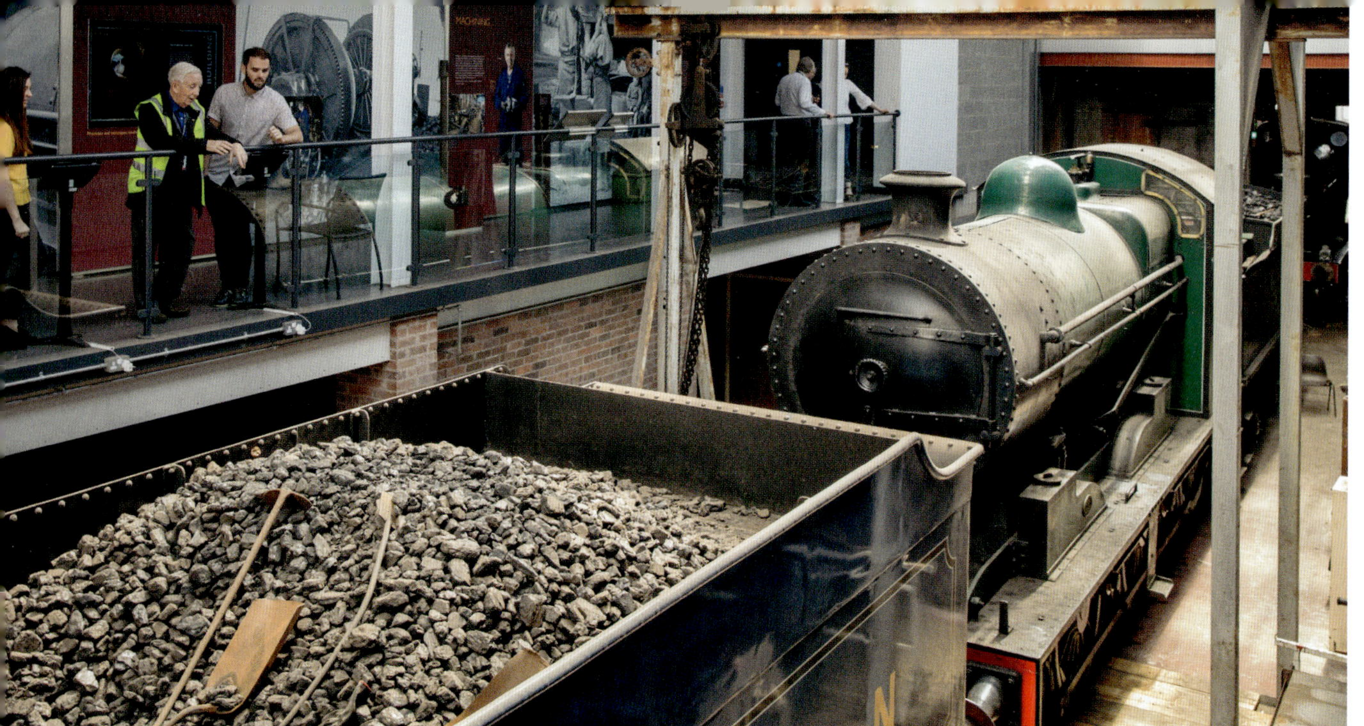

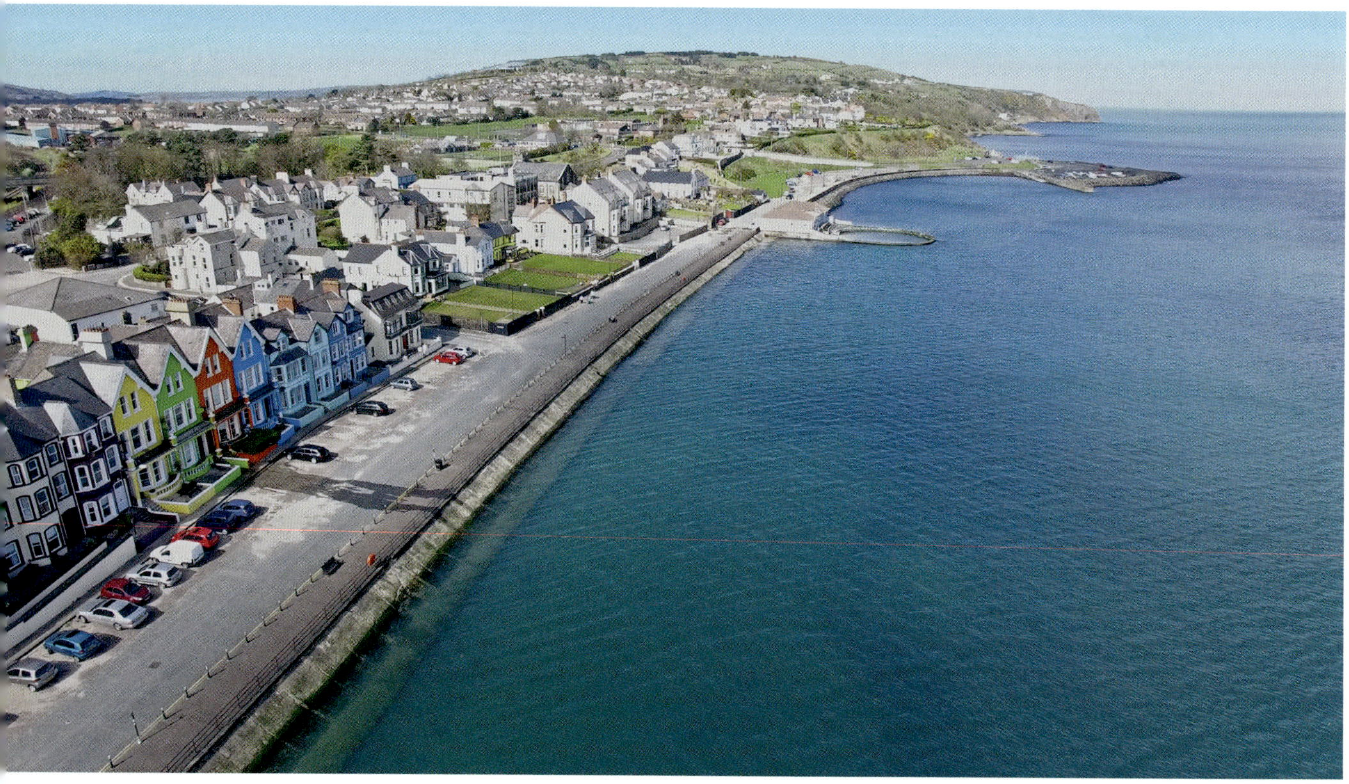

some of whom may still recall the evocative smell of coal smoke trailing back from a steam engine.

Best of all are the steam-train excursions that the RPSI runs from here to destinations like Dublin and Portrush and on seasonal occasions such as Halloween, Easter and Christmas. You can book a walk through Whitehead with Portia Woods of Toast the Coast food tours (who also conducts a great foodie tour of the Causeway Coast) that ends at the Edwardian tea room in Whitehead Railway Museum, where the home-made food is excellent.

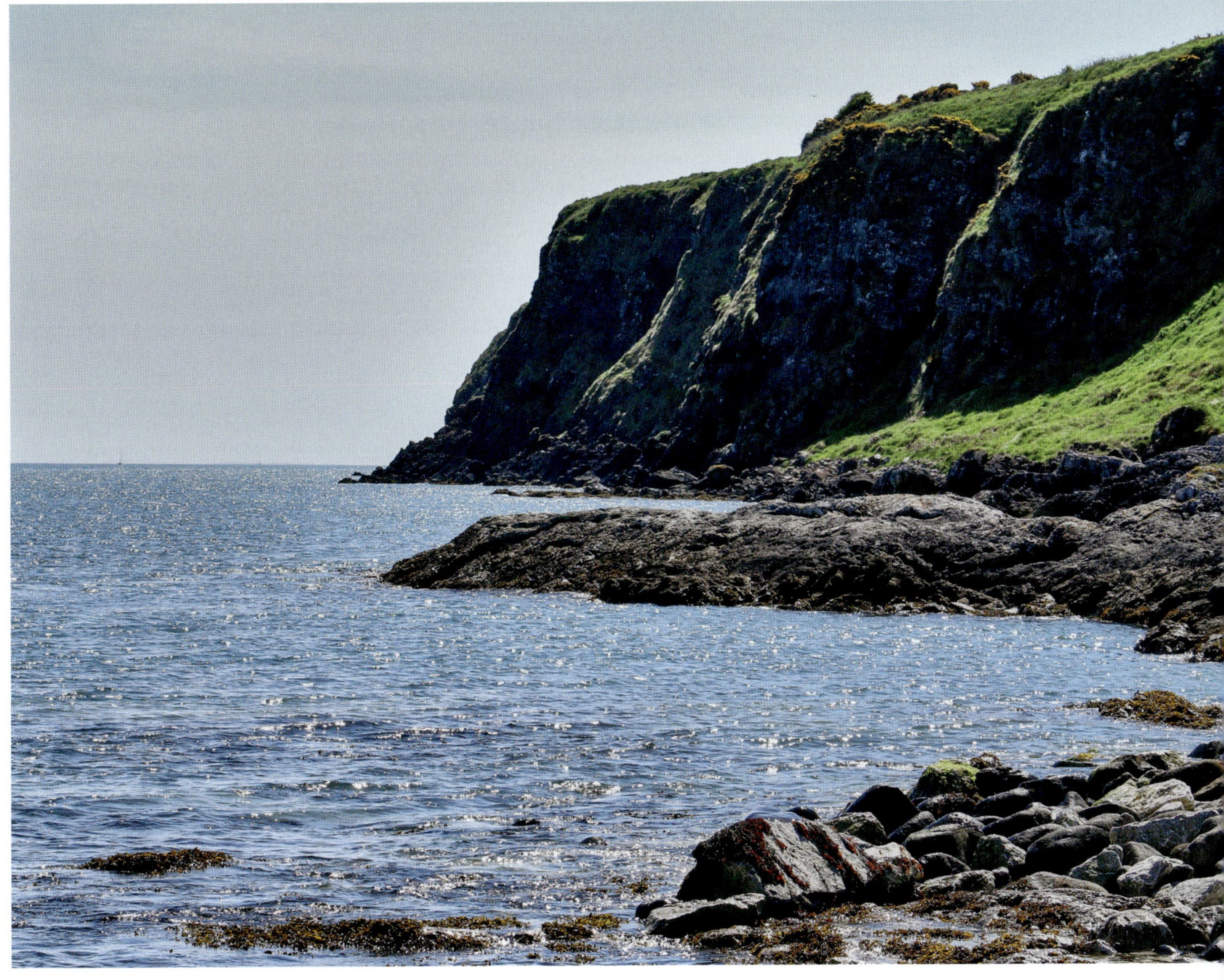

OPPOSITE TOP: WHITEHEAD RAILWAY MUSEUM. OPPOSITE BOTTOM: WHITEHEAD AND THE COAST
ABOVE: ISLANDMAGEE

ISLANDMAGEE

The village of Islandmagee, around the corner from The Gobbins Visitor Centre, has an unusual claim to fame as the site of the mysterious goings-on that led to the last witchcraft trial in Ireland. In 1711, some 20 years after the infamous Salem witch trials, Islandmagee became the centre of attention in Ireland. Although the trial itself was held in Carrickfergus Court, now the museum, most of the eight women accused were from this little village.

The events began with the death of the wife of the local Presbyterian minister. It was said that witchcraft hastened her end and that her bedclothes were arranged in the shape of a corpse by unseen hands. A 'demon' came to one witness in an apparition and forecast the woman's death. Things got worse after her death when her beautiful niece, teenager Mary Dunbar, came to stay in the house.

Among other alleged occurrences was the spectacle of a pillow walking by itself, dressed in a nightgown. Mary, who claimed to have been possessed and suffering hideous convulsions, accused the women, whom she identified, of attacking her in spectral form. They were given one-year sentences, put in the stocks and pelted with stones and rotten fruit. Recently, it was suggested that a plaque to the clearly innocent women be erected at The Gobbins Visitor Centre.

If you want to read more on the Islandmagee witches, there is a fascinating book by Dr Andrew Sneddon on the subject, *Possessed by the Devil: The Real History of the Islandmagee Witches and Ireland's Only Mass Witchcraft Trial*, published by the History Press. A novel – Martina Devlin's *The House Where It Happened* – was based on this episode too.

FAMOUS ICE CREAM AT THE RINKHA

Islandmagee is famous for The Gobbins, the witches and the Rinkha! Just yards away from The Gobbins Visitor Centre, Ross Hawkins is the fourth generation of his family to make wonderful ice creams based on an original family recipe. At the old-fashioned Rinkha Store, the large variety on offer includes the traditional vanilla for which it is famous. If you look around the photos on the wall, you'll be transported back to the days when this store was a leading Northern Irish dance hall, hosting everything from jitterbugging American GIs to swing music and the best of skiffle and showband.

THE GOBBINS

The Gobbins Visitor Centre is the staging post for the remarkable Gobbins Path. After a safety briefing here, a bus will take you on the five-minute ride to this reimagined Victorian walk.

The Gobbins Path was the work of the visionary Victorian engineer B.D. Wise. Chief Engineer of the Belfast and Northern Counties Railway Company, he was one of the first to see the tourism potential of this whole area. Following the extension of the railway from Larne, with its thousands of incoming visitors arriving on ferries from England and Scotland, Wise transformed Whitehead, building a promenade, auditorium and bandstand and importing sand to create a beach.

But it was his creation of The Gobbins Path, said to have 'no parallel in Europe as a marine cliff walk', that truly put the area on the map and made it a destination for this new generation of railway tourists.

Wise, who had already transformed scenic Glenariff, a forthcoming stop on our tour, built a path around the cliffs that passed through and around caves and needed a large number of bridges. Several long tunnels had to be blasted through the rock to link some sections together.

Using the limited technology of the day, it was an incredible achievement. Wise completed the first section of his path in August 1902 and it was an instant international success. However, the cost of keeping the path safe and secure saw it closed in the 1950s, until its multi-million-pound reimagining and reopening in 2015.

The two-mile path (you return the same way) is really for the reasonably fit and able, but for those who can, do! Exposed to the elements, you'll feel the salt water in your face as you take the narrow path around the cliff face, enjoying spectacular views and exploring caves like 'Smugglers', once used to hoard illicit goods such as alcohol and, more surprisingly, salt.

Highlights include the amazing Tubular Bridge, from which you have great views of the Mull of Kintyre, in Scotland; the Man of War, a vast basalt rock above the sea, and the Gallery, where families of the crew would have watched *Titanic* on her sea trials.

At the Aquarium you'll see birds squabbling over fish left by the retreating tide. Indeed, the wildlife – sometimes the birds are within touching distance – is incredible throughout. In summer thousands of birds form vast colonies as they arrive to feed on the spawning herring and mackerel. The fish also bring in porpoises, dolphins, otters and hawks. In August the birds of prey, kestrels and buzzards, arrive. Puffins come here in large numbers to breed too.

OPPOSITE: THE GOBBINS WALK

Check thegobbinscliffpath.com when planning your route to make sure the path is open to the public. The visitor centre and cafe remain open, even when the path is closed for repairs.

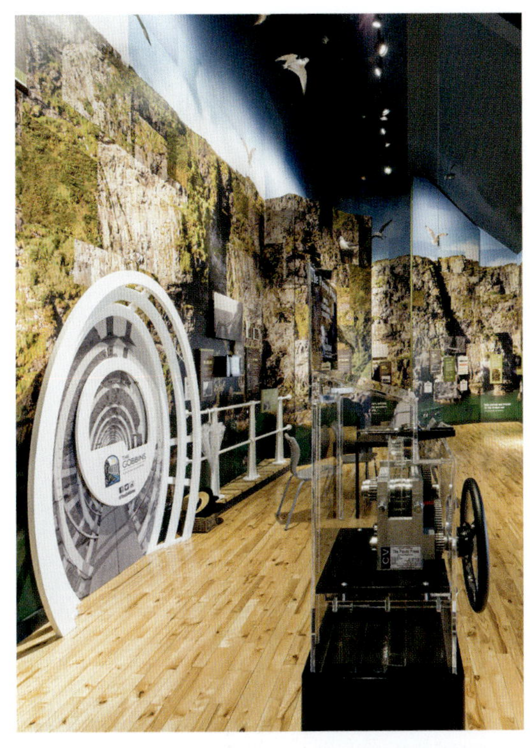

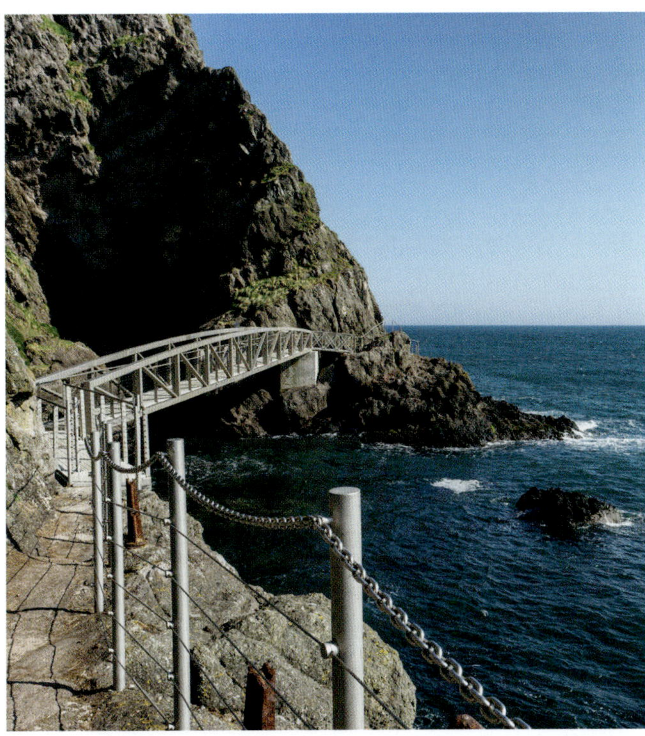

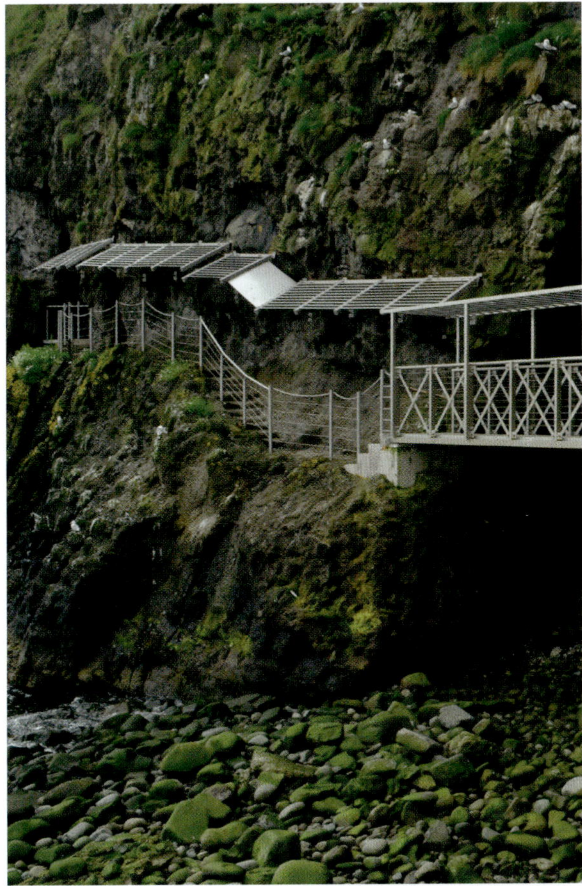

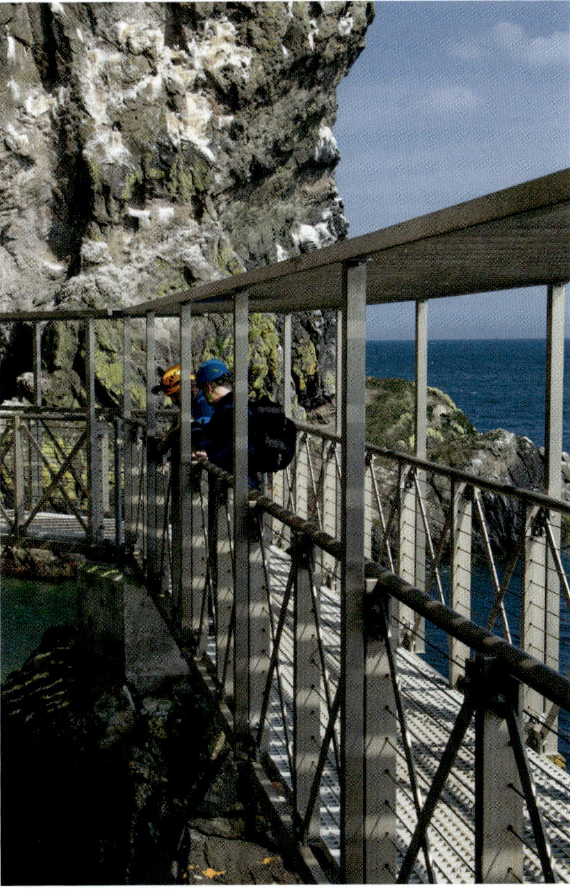

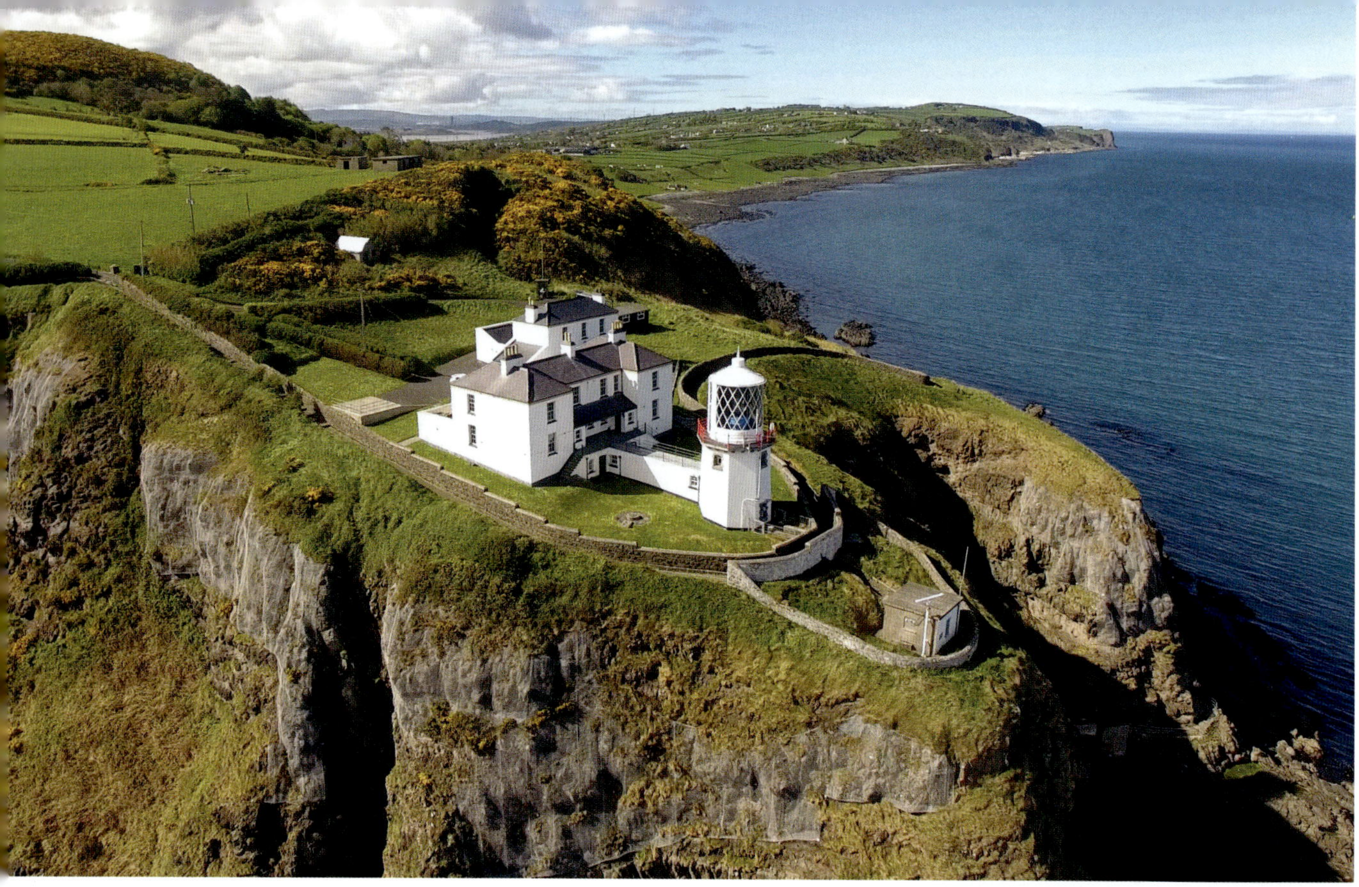

ABOVE AND OPPOSITE: BLACKHEAD LIGHTHOUSE
RIGHT: VIEW FROM A KEEPER'S COTTAGE

ROOMS WITH A VIEW

Fancy an overnight stay with a difference? Just a mile or so from Whitehead is Blackhead Lighthouse. Built in 1902, it's still working but now fully automated, so its old lighthouse keepers' cottages are no longer needed. Beautifully restored as self-catering accommodation, they offer the most atmospheric self-catering experience you could want. Just imagine the views on long summer evenings.

If you're lucky, there are four kinds of dolphins you might spot in the waters below – Risso's, bottlenose, common and Atlantic white-sided – not to mention minke whales.

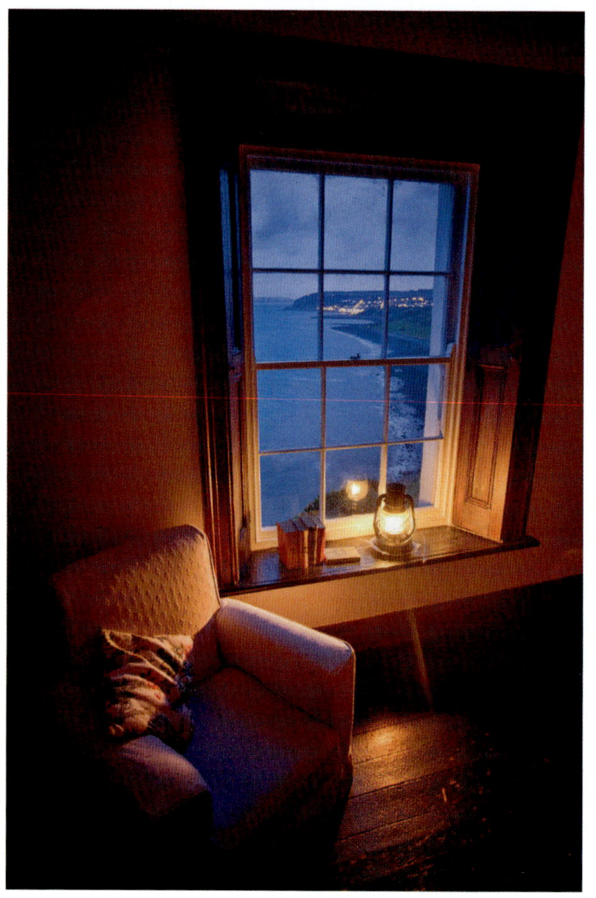

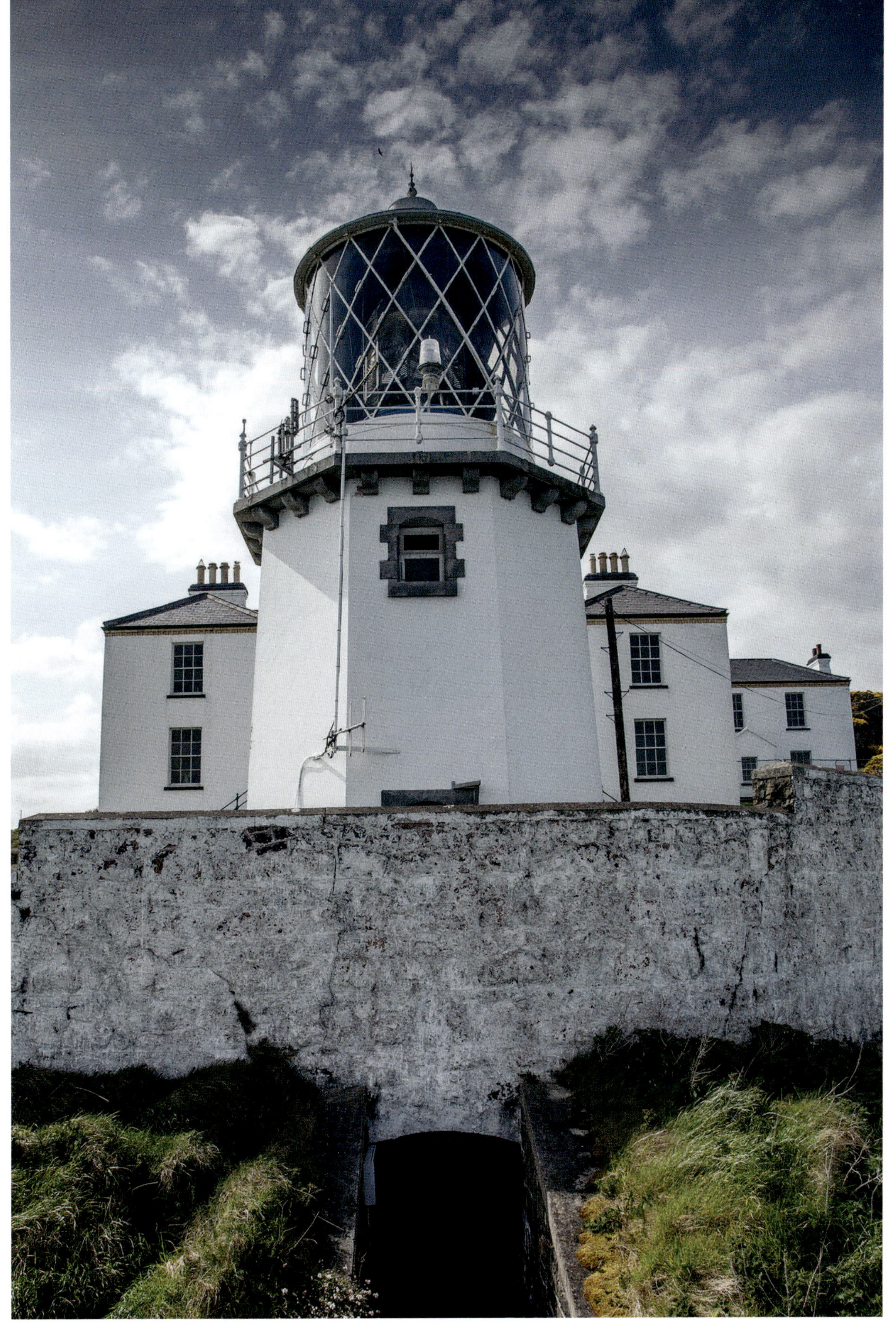

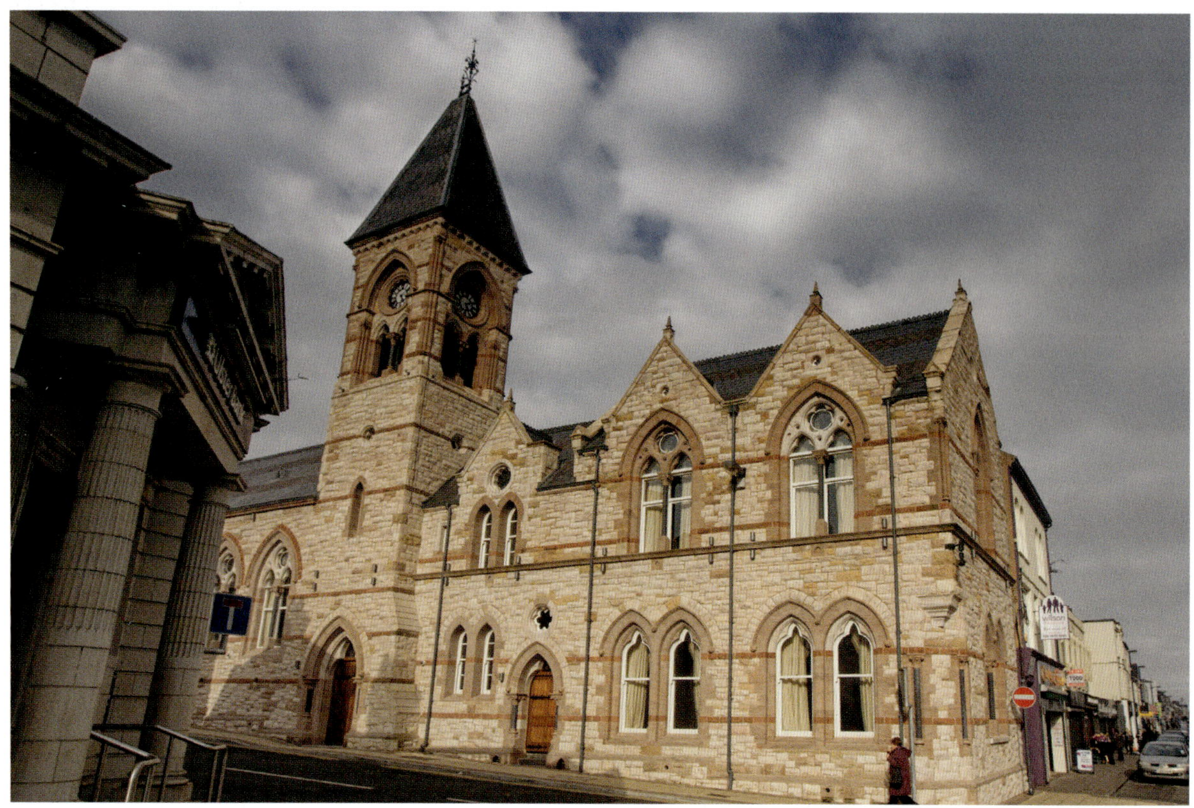

THE ANCIENT SEAPORT OF LARNE

It was the growth of this 900-year-old port during the golden age of steam travel that helped open up the Causeway Coastal Route in Victorian times. Many plantation settlers landed here in the 17th century and many people also left from here in the regular waves of emigration from Ireland to the US, Australia and Canada.

Foodies might want to stop off at the famous Ann's Pantry in Main Street, which has won endless prestigious Great Taste Awards. This family bakery epitomises everything great about local food – including its distinctive breads, like potato bread.

From Larne, it's just a 20-mile detour to Slemish Mountain, where Ireland's patron saint, St Patrick, tended livestock for six years. There will be an option to go to Slemish later in the journey, but travelling there from Larne is probably the quickest way.

THE GLORIOUS COASTAL ROUTE

It's just after Larne that the Causeway Coastal Route truly gets under way. Just outside the edge of Larne Town Park on the Coast Road, about half a mile before the Black Arch, a small memorial sculpture overlooks the Irish Sea. It reads 'Antrim Coast Road constructed 1832 to 1842 by the Men of the Glynnes [Glens] under the direction of William Bald'.

Before the coastal road opened in 1842, the Causeway Coast and Glens had been isolated from the rest of Ireland because of the poor quality of the often hazardous roads. Indeed, it was much easier for those living along the coast to reach Scotland by boat than Belfast by road.

William Bald, the Scottish engineer tasked with building the road, faced a gigantic challenge. The spectacular geography of the coast made the construction of a road with the limited technology of the time both dangerous and, at times, near impossible.

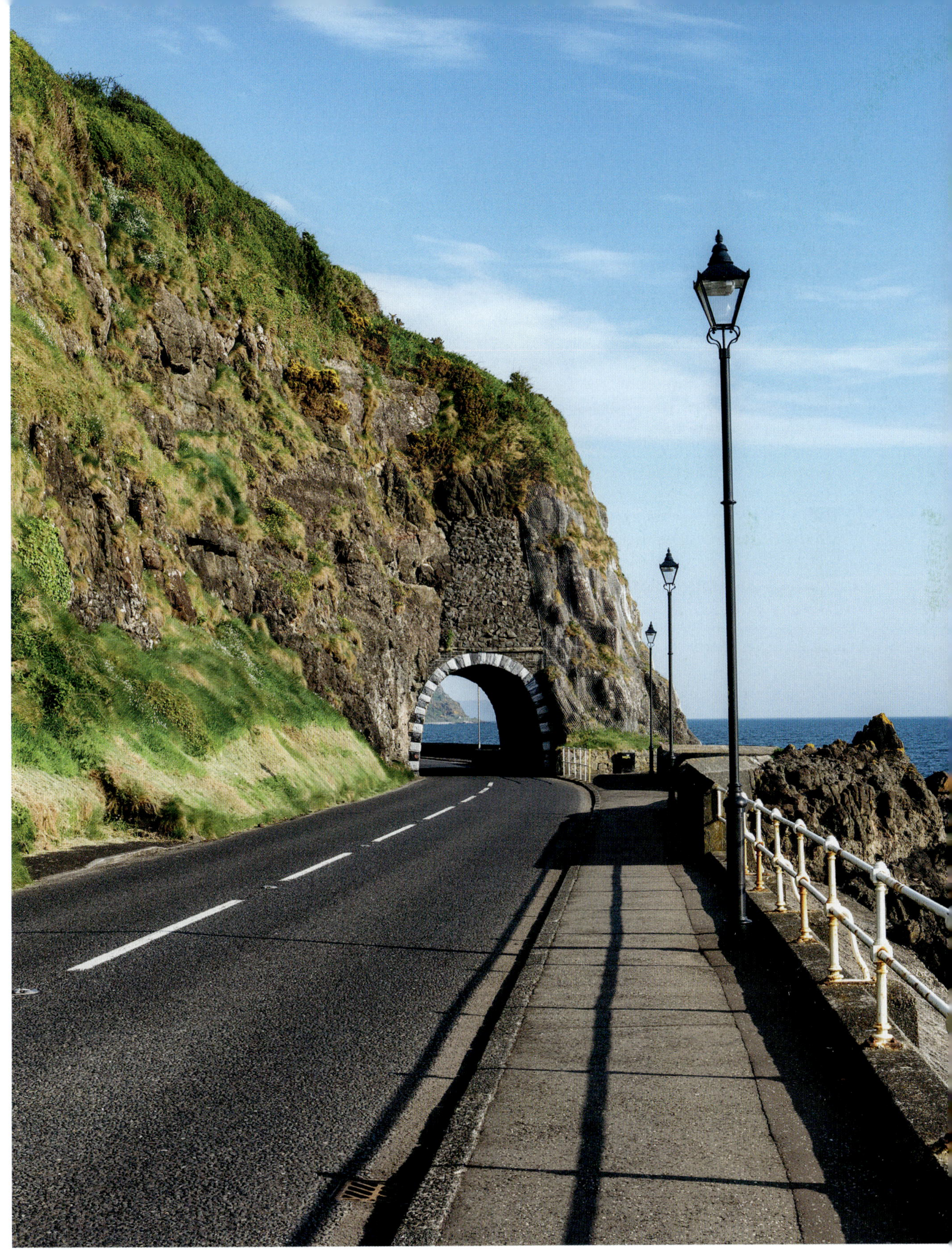

OPPOSITE: THE TOWN HALL, LARNE. ABOVE: APPROACHING THE BLACK ARCH

He marshalled hundreds of local men to forge a way through a huge extent of rock and steep hills of moving clay banks, not to mention the mass of faulted limestone that lay beneath the depths of basalt.

To do so, Bald employed new techniques, such as exploding headlands, using the rock left over to create sea defences. '30,000 cubic yards of rock,' he reported in 1834, 'have been hurled down on the shore almost entirely by blasting, which has been executed by care and judgement.'

As you leave Larne behind, the scenery begins to change. The intensely blue (on a sunny day!) waters are close to your right, with views of Scotland a constant feature. There's a sense of wildness too, not unlike the west of Ireland. There are strange rock formations on both sides, and headlands appear and disappear in the distance as the road veers around.

CARNFUNNOCK COUNTRY PARK

Before we reach our next stop, Ballygally, there's an option to stop at Carnfunnock Country Park. An elegant estate that dates back to 1825, it has much to offer a visitor, including a beautiful walled garden, ice house, maze and Norman motte. There's even a sandy beach. Marked ways take you through diverse woodland.

BALLYGALLY

SPIRITS, SIEGES AND THE *GAME OF THRONES* DOOR

The village of Ballygally is best known for having the oldest building still lived in in Northern Ireland, and its *Game of Thrones* connections. Park at the car park by the water, overlooking the small beach that is opposite Ballygally Castle, a hotel where you can enjoy a relaxing glass of wine or maybe an afternoon tea, and take a short ghost tour while you are there.

Ballygally Castle was constructed in the turbulent early decades of the Plantation of Ulster. Designed for defence by its Scottish owner, James Shaw, its thick walls are studded with loop holes. These were much needed in 1641, when the Gaelic Irish rose up against the English and Scots who had been settled on their land. Next to the castle's original doorway, you can see the musket holes that were used to keep the attackers at bay.

Take a quick dander around the original wing of the hotel (it was extended by current owners the Hastings Group). Up some narrow steps in the tower you may encounter the ghost of poor Lady Isabella, James Shaw's wife, in the room in which he allegedly locked her up. It seems he only married her to produce an heir: this duty achieved, he had her incarcerated at the top of the castle, from where she jumped to her death.

You can visit her room, now known as the Ghost Room. Psychics have recorded strange goings-on there, and guests are not allowed to stay in the room anymore. Another ghost is said to knock on doors in the middle of the night. Guests have also reported the rustling of silk in empty corridors.

Before the Hastings Group took over the castle in 1966 it belonged to carpet king Cyril Lord, who opened it as the Candlelight Hotel.

It is said that stones were taken from the ruins of nearby Cairn Castle for the building of Ballygally Castle. The building that gave this area its name, Cairn Castle may have been originally built by an Anglo-Norman, Duncan Fitzgilbert, in the 13th century. One legend attaching to it, however, claims it was built by the King of Antrim to confine his beautiful daughter from the advances of an unwelcome suitor.

Today the area around where the castle would have stood is best known as a location for another medieval fantasy, *Game of Thrones*.

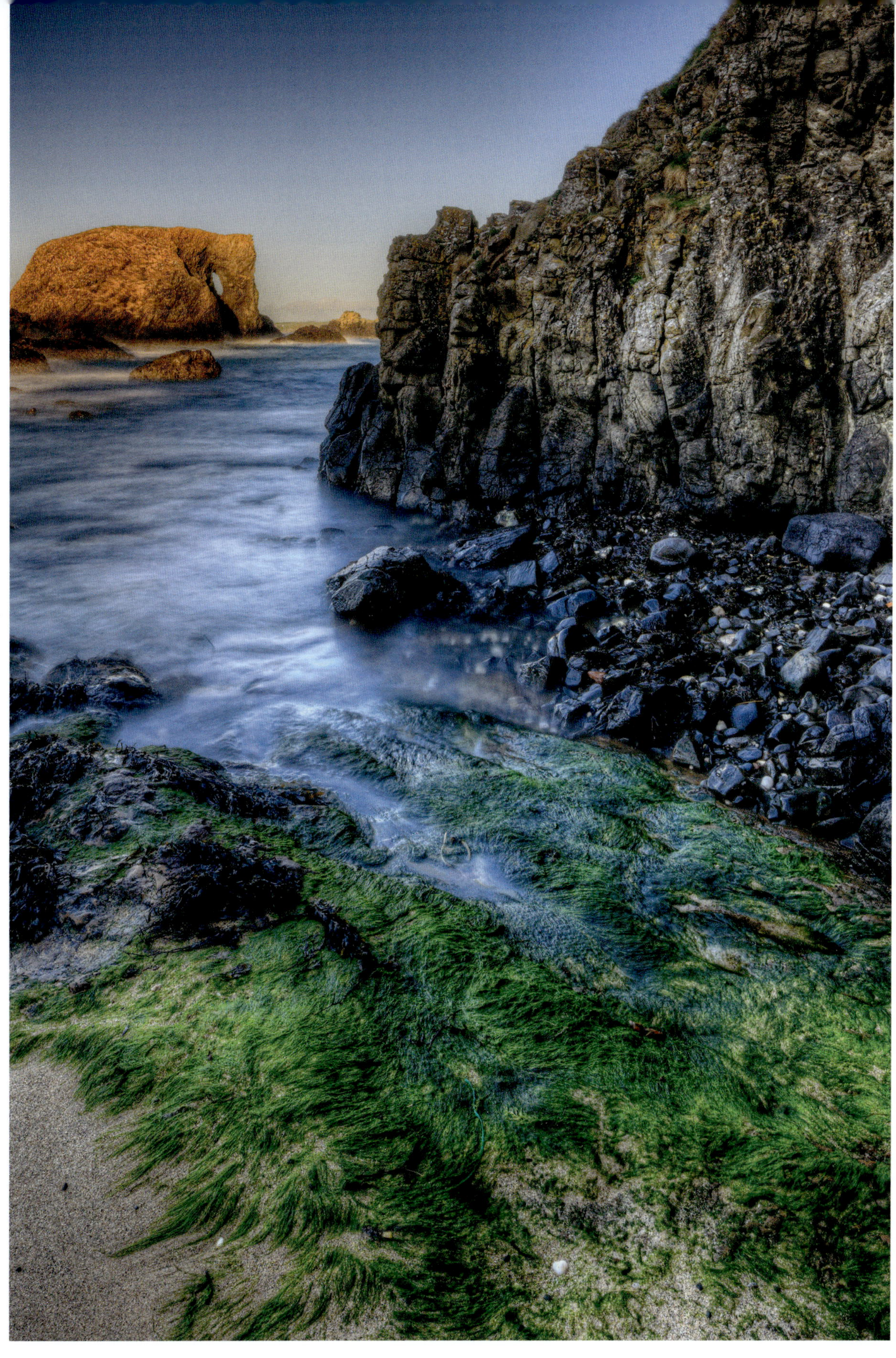

ELEPHANT ROCK, BALLINTOY

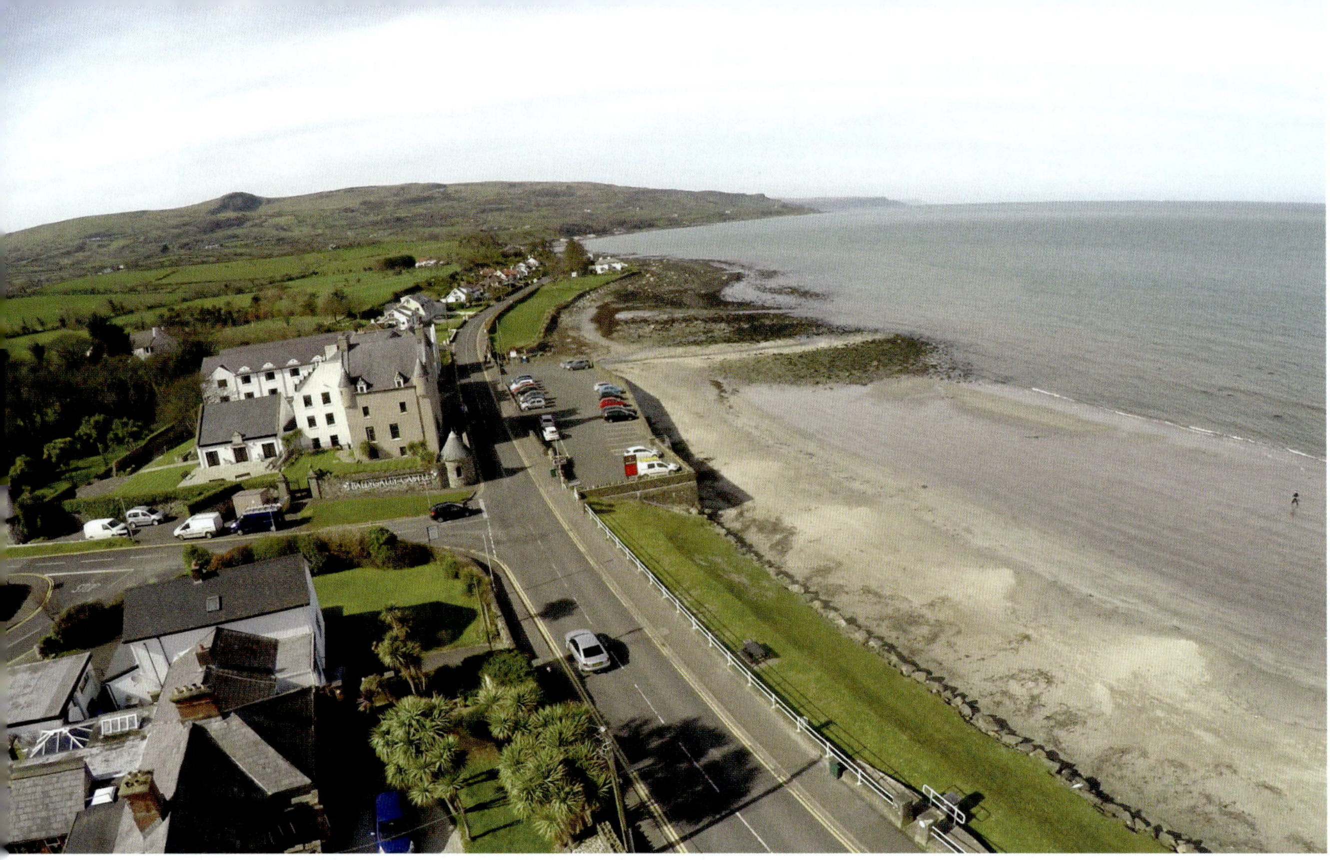

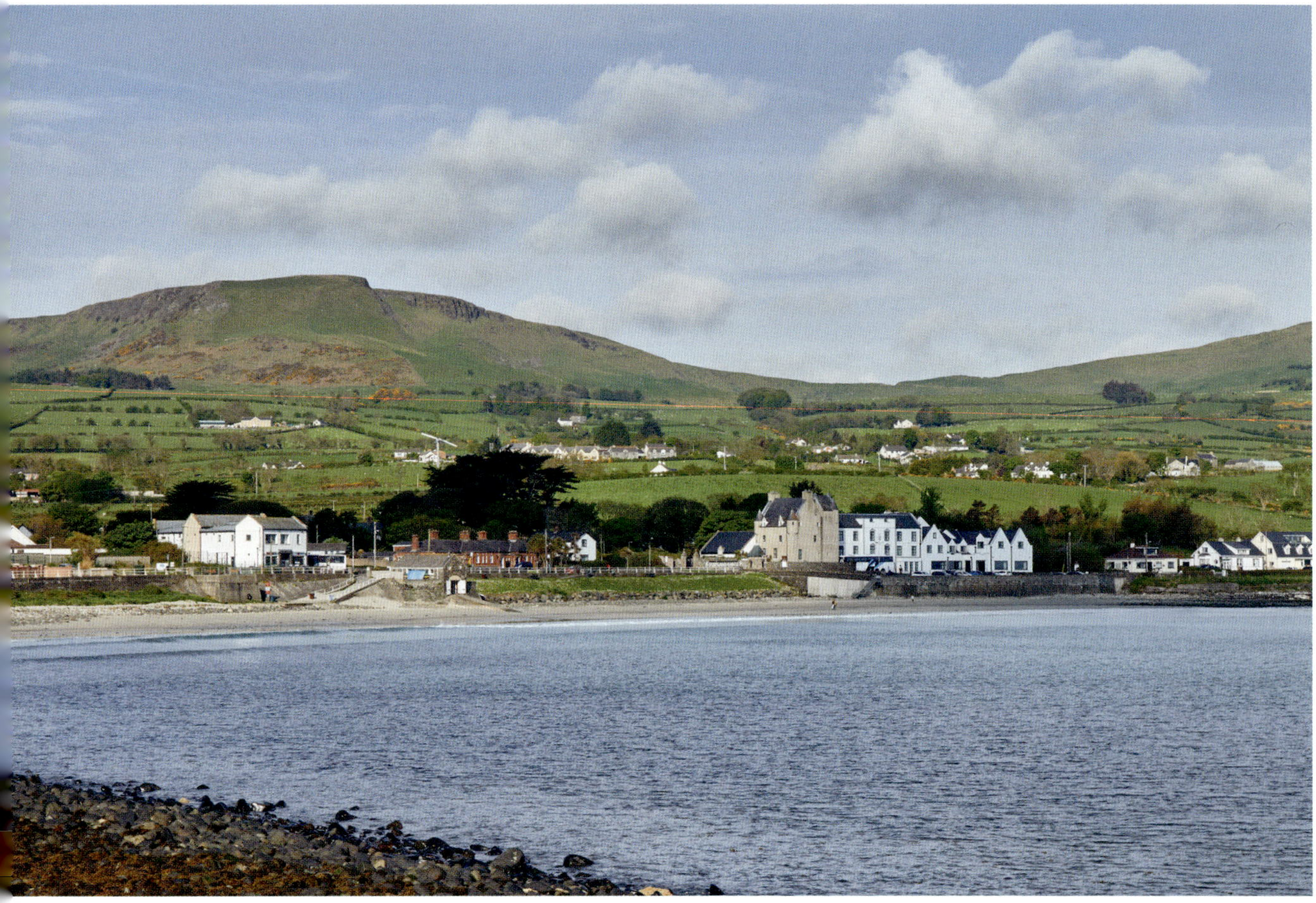

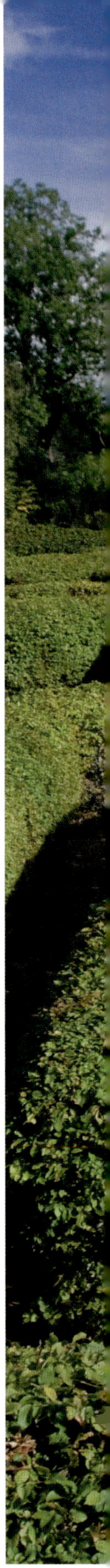

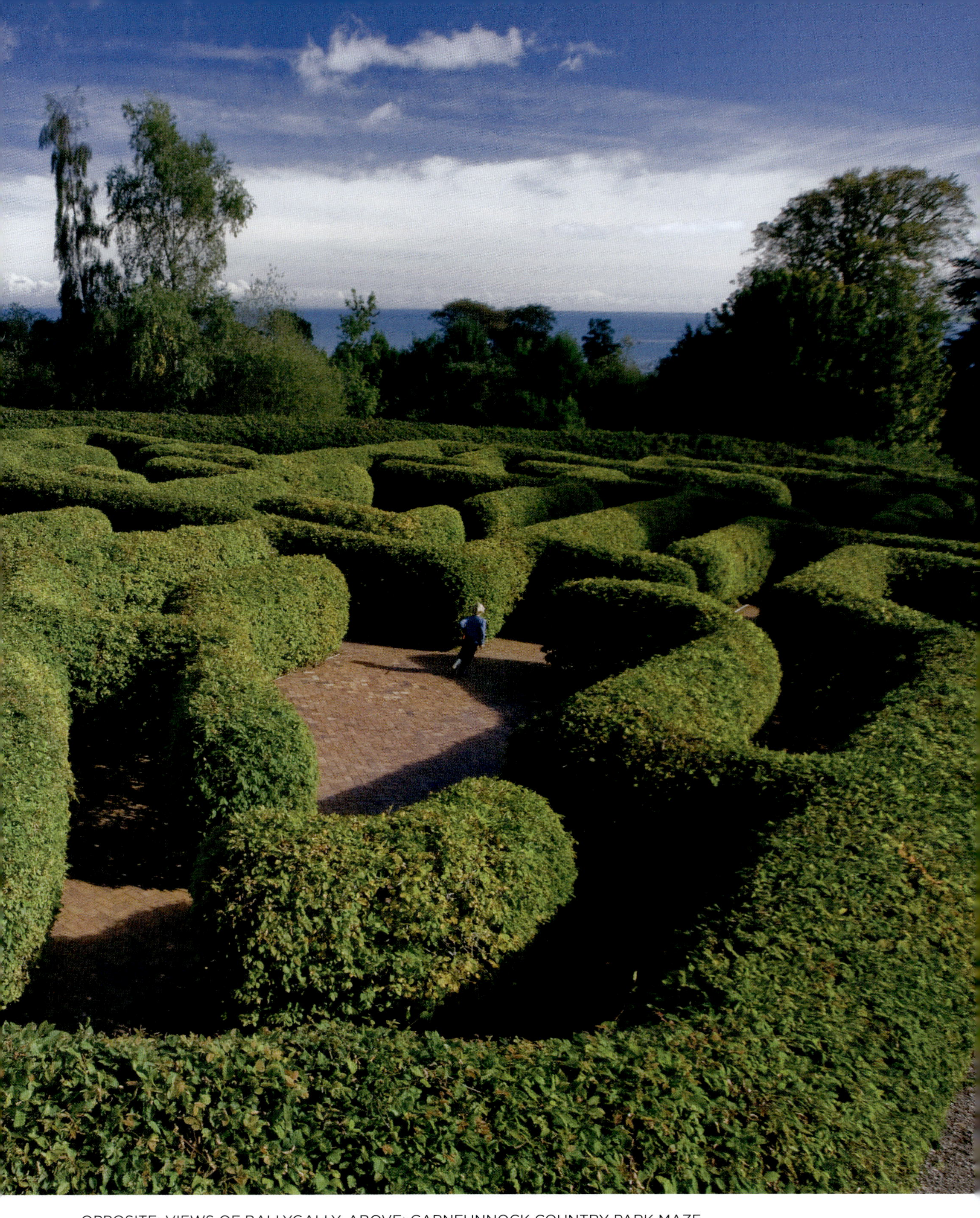

OPPOSITE: VIEWS OF BALLYGALLY. ABOVE: CARNFUNNOCK COUNTRY PARK MAZE

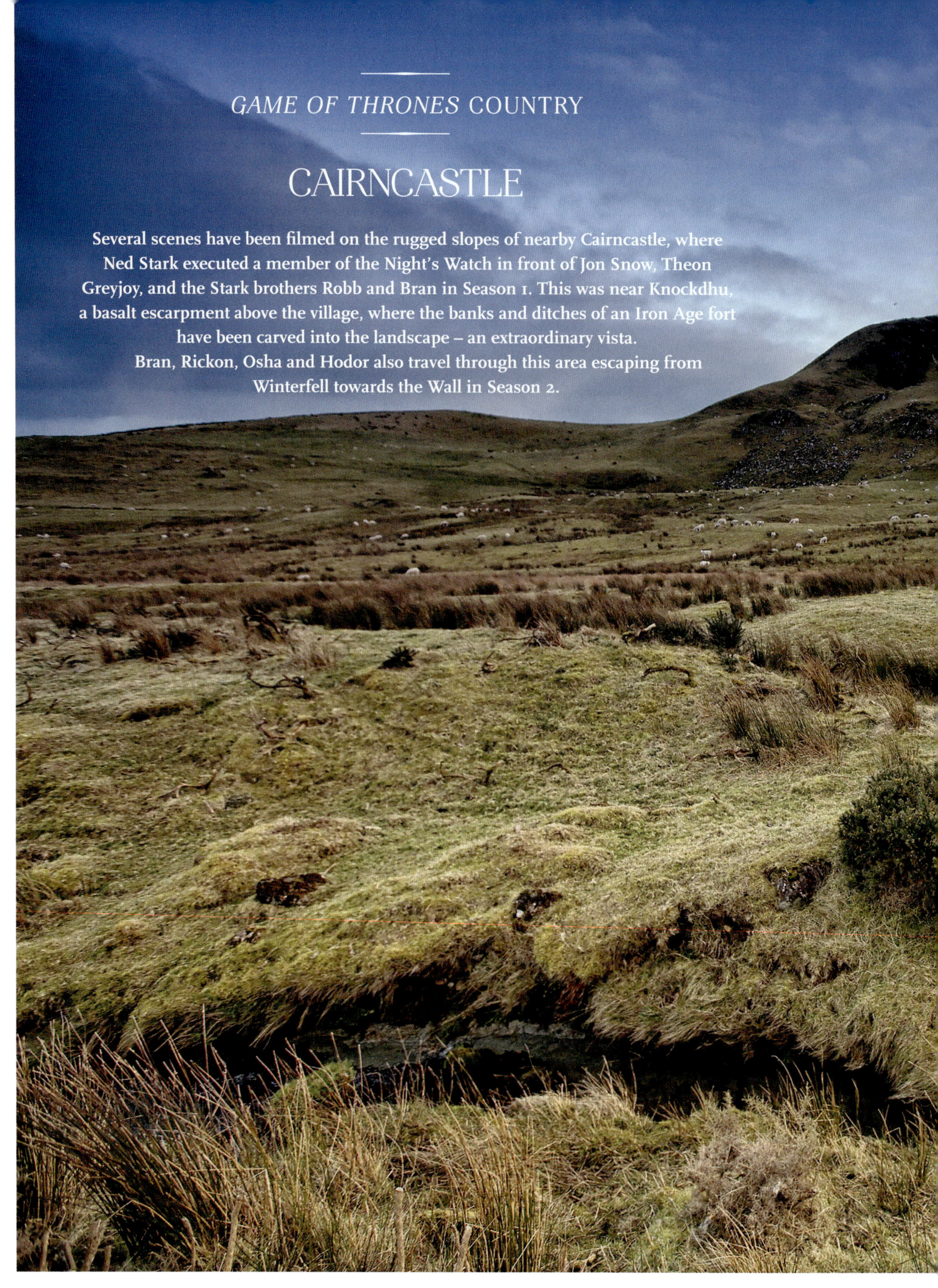

CAIRNCASTLE

Several scenes have been filmed on the rugged slopes of nearby Cairncastle, where Ned Stark executed a member of the Night's Watch in front of Jon Snow, Theon Greyjoy, and the Stark brothers Robb and Bran in Season 1. This was near Knockdhu, a basalt escarpment above the village, where the banks and ditches of an Iron Age fort have been carved into the landscape – an extraordinary vista.
Bran, Rickon, Osha and Hodor also travel through this area escaping from Winterfell towards the Wall in Season 2.

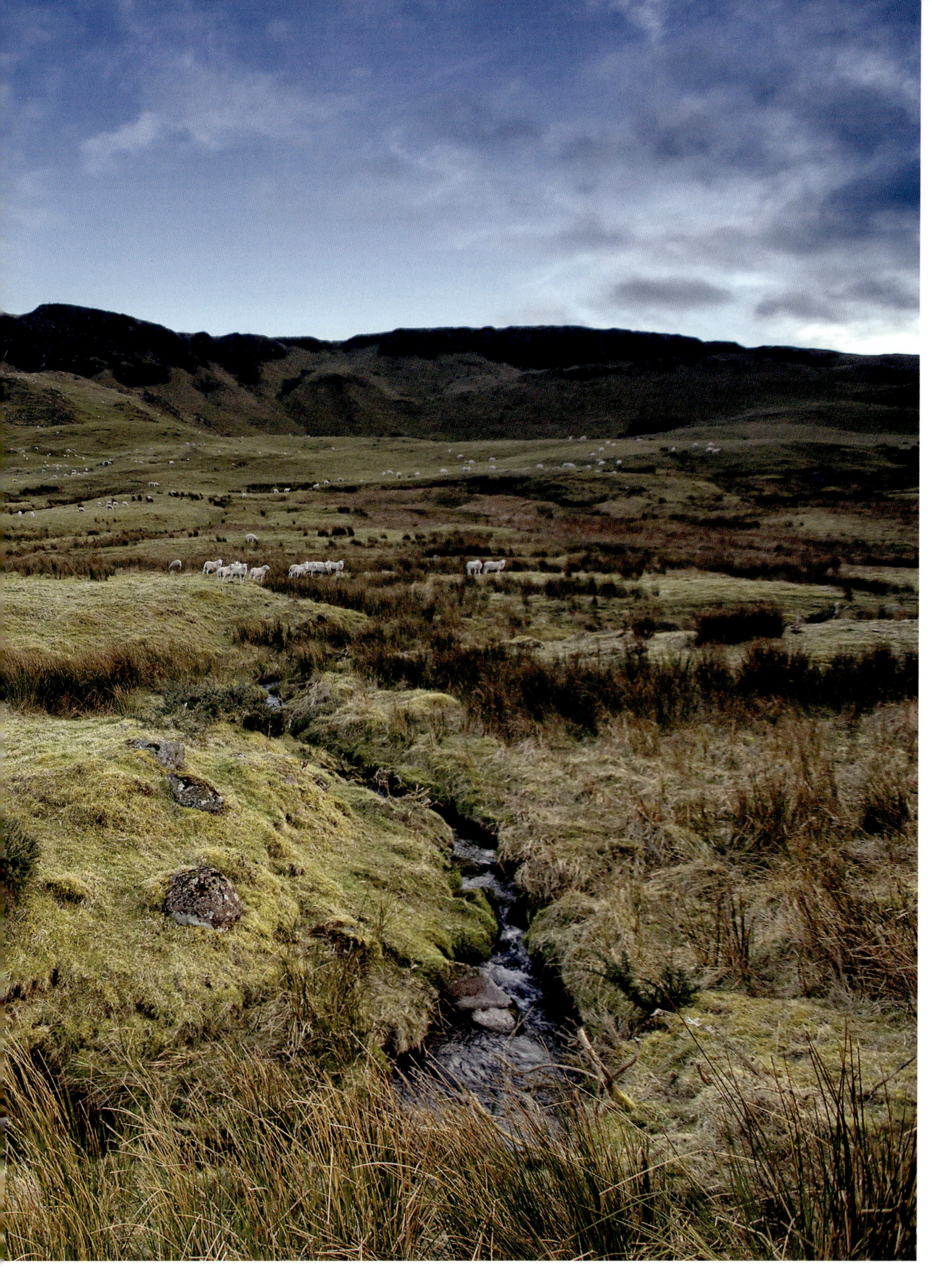

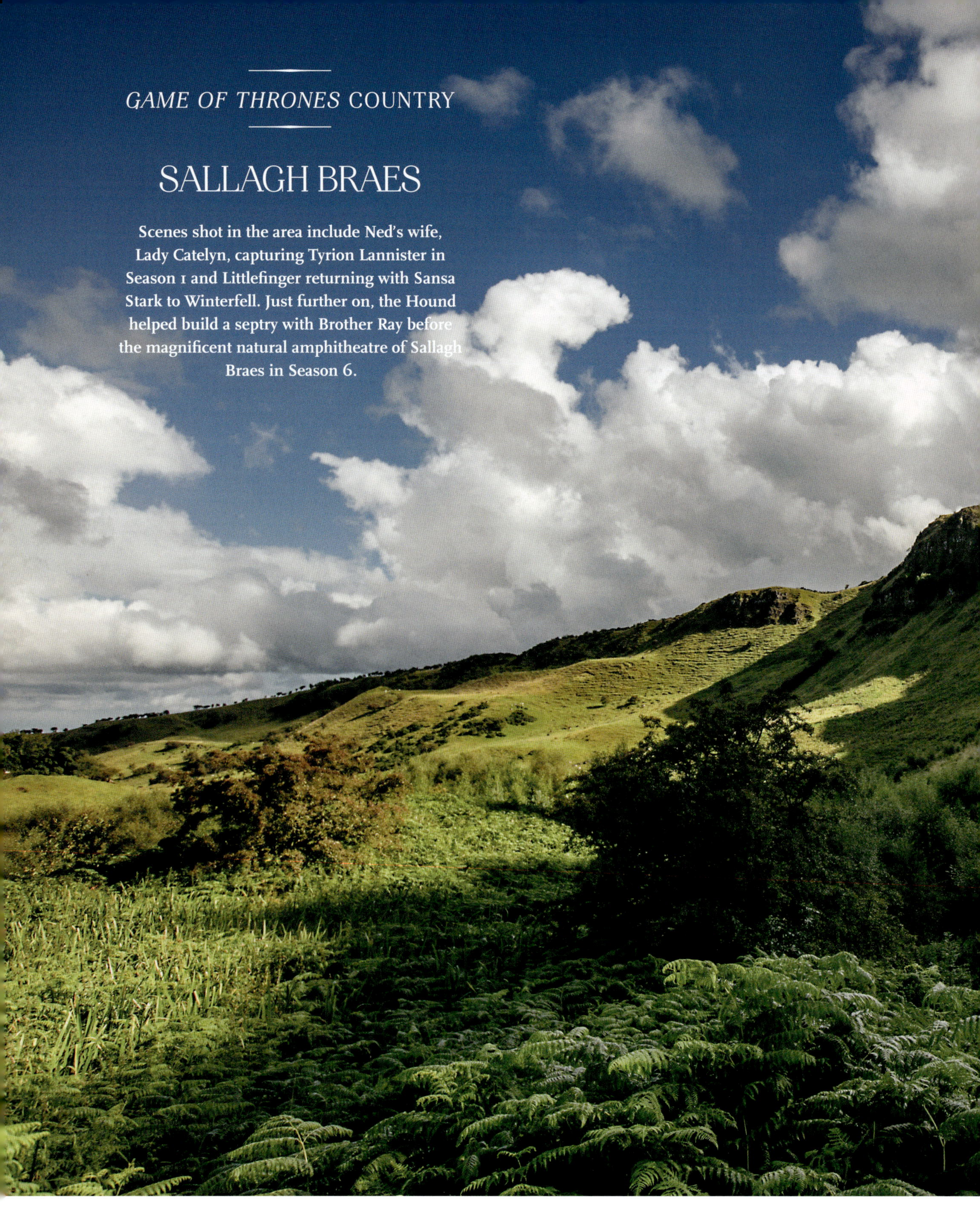

GAME OF THRONES COUNTRY

SALLAGH BRAES

Scenes shot in the area include Ned's wife, Lady Catelyn, capturing Tyrion Lannister in Season 1 and Littlefinger returning with Sansa Stark to Winterfell. Just further on, the Hound helped build a septry with Brother Ray before the magnificent natural amphitheatre of Sallagh Braes in Season 6.

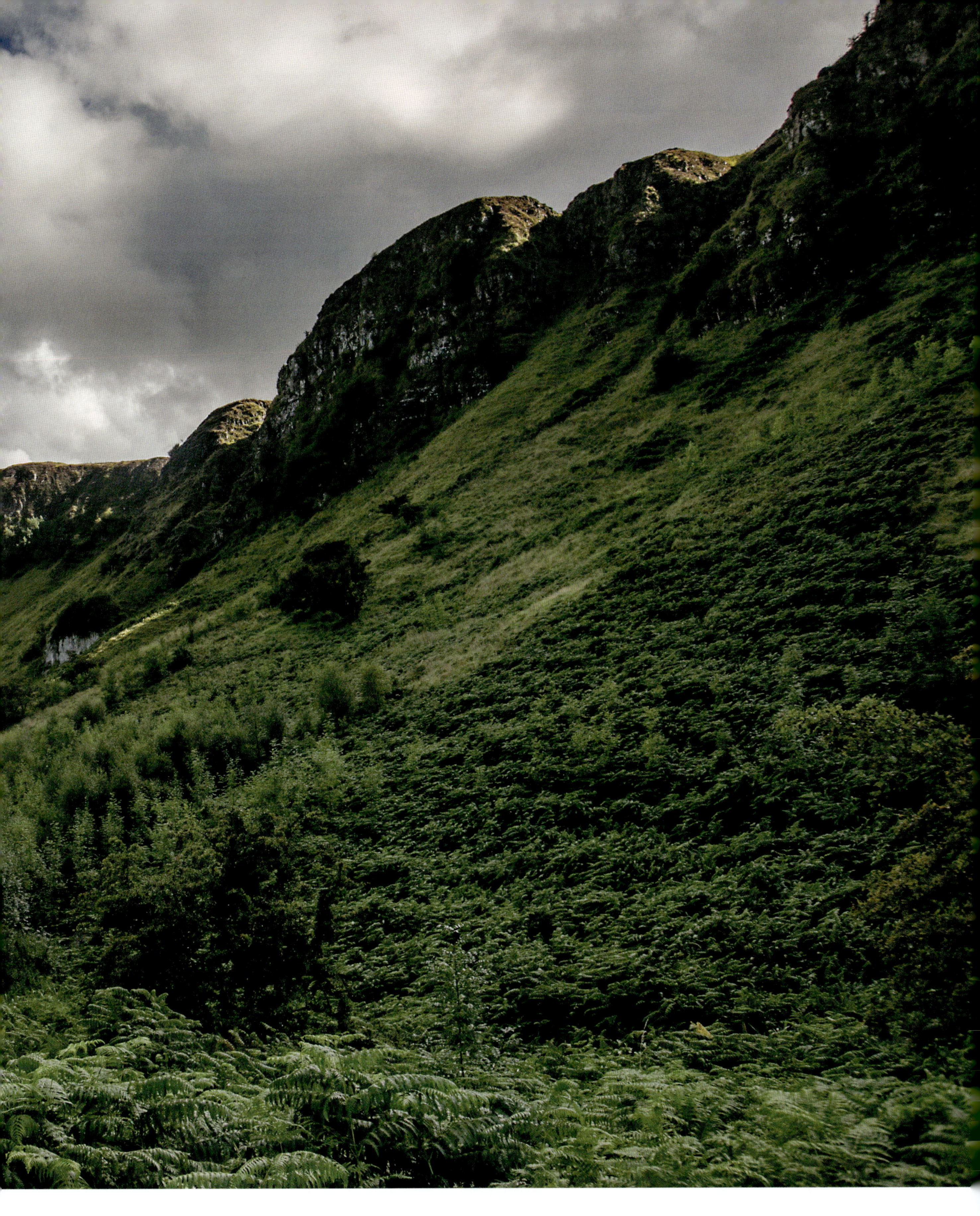

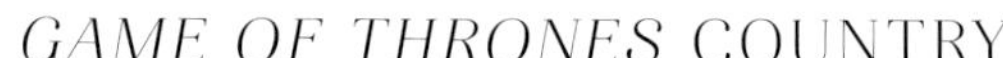

Ballygally Castle

Ballygally Castle is one of the 10 hospitality outlets in Northern Ireland that feature a *Game of Thrones* door. Theirs is No. 9, which depicts the famous battle between House Stark and House Bolton in Season 6 and features the crests of the two houses, Ramsay Bolton's hungry dogs and Winterfell Castle.

The hotel also hosts a *Game of Thrones* afternoon tea and banquet (if ordered beforehand), featuring such delights as a Dothraki trifle with mini dragon's egg, John Snow cakes and Baratheon bread, and a Westeros tomahawk steak served on a wooden platter with a Valyrian steel-inspired carving knife.

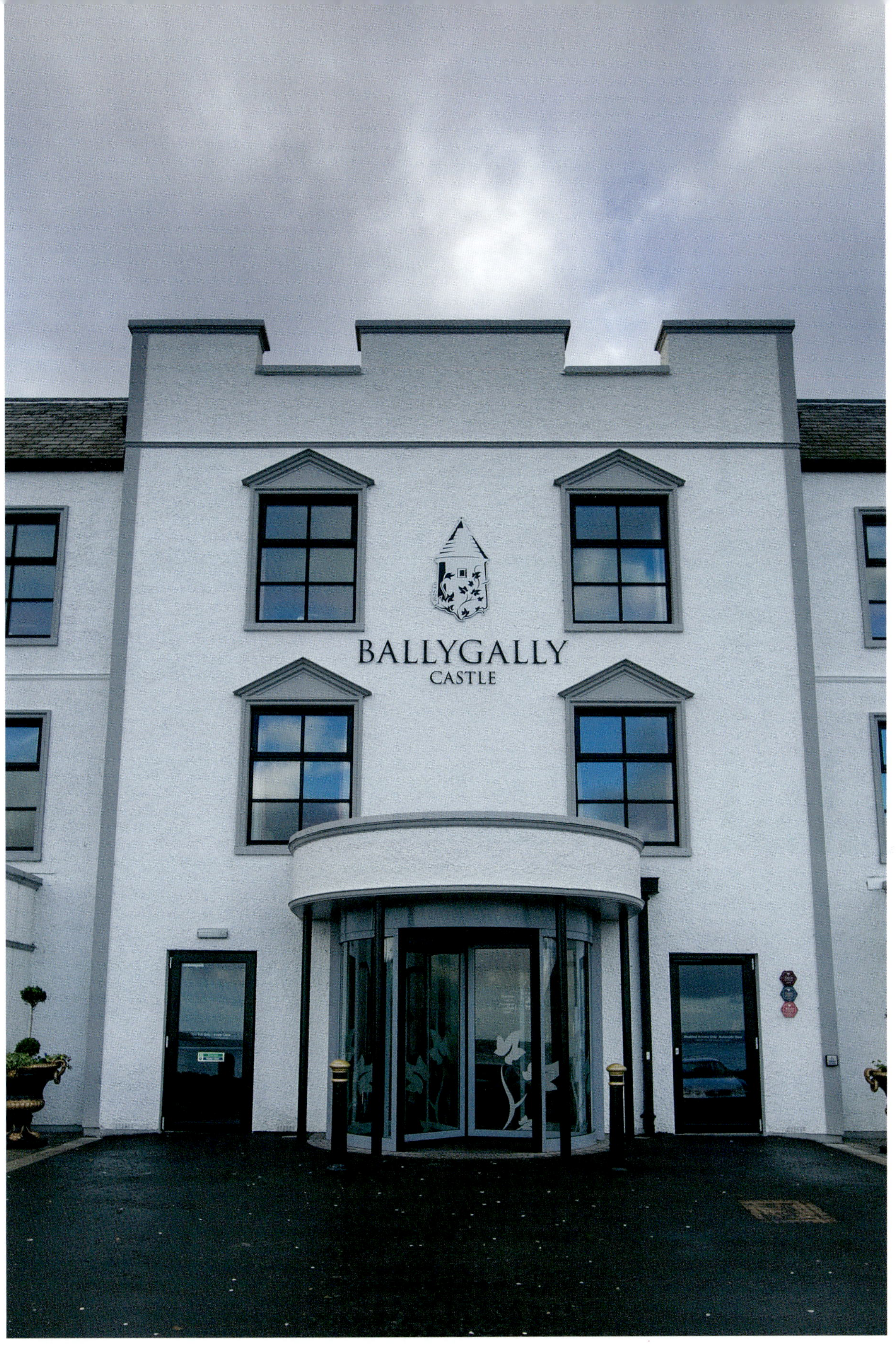
BALLYGALLY
CASTLE

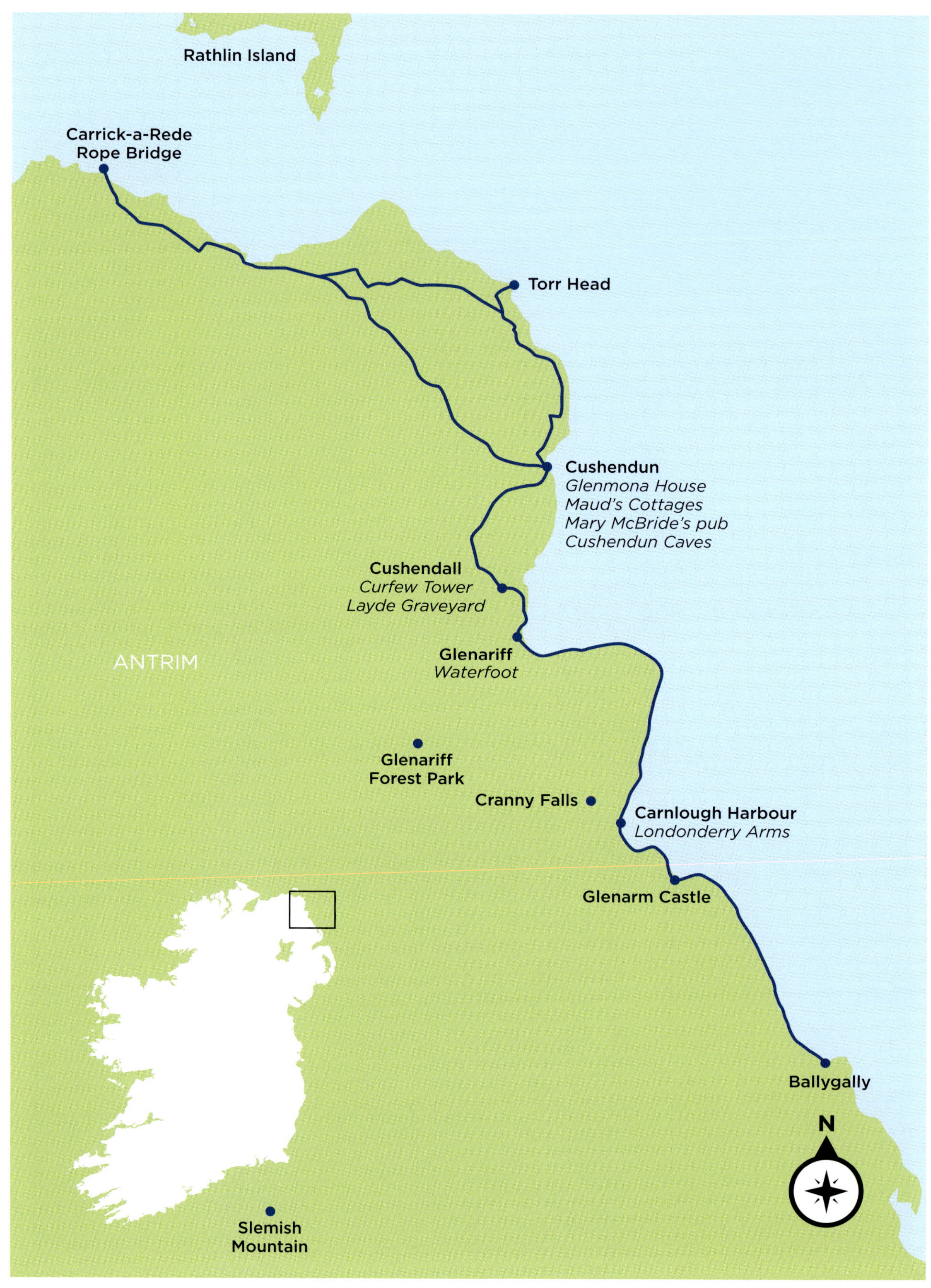

Rathlin Island
Carrick-a-Rede Rope Bridge
Torr Head
Cushendun
Glenmona House
Maud's Cottages
Mary McBride's pub
Cushendun Caves
Cushendall
Curfew Tower
Layde Graveyard
Glenariff
Waterfoot
ANTRIM
Glenariff Forest Park
Cranny Falls
Carnlough Harbour
Londonderry Arms
Glenarm Castle
Ballygally
Slemish Mountain
N

THE GLORY OF THE GLENS

Onwards now towards the wonderful Glens of Antrim, an Area of Outstanding Natural Beauty that strangely remains one of the least-known gems on the island of Ireland. On this route we pass all nine glens, but further exploration is recommended if you can find the time. From south to north, they are Glenarm, Glencloy, Glenariff, Glenballyeamon, Glenaan, Glencorp, Glendun, Glenshenk and Glentaisie.

This stage takes us to the magnificent Glenarm Castle and the picturesque Victorian harbour of Carnlough and detours to a tranquil forest with walks past cascading waterfalls and Ireland's most spiritual mountain, Slemish, once home to St Patrick.

Cushendall is at the heart of the famous Glens' traditional music scene, and lovely Cushendun is one of the most atmospheric villages on the island of Ireland.

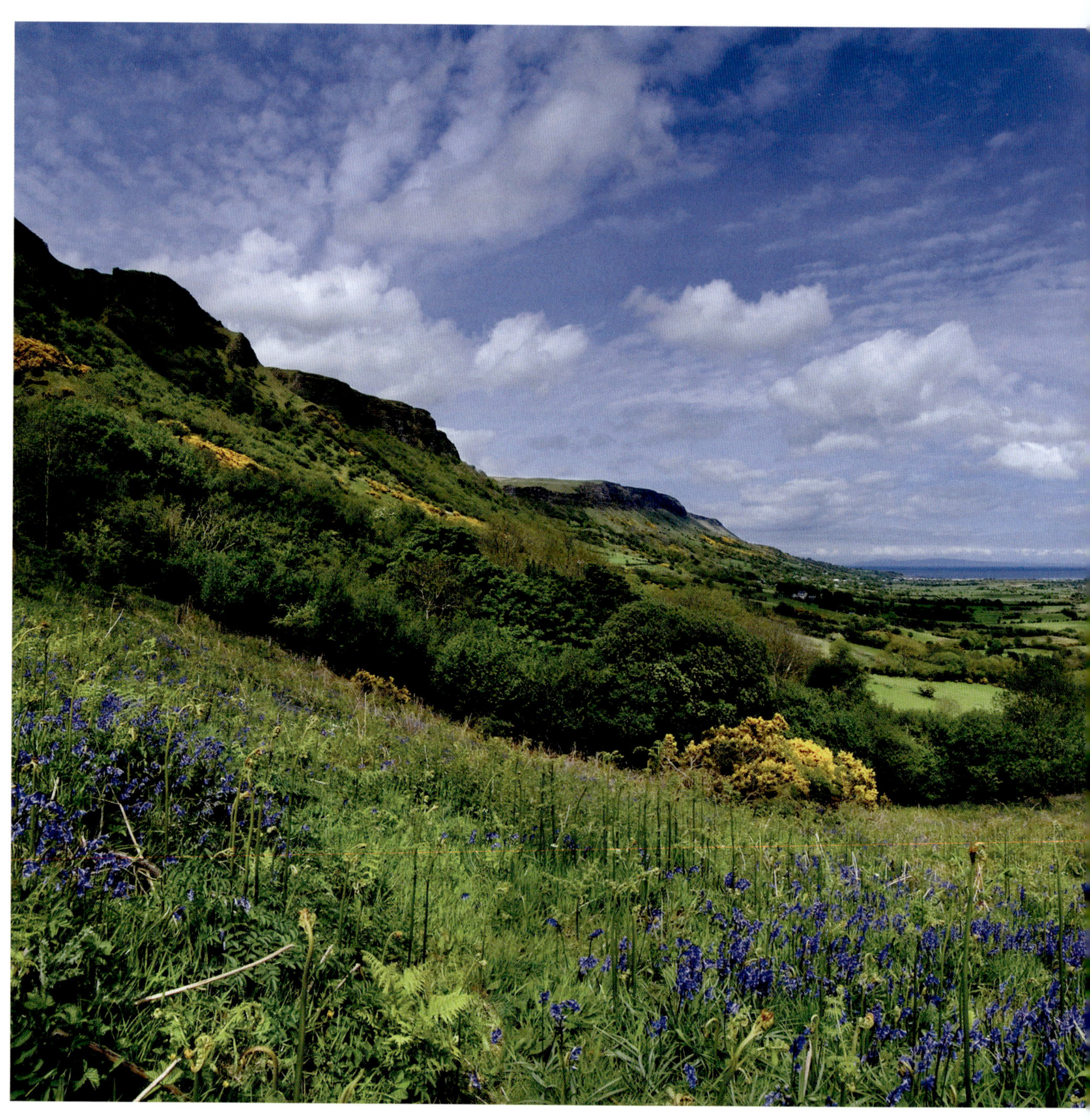

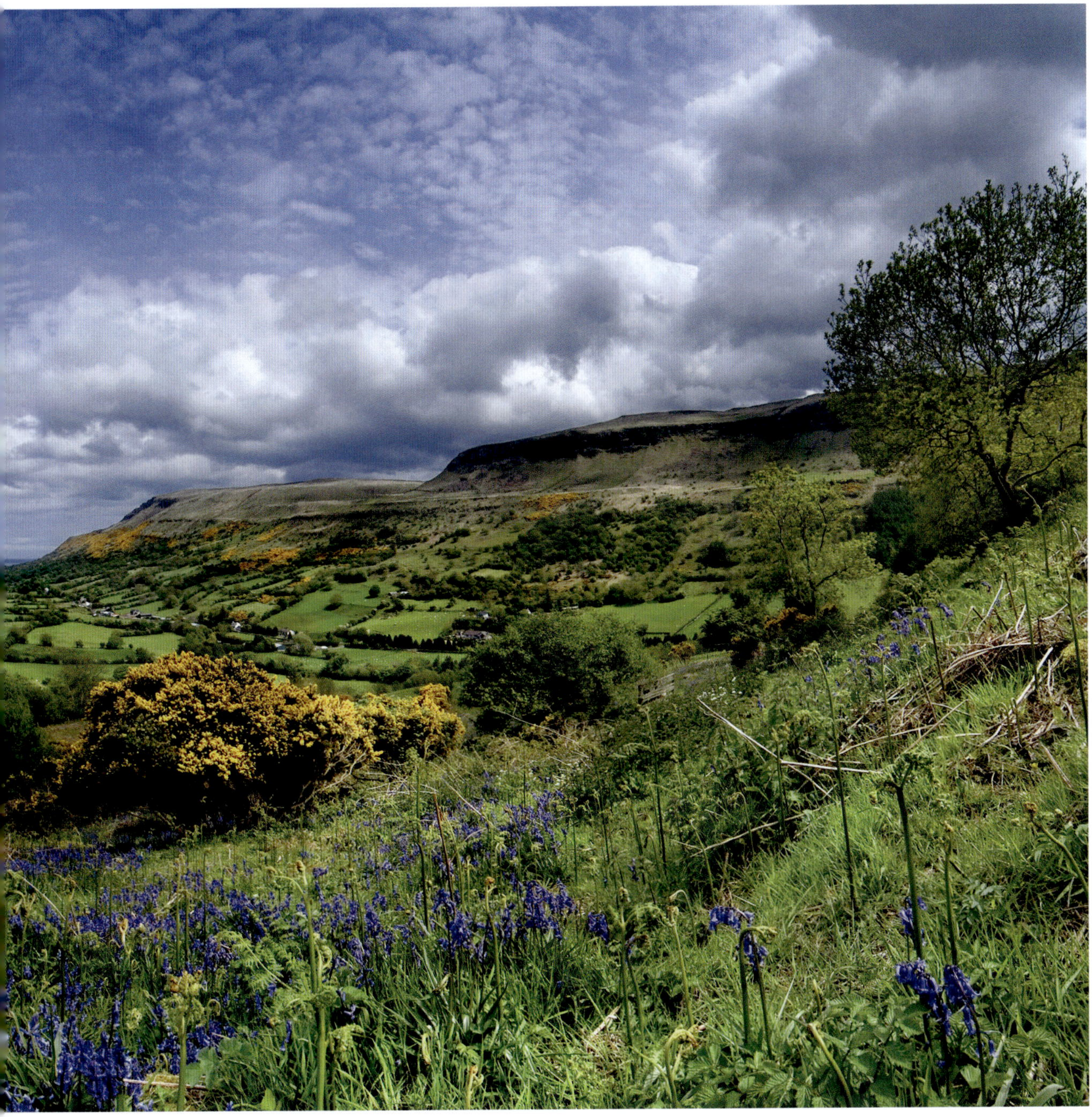

THE GLENS IN ALL THEIR GLORY

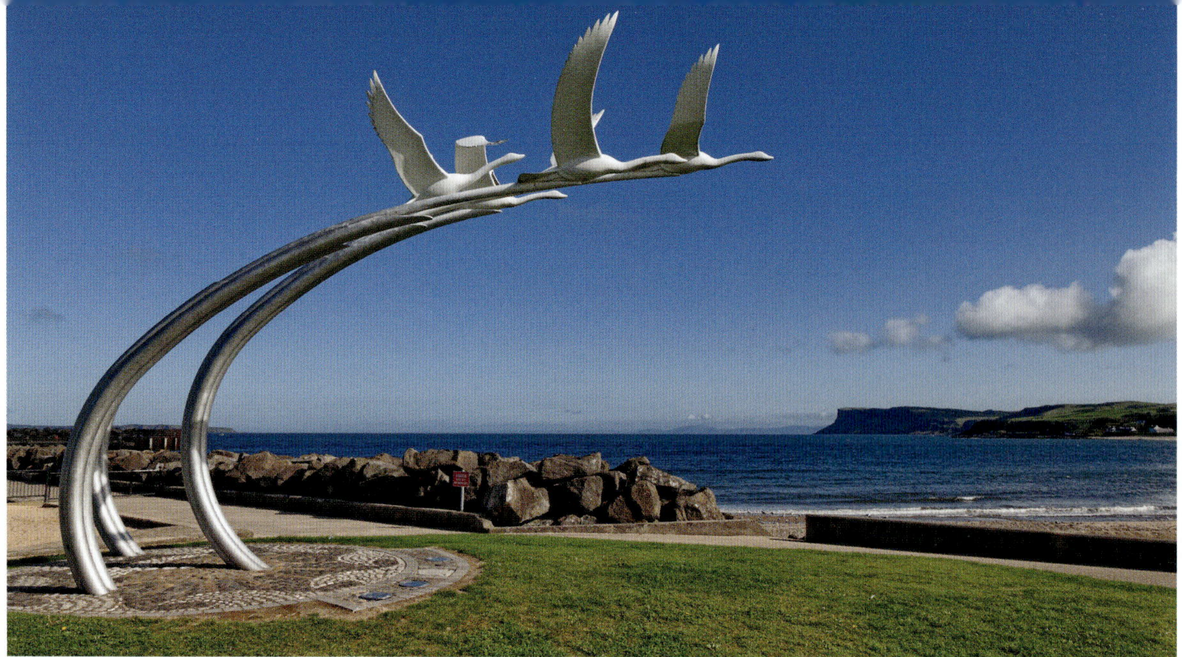

FOLKLORE OF THE GLENS

The Glens of Antrim is an area rich in myths and folklore, music and storytelling.
This is an astonishingly beautiful part of the world, but visitors don't just come to see the amazing landscape – they also want to hear the stories associated with it. There's a story in almost every stone here. Local people still have a strong connection to the land and its tales, and wouldn't cut down a fairy thorn-bush.

The Children of Lir, transformed into swans, spent 300 years on the Sea of Moyle, just off Ballycastle. They say Deirdre of the Sorrows returned from Scotland to the same area, and that the grave of the warrior poet Oisín, Finn McCool's son, lies in a Stone Age tomb in Glenaan.

The story goes that Oisín was lured to Tír na nÓg, the land of eternal youth, by a beautiful woman named Niamh. He was told that if he returned he would surely perish. But he could not keep away from the beauty of the Glens, and did indeed die when he came back to Glenaan.

People love to hear how places got their names. For instance, the beautiful Glendun ('dun' comes from the Irish for 'brown') was named when a girl came across an old woman washing little fairy war-shirts in the river, preparing for a battle in Scotland.

'How will I know if they win?', asked the girl. 'If we win, this river will run clear; if it is brown we will have lost, for the water will be stained with our blood', the woman replied.

Next day the river ran brown, and it has done so ever since. The fairies were never seen there again, and today the village is still called Cushendun (Foot of the Brown River).

The céilí tradition is still thriving here. I host a session every Saturday night where people tell stories, sing songs and play tunes. For there's stories in songs and stories in tunes too. Traditional singing and music continue to be very strong in the Glens.

Liz Weir, Irish storyteller. www.lizweir.net/www.ballyeamonbarn.com

Liz Weir's Ballyeamon Barn is situated overlooking Glenariff Forest Park. The barn offers hostel accommodation, a private apartment and regular storytelling and music sessions. Liz also organises storytelling workshops and can arrange local walking guides, horse riding, yoga and 'pamper' sessions for visitors.

MUSIC OF THE GLENS

There are few more exhilarating experiences, even on this journey, than a night of superb traditional music in an Irish pub. The Glens is renowned for such sessions and, fortunately, the finest of these are to be found along our route.

For all the gratitude we must feel towards engineer William Bald and his extraordinary achievement in building the coastal road and opening up this wonderful area, it was actually the absence of such a road for so long that allowed the Glens to retain its unique Gaelic culture. Before the arrival of the road and the influx of visitors, the tightly knit communities of the area had developed a thriving cultural life, from dancing, arts, crafts and music to hurling, a Gaelic sport with ancient origins played at lightning-fast pace with a stick (hurley) and a ball (sliotar). Irish was widely spoken as a first language.

One reason this traditional culture continues to this day is the Feis na nGleann, which was first held back in 1904. It was founded by a group of people who were determined to preserve the culture of the area, which was then in some danger of dying out.

A popular movement known as the Gaelic Revival, spearheaded by literary figures like the great Irish poet W.B. Yeats, had been organised to renew pride and interest in the Irish language and Irish culture in the late 1800s.

The Feis na nGleann was instigated by an influential group of largely local people. Not least among these was the remarkable figure of Ada McNeill, English-born first cousin of staunch unionist Ronald John McNeill, Baron Cushendun. Her friend Roger Casement, whose family house, Magherintemple, is just outside Ballycastle, was another supporter of the Feis. Casement was executed for treason after trying to smuggle arms to Ireland to support the Easter Rising of 1916. Eoin MacNeill from Glenarm, who gave the order to countermand the Easter Rising following the capture of those arms, was also an important influence on the Feis.

The first Feis took place in Glenariff in June 1904, and popular competitions were held to encourage the development of Irish music locally.

Today, organisations like Baile an Chaistil Comhaltas Ceoltoiri Eireann in Ballycastle, the Glens of Antrim Comhaltas Branch (Comhaltas Glinnte Aontroma) in Cushendall and the Counties Antrim and Derry Country Fiddlers Association oversee the continuing mission to preserve the traditional music of the region.

You can enjoy this wonderful cultural heritage in a number of ways. The Feis na nGleann is held each summer at venues in Ballycastle, Cushendall and the vicinity. Traditional music is an important feature of the Rathlin Sound Maritime Festival, held each May/June at Rathlin Island and Ballycastle.

As for those exhilarating sessions, there are three stand-out locations along the route, all of which can be enjoyed throughout the year. On Wednesday nights the place to be is O'Connor's Bar in Ann Street, Ballycastle, where the millennia-long Scottish influence on the Glens can be clearly heard in the music. On Friday nights, there's a famous session at the House of McDonnell on Castle Street in Ballycastle, one of the oldest pubs in the Glens. In Cushendall, renowned as the heart of Glens culture, you can enjoy sessions on Fridays, Saturdays and Sundays at Johnny Joe's in Mill Street, run by the McCollam family since the 1800s (now run by Joe, son of Annie McCollam, and Sheila Blaney).

GLENARM

In past centuries this coastline would have been dotted with endless nets to capture Atlantic salmon on their return to their native spawning grounds. Today, there is really just one such enterprise; however, it is world-famous for the quality of its smoked salmon.

As you drive into Glenarm, look towards the sea and you may catch a glimpse of the floating salmon nets of Glenarm Salmon Fishery, providers of organic smoked salmon to leading restaurants and shops in the UK. Only just, though. In 2007 their stocks were nearly wiped out by a vast army of mauve stinger jellyfish, apparently some way off course. It is said that three miles of water was nothing but red and purple, reflecting the sheer density of the stingers.

If you've time to explore the village, which claims to be the oldest in Northern Ireland thanks to a 12th-century charter, park near the white limestone harbour on the right.

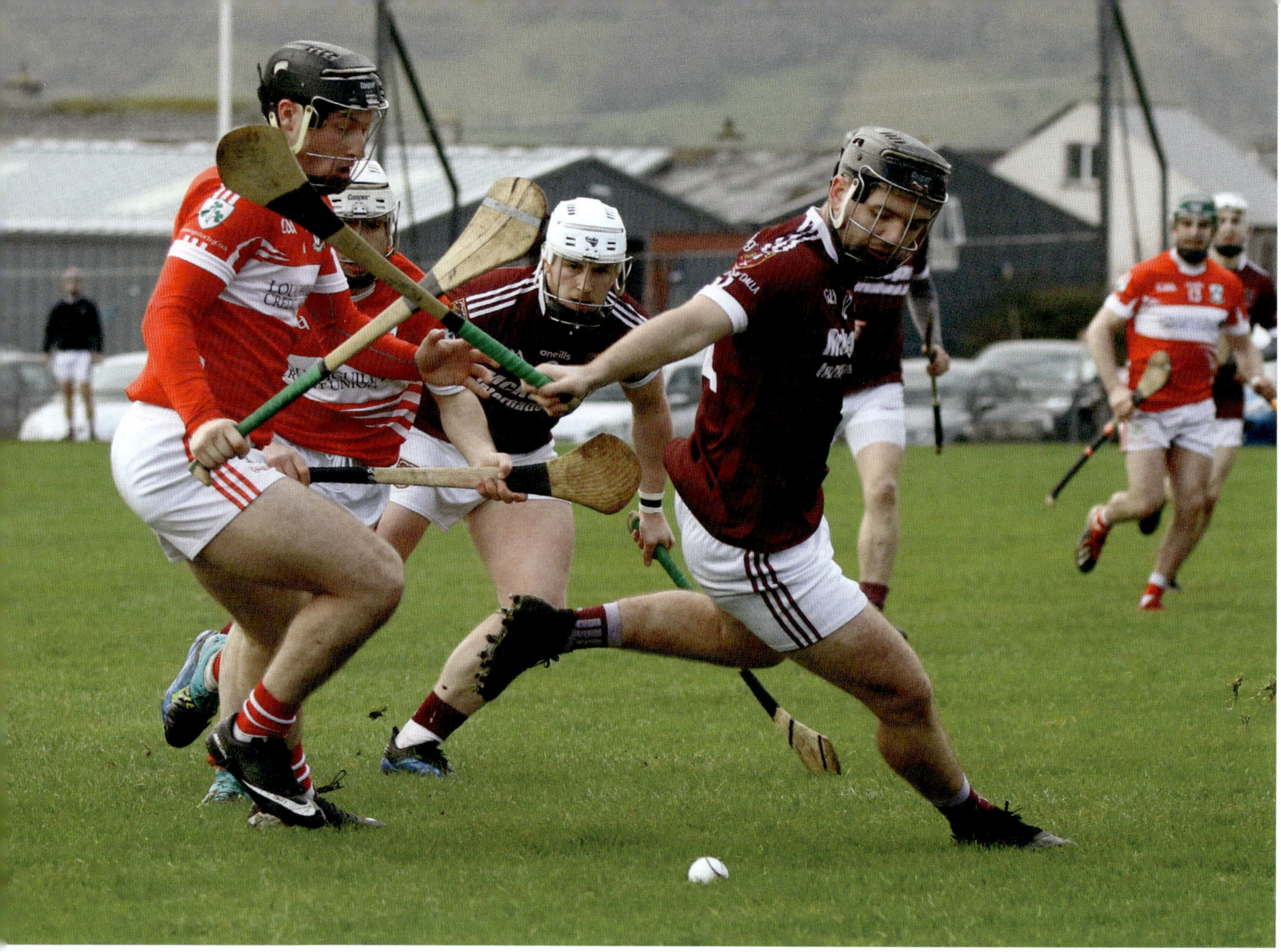

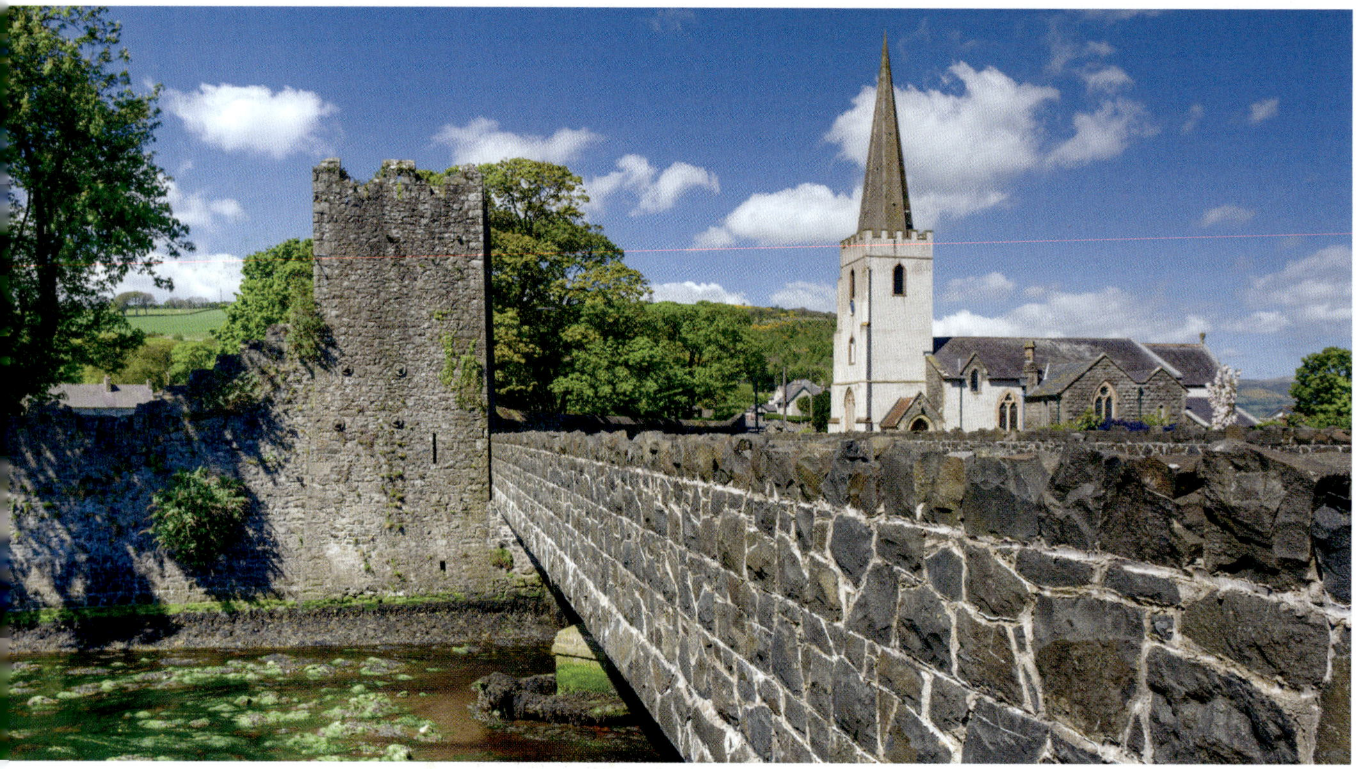

TOP: A HURLING MATCH BETWEEN LOUGHGIEL SHAMROCKS AND CUSHENDUN. BOTTOM: GLENARM

Steenson's Jewellery

Make your first stop in Glenarm the jewellery workshop belonging to Bill and Christina Steenson – a must for lovers of beautifully crafted jewellery and *Game of Thrones*, for which they produced many wonderful pieces, including Joffrey's crown. They are happy to let you see their craftspeople at work; also inspect some of the replica pieces relating to *Game of Thrones*. You can buy pendants and brooches inspired by the TV series. How about a direwolf, House of Targaryen or Lannister pendant?

HOME OF THE MACDONNELLS

Beautiful Glenarm Castle has been home to the MacDonnell clan for many centuries. It's still owned by the family, currently under the stewardship of Viscount and Viscountess Dunluce, Randal and Aurora MacDonnell, who have transformed the grounds into a much-loved attraction.

The MacDonnell family were once 'Lords of the Route', and though this didn't refer to the Causeway Coastal Route (it actually meant the 'Rout' – the private army of their predecessors, the McQuillans), the territory they owned covered much of the same area.

There has been a castle here since 1242, but it was nearly three centuries before the MacDonnell clan claimed it for their own. They built a castle in 1636 but it was soon burned down by an invading Scots army – a not untypical occurrence in those turbulent times.

For a while the MacDonnells returned to Dunluce Castle, towering over the Atlantic along the coast from here and whose ruins we will see later. It is said that they only left after their kitchen hurtled into the crashing waves below, taking some members of staff with it!

It was the Fifth Earl who transformed the ruined Glenarm Castle into one of Ireland's finest palladium houses in the mid-1700s.

And with some refinements, extensions and redevelopments, that's pretty much what we see today. You can walk around it on the Castle Trail and even visit on selected dates. Groups of 10 or more can book tours.

Pride of place, though, goes to the beautifully restored early 1800s walled garden created by Randal's ancestor, Countess Anne – four acres of tranquil paths and wildly colourful plants and flowers. The castle can be glimpsed from the man-made mound here, as well as the fruit trees and the beautiful glen beyond.

The Walled Garden Tea Room, elegantly fashioned from the old mushroom house, is worth a visit. Glenarm Shorthorn Beef, among the finest you can taste, produced by the MacDonnells is served here (and available to buy), as is Glenarm smoked salmon, from the company rebuilt with the involvement of the MacDonnells. It may be worth buying it here too, as the next nearest option is Harrods!

Before you leave Glenarm, it's a worth a quick visit to the 18th-century St Patrick's Church, the oldest Gothic-style church of its kind in Ireland, which features some lovely stained-glass windows. It was built in the 1760s on the site of a 15th-century Franciscan friary, of which sadly little remains.

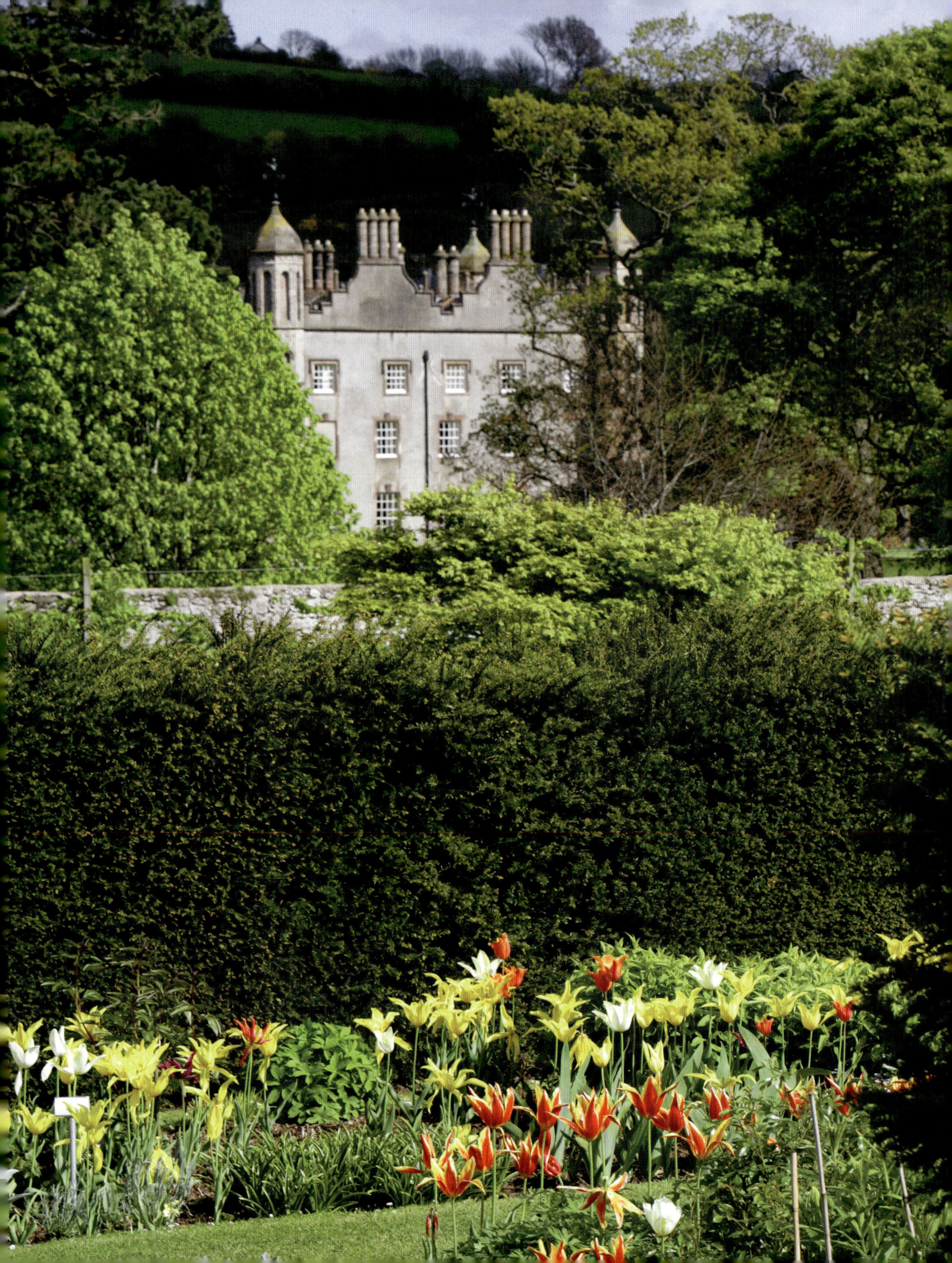

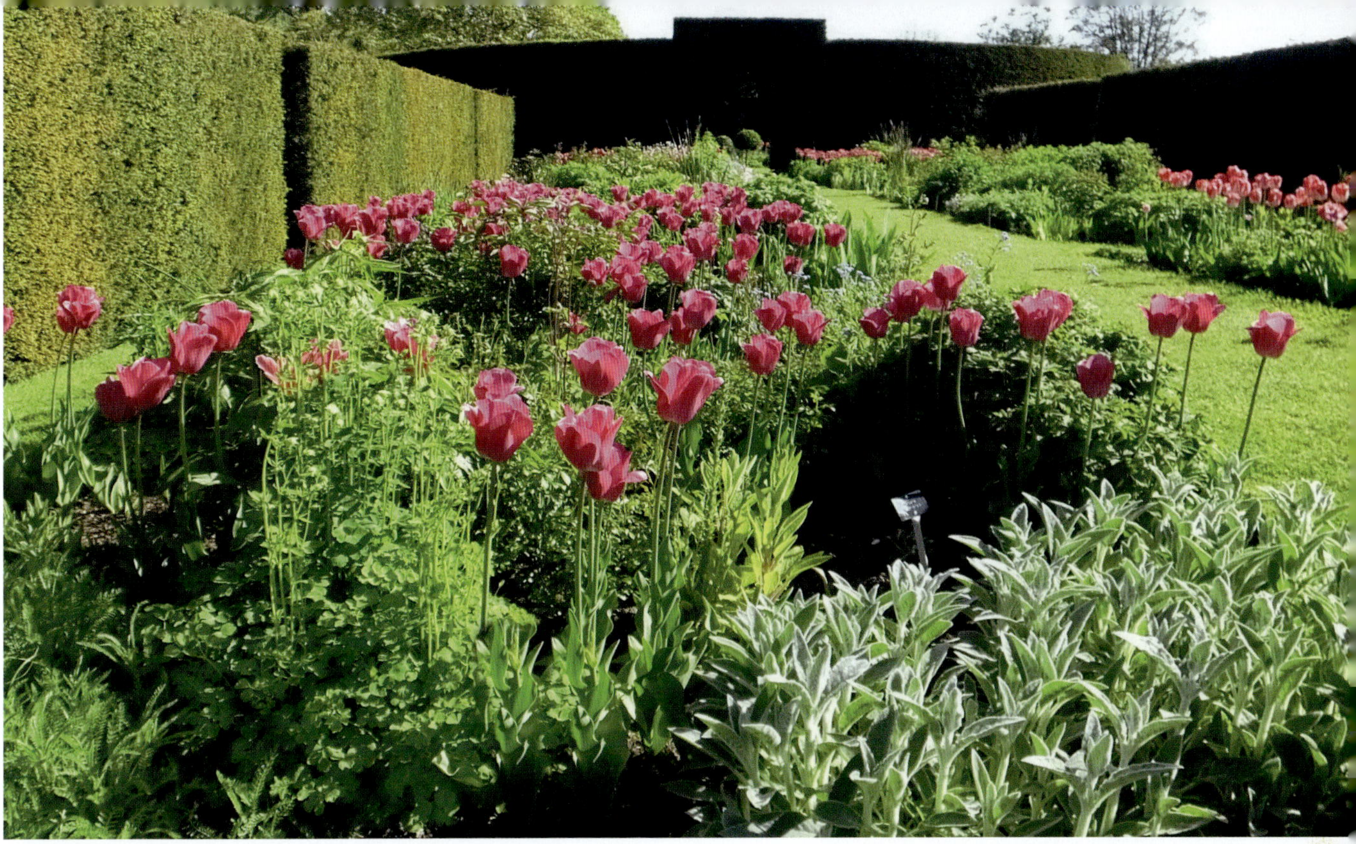

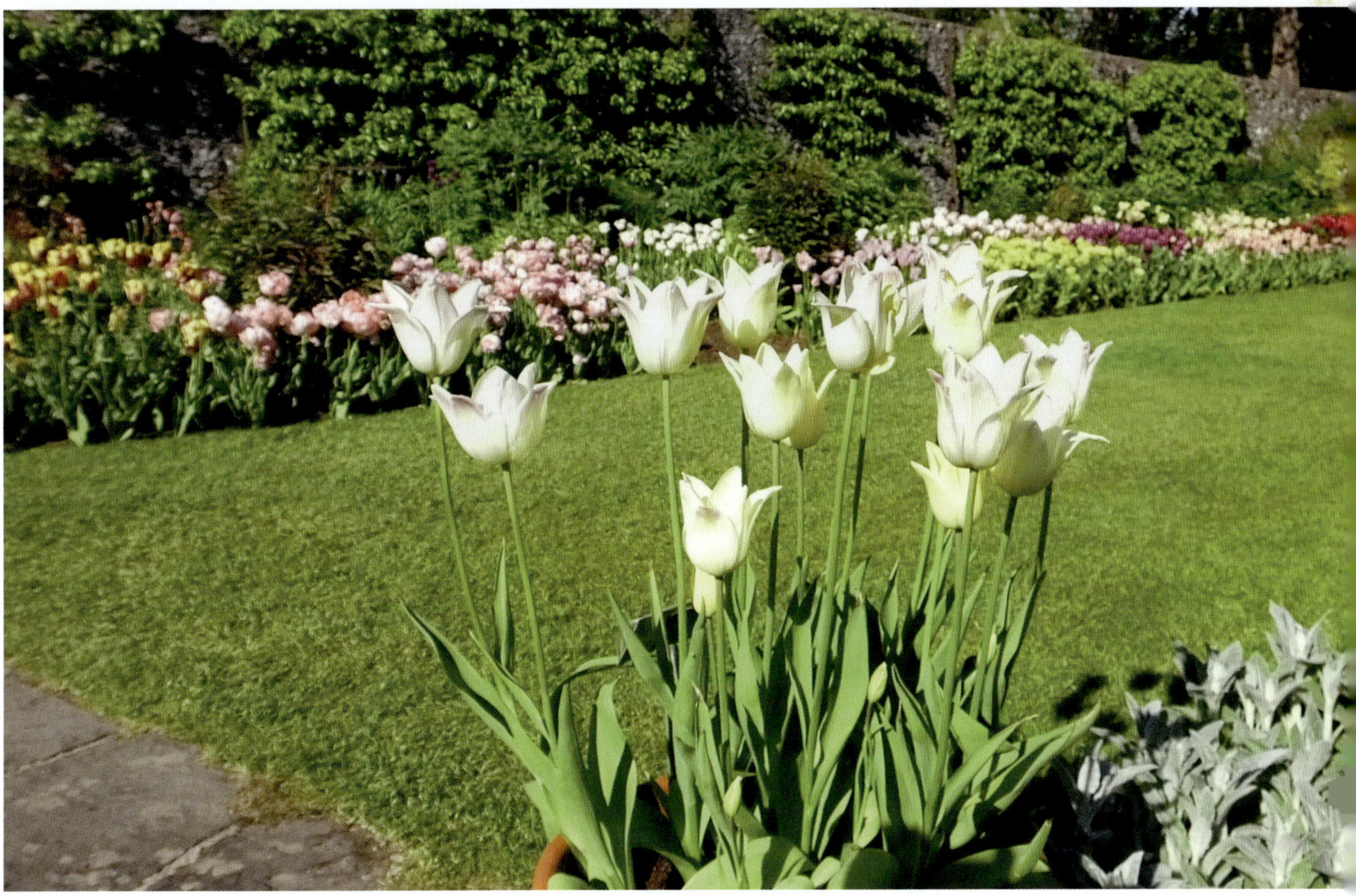

GLENARM CASTLE, WHICH HOSTS A POPULAR
TULIP FESTIVAL

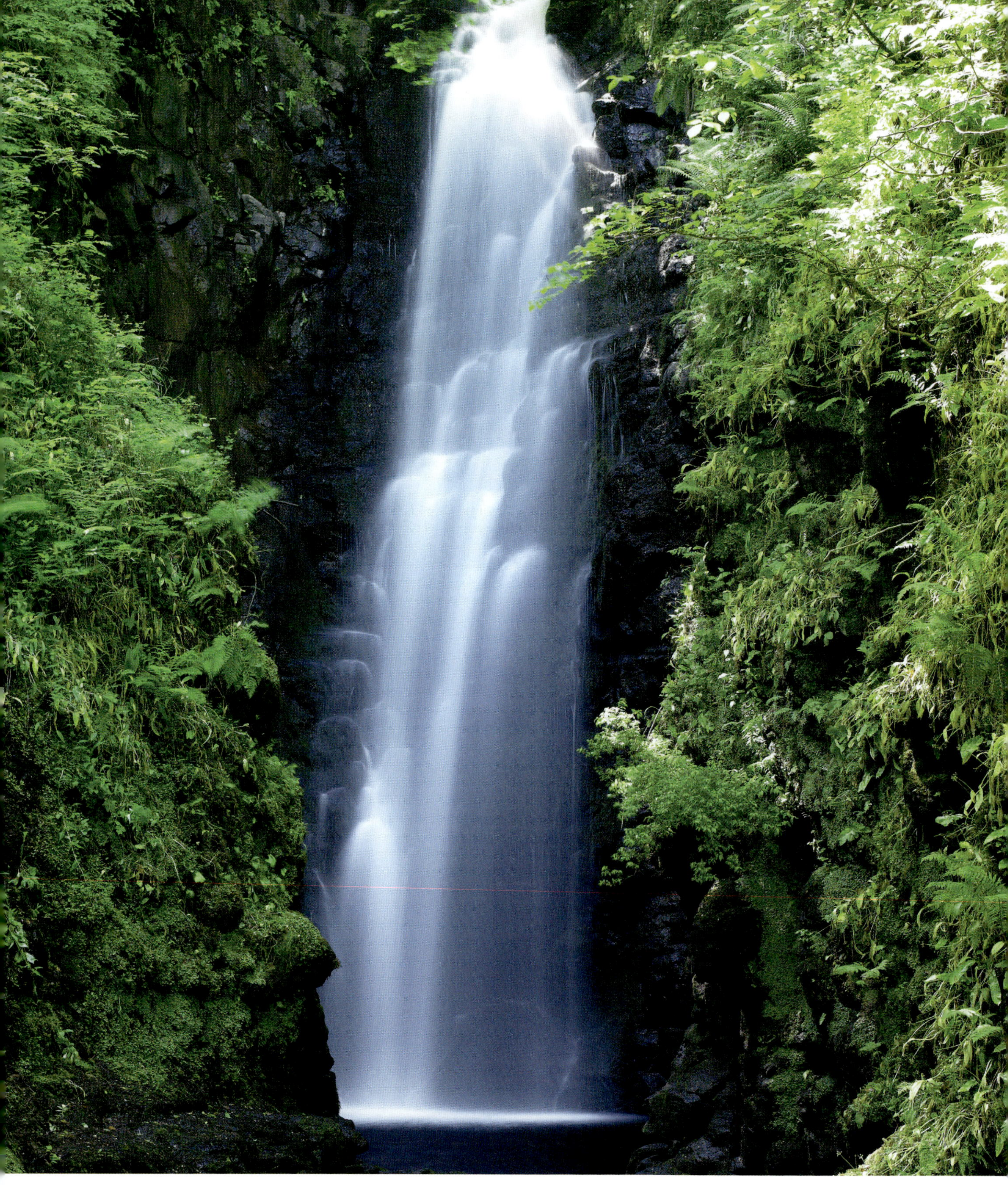

CRANNY FALLS

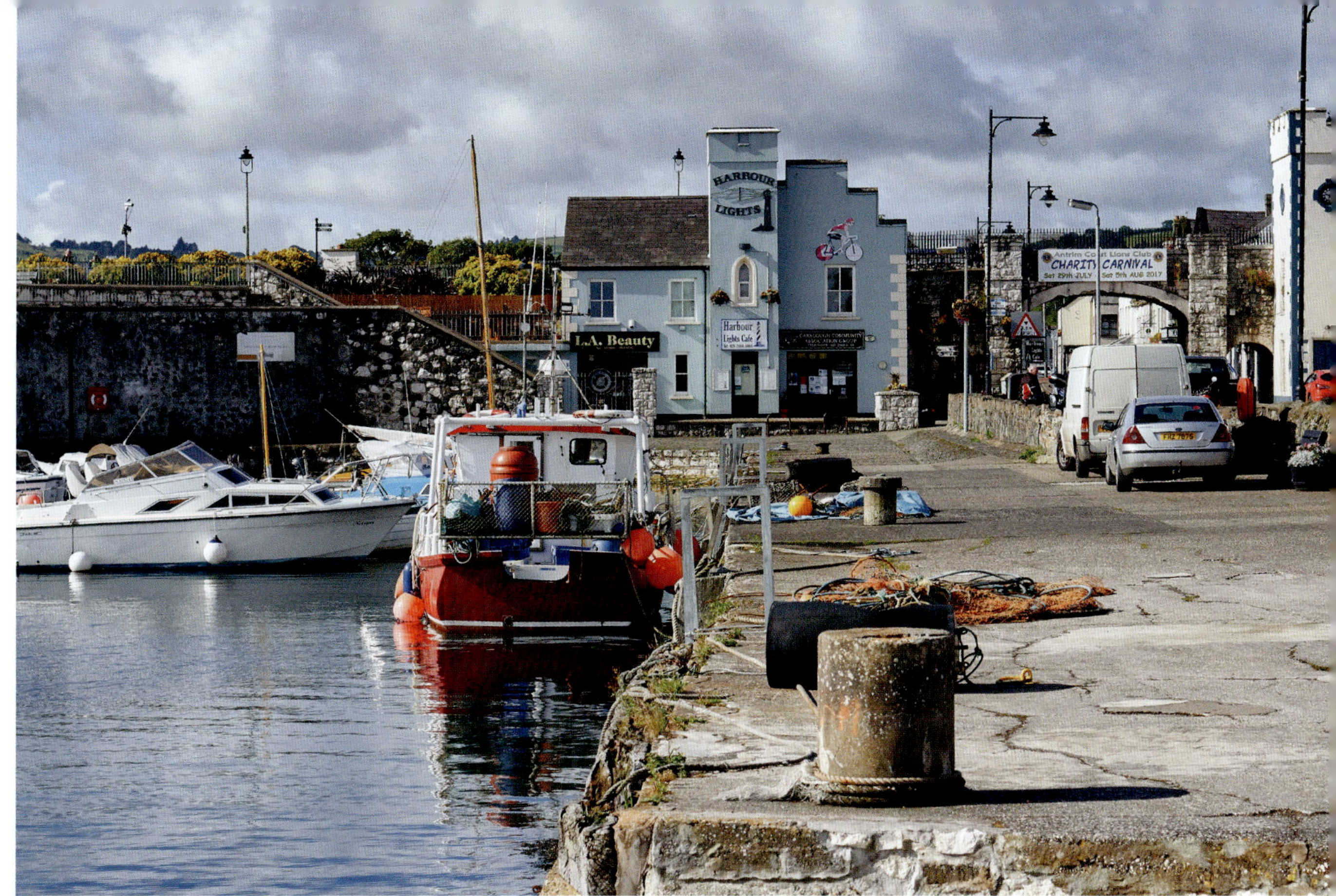

CARNLOUGH HARBOUR

CARNLOUGH

CHURCHILL'S INN AND AYRA STARK'S DUCKING

The lovely little harbour here was developed by Lord and Lady Londonderry in the 1850s (the latter having inherited this land as a member of the MacDonnell family). They used the harbour to export the local limestone and built a railway to bring it down to the ships. Climb up the steps overlooking the harbour and you can follow the path of the track up to Gortin Quarry, ending at the spectacular Cranny Waterfall.

You can check out the history of the town – birthplace of football manager Brendan Rodgers – at an exhibition in the Hub, the old Town Hall, opposite the small harbour. There you'll learn about the transformation Lord and Lady Londonderry created, turning a sleepy village into a thriving industrial enterprise. Its opening hours are limited to weekend afternoons.

Lady Londonderry also built the Londonderry Arms, which for some generations has been owned by the O'Neill family. If you're lucky, owner Denise or her father Raymond will tell you some of the hotel's history, such as its close association with Ireland's most famous racehorse, Arkle, the long seat in the Churchill Lounge that had been destined for *Titanic* and the many connections to one-time owner of the hotel Winston Churchill.

Enjoy a lovely lunch here – maybe an open Glenarm organic smoked salmon sandwich on wheaten bread made daily to the secret O'Neill's family recipe – in one of their delightful antique-filled Georgian rooms.

If you time your visit for May, it might coincide with the annual Round the Rock competition, which features the popular local tradition of gig racing. Designed by local builders and crewed by four oarsmen (traditionally local fishermen), gigs are light, fast narrowboats that were originally used to meet arriving schooners. These races have drawn big crowds for centuries.

CARNLOUGH HARBOUR/BRAAVOS

Local fisherman Davy Smyth's boat tours leave from the same stone steps Arya Stark ascended in Season 6 after being stabbed by the Waif and diving into the water in Braavos. If you want a fuller account of that day, pop in to the nearby Londonderry Arms to sample their famous collection of Irish whiskeys, and ask to be shown the chair Maisie Williams, who plays Arya Stark, sat on between filming. You'll know it – she wrote a message on the back!

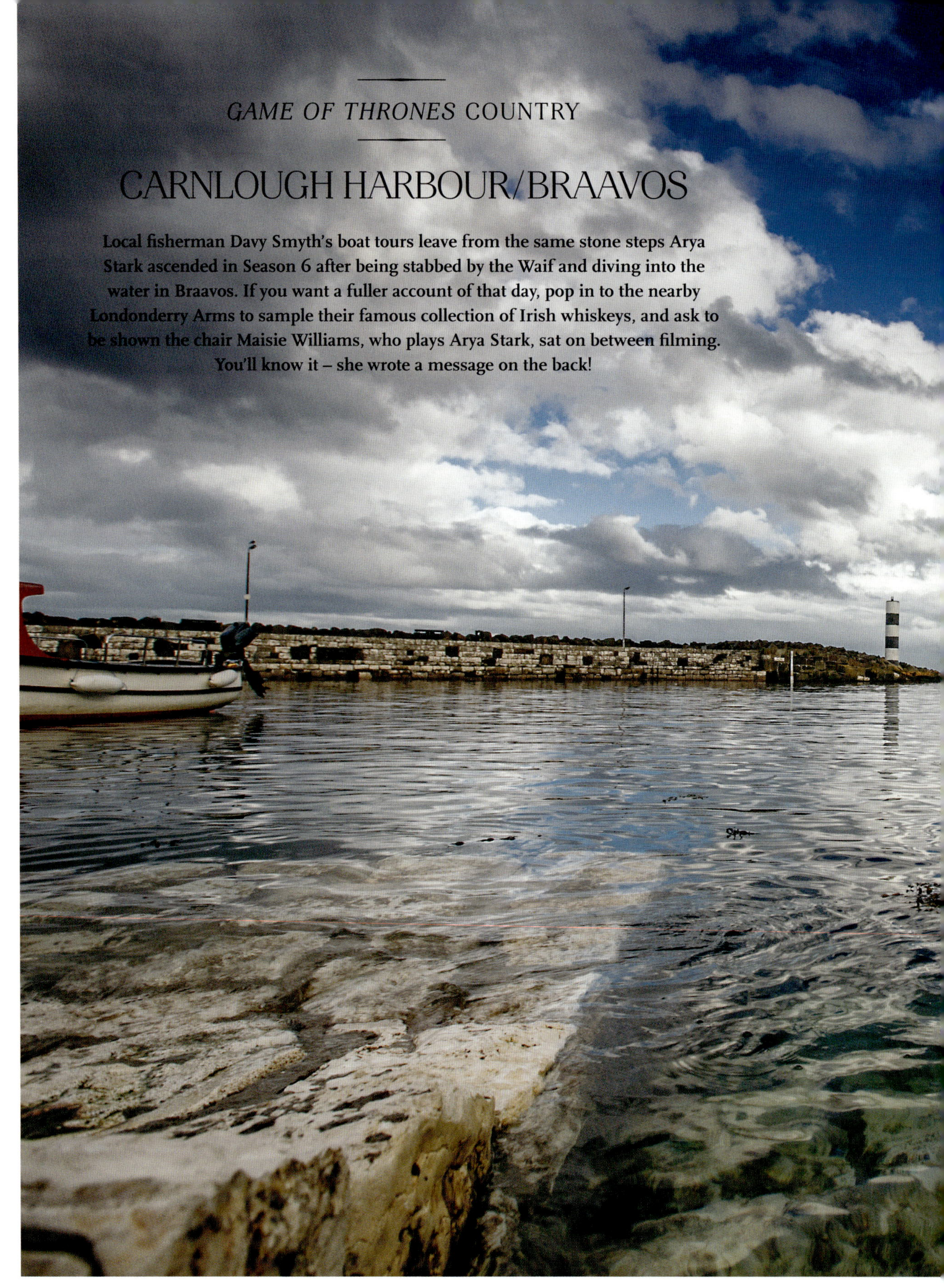

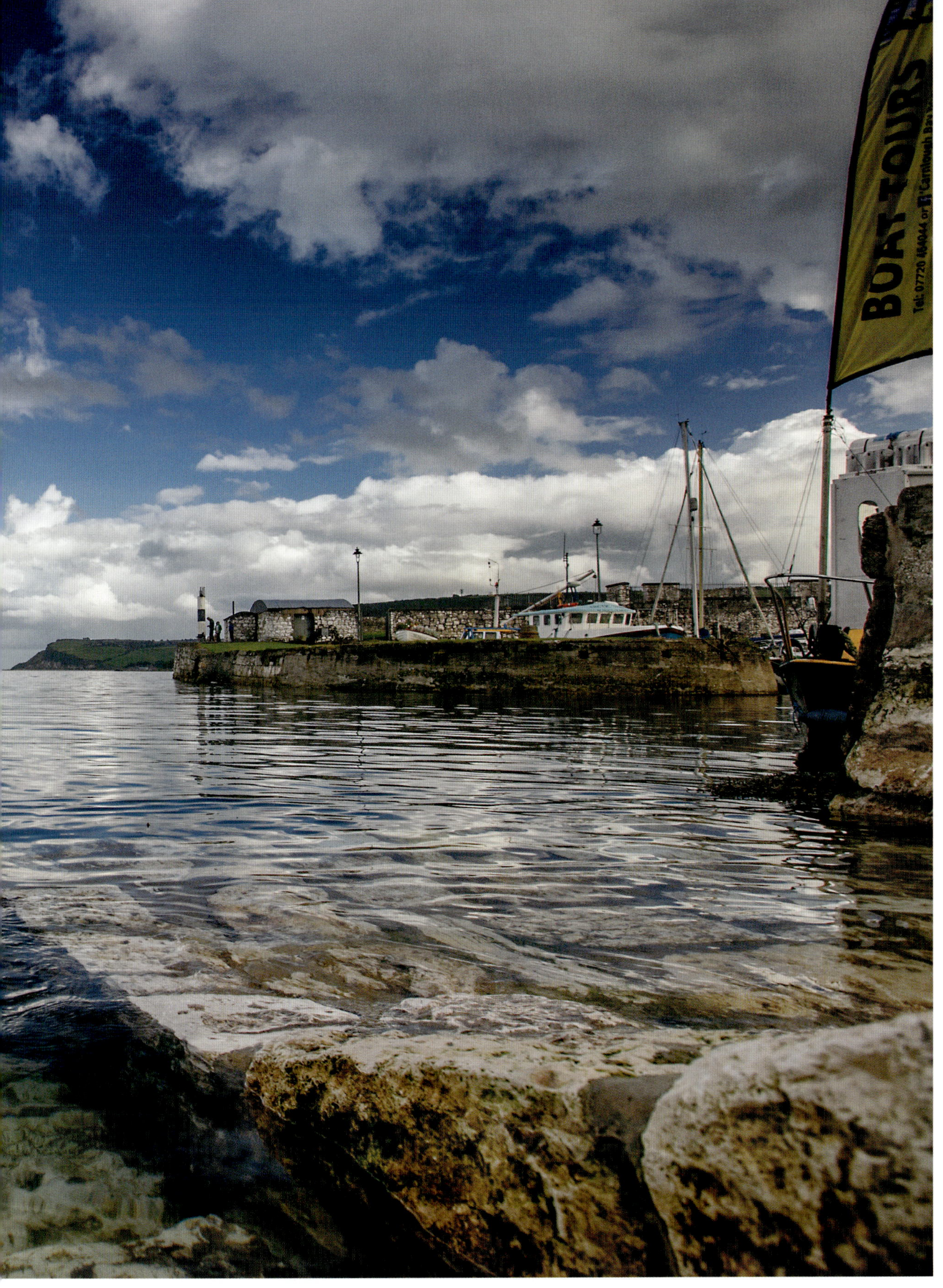
BOAT TOURS
Tel: 07720 484044 or f Carnlough Bay

RUNESTONE

Galboly was the location for Runestone in *Game of Thrones*. Here, in Season 5, Sansa Stark and Petyr Baelis (Littlefinger) visit Lord Yohn Royce and watch the young Robin Arryn practise his swordmanship. Runestone also features in Season 6, when Littlefinger convinces Robin to take an army to Winterfell to help Sansa Stark.

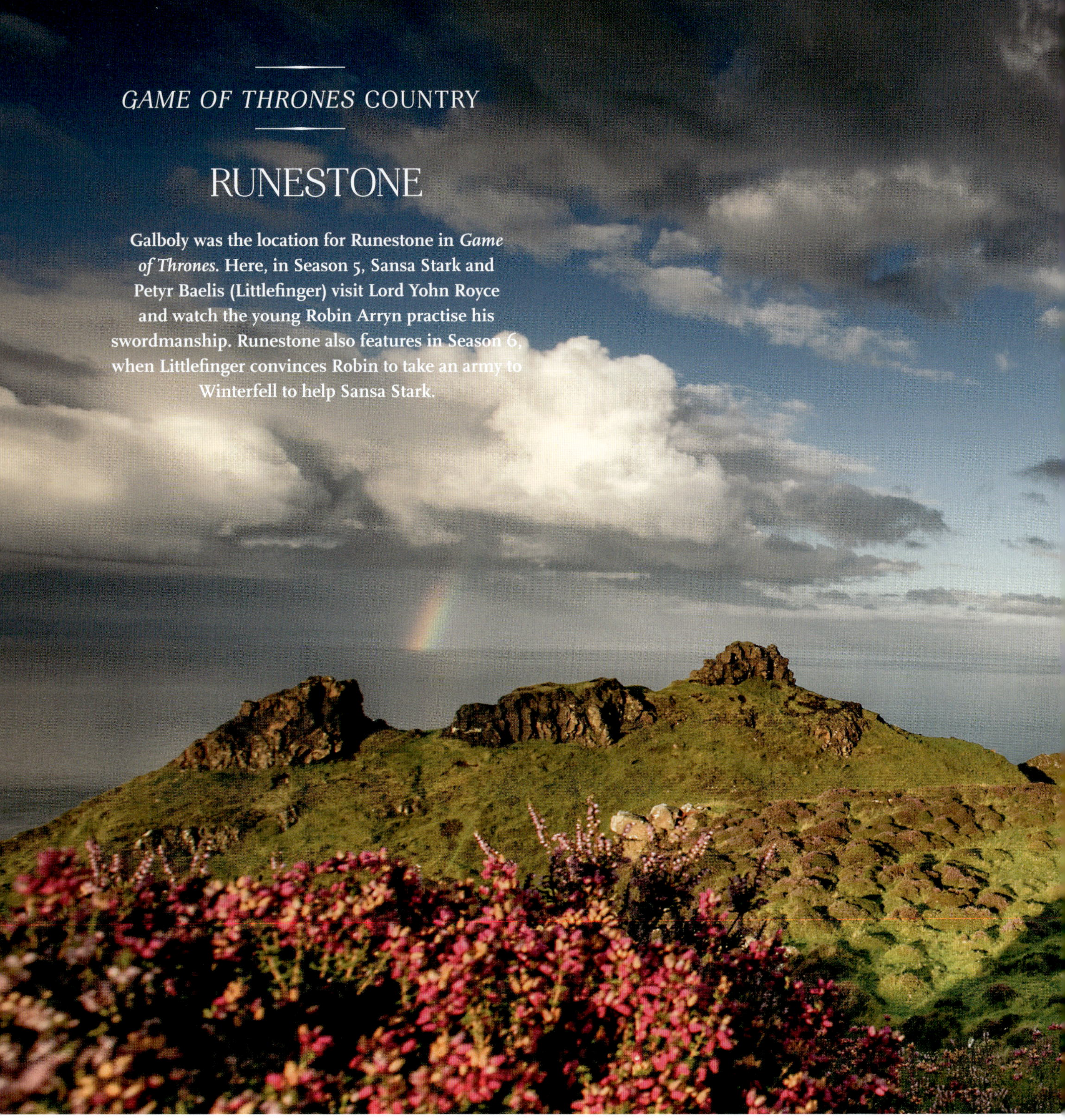

GALBOLY, THE HIDDEN VILLAGE

This is one of the most haunting places you will discover on this route, and one of the hardest to find. Even at its height this tiny village was isolated. Today, the substantial ruins, in a beautiful location in hills beneath the Garron Plateau, seem from a lost world. The closest village is Glenariff, but that doesn't help much – best to ask a local for instructions.

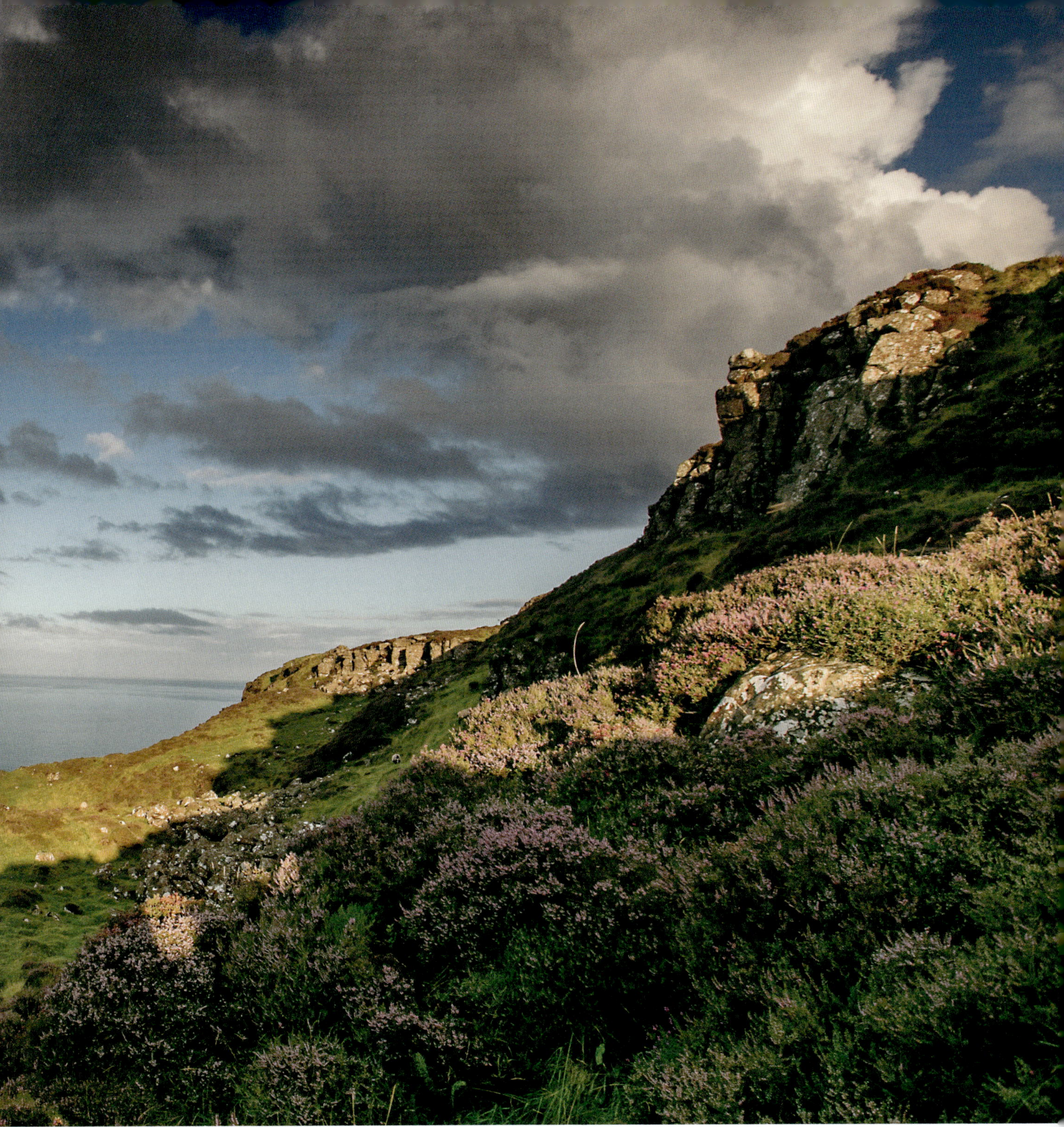

Galboly's last inhabitant was in situ quite recently, but its peak would have been in the early 1800s, when over 60 people lived here. Find it on a sunny day and you will truly feel its magic – not just a hidden village but a lost world. Please note that this is private property and can only be accessed with the owner's permission.

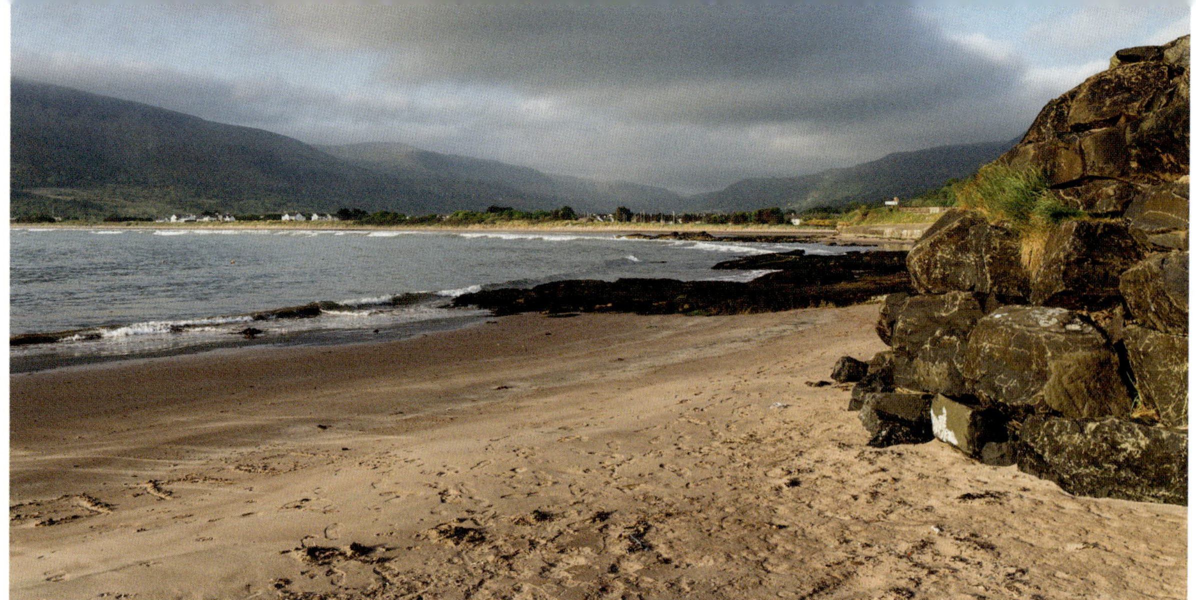

GLENARIFF

As we head for Glenariff/Waterfoot, two villages that have more or less merged into one, look out for hedgerows covered in striking red fuschia and yellow gorse, meandering bays and harbours, tiny hamlets and sheep grazing on hills.

Just before you reach the village of Glenariff, you will pass the White Arch. Actually it is no longer an arch but two sides of one, on either side of the road, that once supported the bridge that carried the railway track of the Glenariff Iron Ore and Harbour Company railway to the water. Waterfoot, by the way, is renowned for its lovely mile-long beach.

GLENARIFF FOREST PARK

A detour from our route, but surely worth it! B.D. Wise, the engineer who created The Gobbins, was responsible for developing this tranquil area as a tourism resort with a series of innovative features, including scenic paths and rustic bridges. He even built a tearoom with a dedicated dark room for photographers!

The exhibition here could do with an upgrade – in another country, this would be dressed up as a major tourist attraction – but perhaps that is part of its charm. The park covers around 1,000 hectares and a variety of scenery from wooded glades to waterfalls and lakes. It's possible to swim in some locations too.

Finest of the walks here is the three-mile Waterfall Walk, for which you follow the way-marked trail down the steps, along the boardwalks through Glenariff Nature Reserve. Walk through the river gorge and past spectacular cascading waterfalls. You can stop at the original tea house built by Wise, now known as Laragh Lodge, before returning to the car park.

SLEMISH MOUNTAIN: THE HOME OF IRISH SPIRITUALITY

Slemish Mountain is another wonderful location off the Causeway Coastal Route that is near enough to merit a detour. A short drive from the pretty village of Broughshane, you can leave the car in Slemish Car Park, to begin your ascent to the summit of 'Patrick's Mountain'. Here, Ireland's patron saint, St Patrick, tended sheep after being kidnapped by pirates under the leadership of Niall of the Nine Hostages. For six lonely years the young Patrick walked these slopes, tending livestock for a local herder.

From the summit, 1,500 feet above sea level, you can easily imagine the influence of this isolated beauty on Patrick's spirituality. You can see the Antrim and Scottish coasts, the rolling Antrim Hills, Lough Neagh and the rugged Sperrin Mountains. Here, following his vision of the angel Victoricus, Patrick began his path towards his life's work, converting the Irish to Christianity.

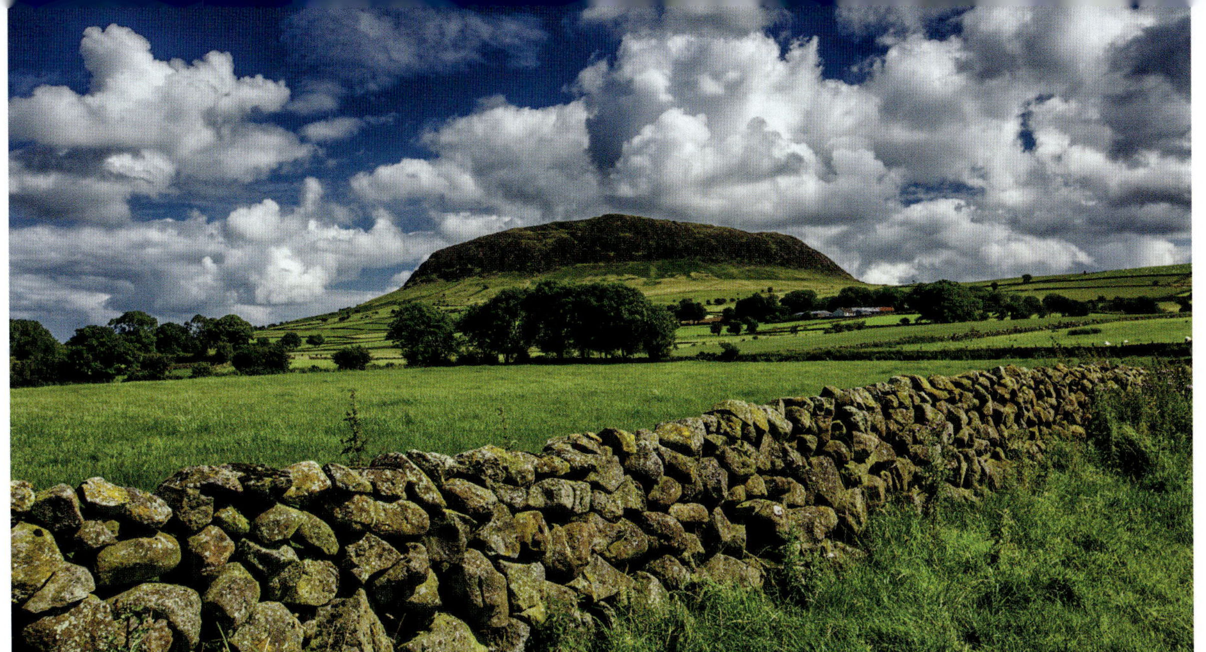

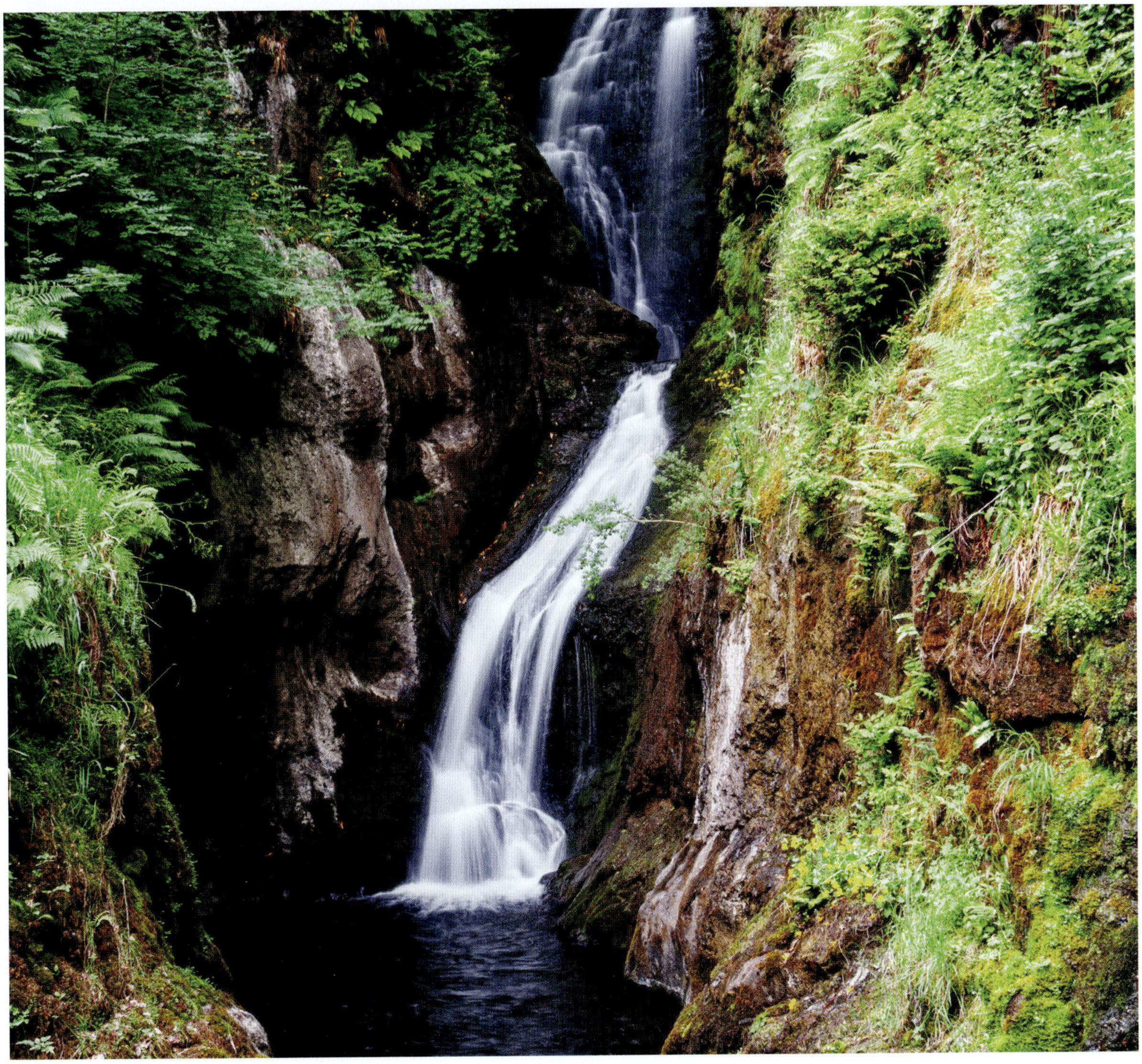

TOP: SLEMISH MOUNTAIN. BOTTOM: GLENARIFF FOREST PARK

SHILLANAVOGY VALLEY/ DOTHRAKI SEA

Today Slemish has a more contemporary claim to fame. The mountain overlooks beautiful Shillanavogy Valley, recreated as the Dothraki grasslands in *Game of Thrones*. Here, in Season 1, Daenerys Targaryen and her brother Viserys, Ser Jorah Mormont and the Dothraki horsemen ride through the grasslands of Essos en route to Vaes Dothrak.

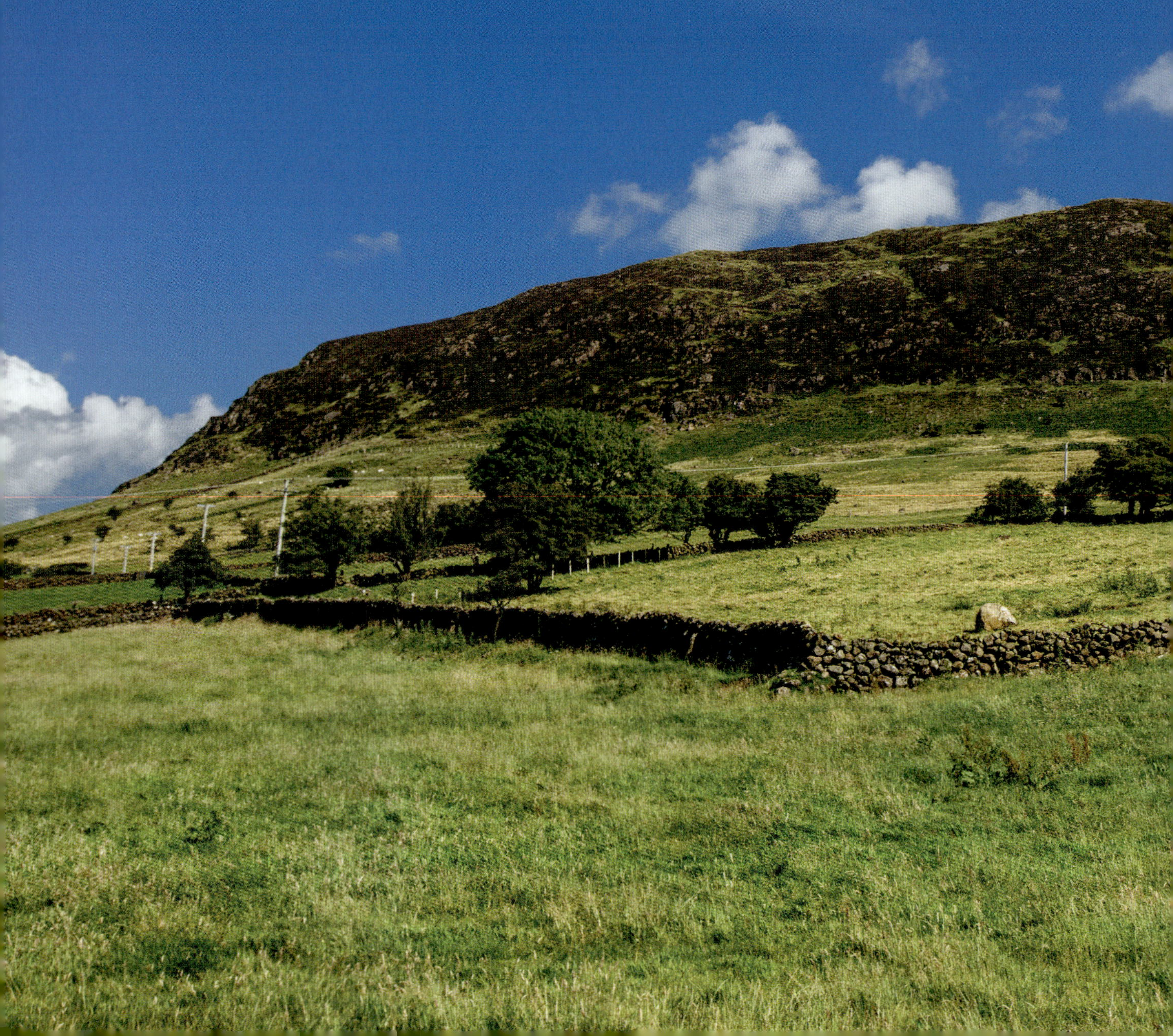

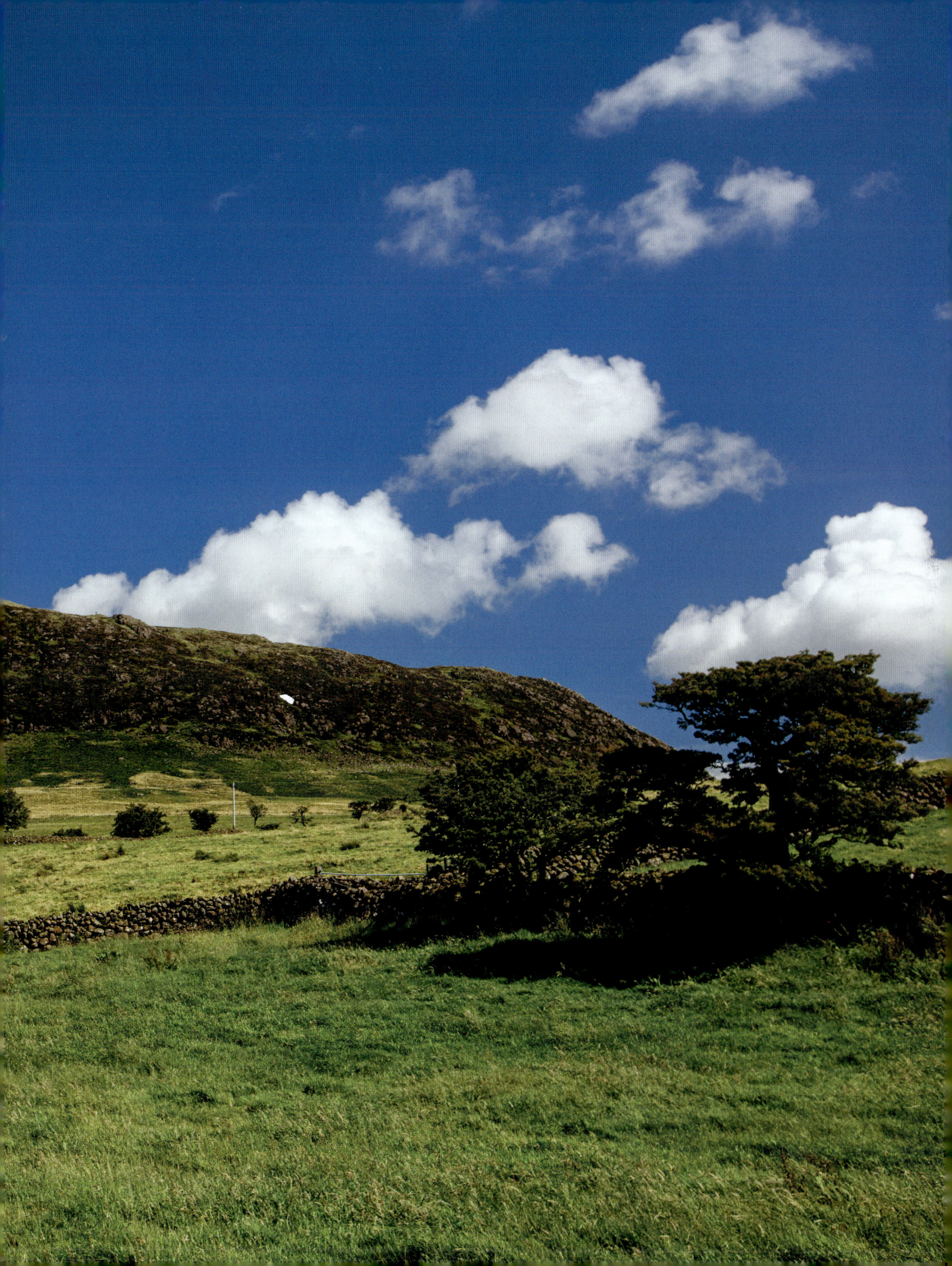

CUSHENDALL

I have seen nothing in Ireland so picturesque as this noble line of coast scenery.
(William Makepeace Thackeray)

En route to this important Glens village, we pass through the famous Red Arch. It was created in 1817 by the man who did so much to develop this atmospheric village, Francis Turnley, to improve access on the then nearly impassable coastal route.

Above the arch, though out of sight (if travelling south to north), are the remains of what was an important strategic castle in medieval times, Red Bay Castle. Dating back to the 13th, century it was rebuilt by the MacDonnells in the 1500s before being destroyed by Cromwell's troops in 1662.

Views across to nearby Scotland remind us that until the coastal road was built, it was so much easier to travel 20 miles across the water than on land to local market towns that locals would offer people a 'sail', rather than a 'lift'. The area was once part of the ancient kingdom of Dalriada, which included much of Western Scotland, and Scottish immigration in the 1600s had a huge impact on the Glens.

Once one of the most isolated areas of Ireland, it was in Cushendall in the early 1800s that Francis Turnley built the first hotel in the region, the Glens of Antrim in Shore Street, soon after he bought the village.

Turnley had made his fortune working for the East India Company in China. When he returned he bought Cushendall and the land around it and set about transforming the village. He also expanded the harbour and improved the almost impassable coastal route locally.

Among his legacies to the town is the Curfew Tower, which he built 'as a place of confinement for idlers and rioters'. It takes its name from a bell it housed until the 1940s, which sounded a curfew at 9pm – the time respectable people were expected to be indoors!

Today, the small town is alive with visitors in the summer, walking its four original streets with their colourful Georgian buildings and enjoying nightly traditional music in its pubs.

LAYDE GRAVEYARD

Romantics should seek out the ancient stone cross at the entrance to the Layde graveyard just outside the village off a tiny country road, where the ruins of Layde Church are still visible. It is said that that the hole in its circular top might have been used in pagan marriages in ancient times. Couples joined hands though the hole to signify their love. After a year and a day, if the relationship did not work, they could return to the stone, reverse their vows and go back to being single! Pregnant women also used the stone. They passed the clothes meant for the new baby through the hole and prayed for an easy birth.

The graveyard is full of old stones, some of which belong to the MacDonnell family. Their coat of arms is marked on the stones near the church door.

MOUNTAINS OF THE GLENS

From Cushendall you can see Lurigethan Mountain, an ancient volcanic plug which features the remains of a large promontory fort that may date from the Iron Age. Just outside the village the round steep-sided hill is the fairy hill, Tiveragh. Also nearby is Tievebulliagh Mountain, where in ancient times porcellanite – used for axes – was mined to be traded throughout Britain and Ireland, and possibly elsewhere.

OPPOSITE TOP: RED BAY CASTLE. OPPOSITE BELOW LEFT: LAYDE GRAVEYARD. OPPOSITE RIGHT: CURFEW TOWER, CUSHENDALL

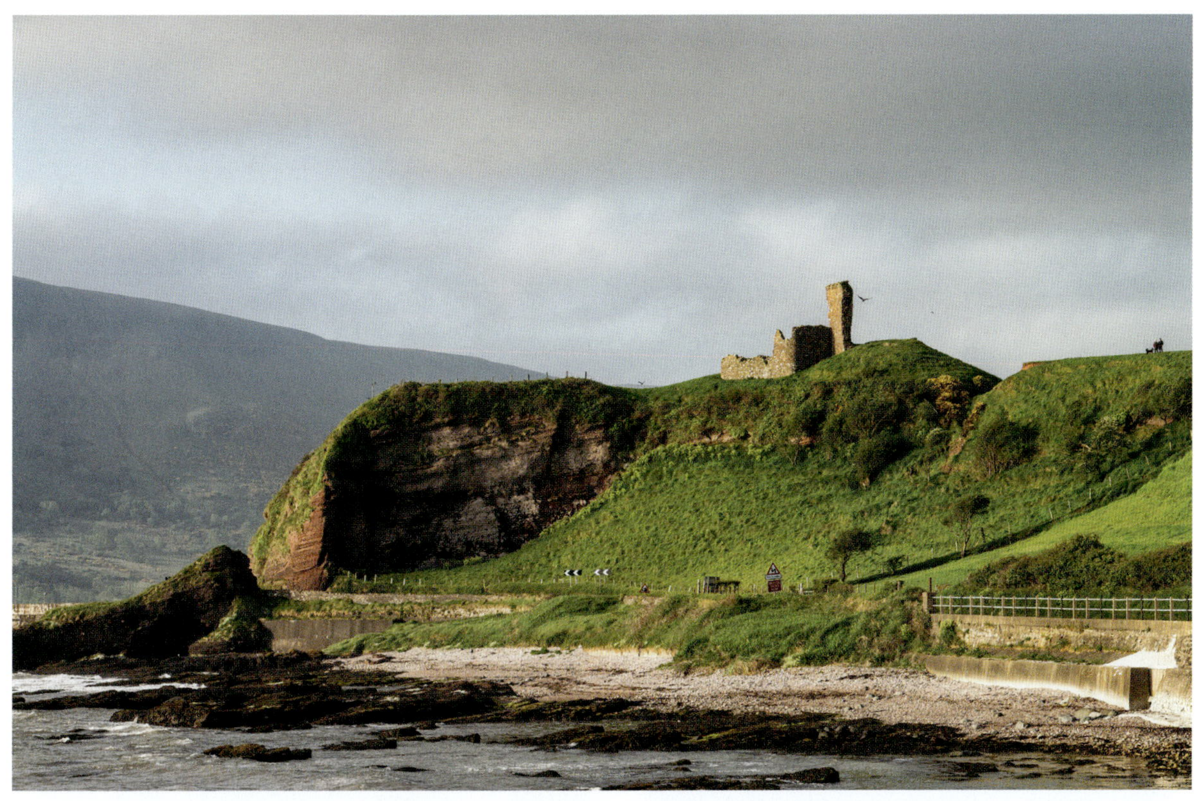

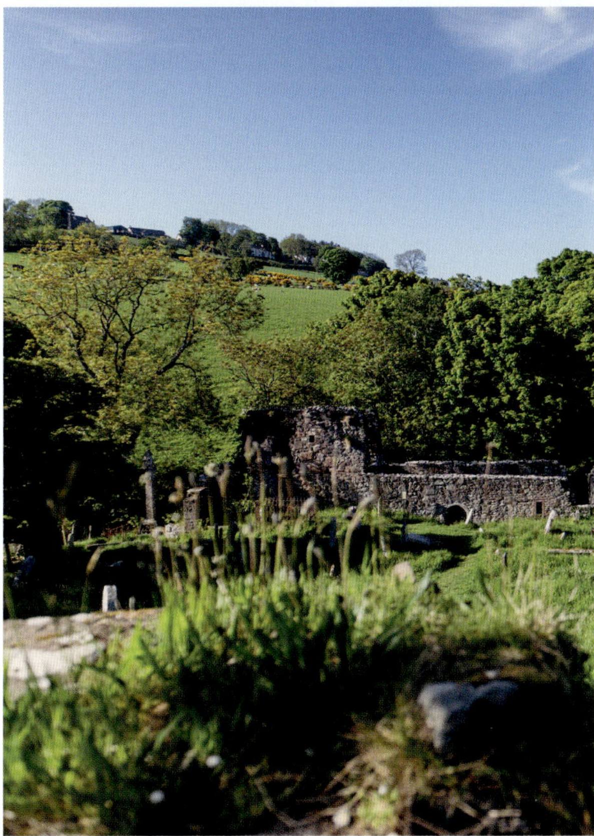

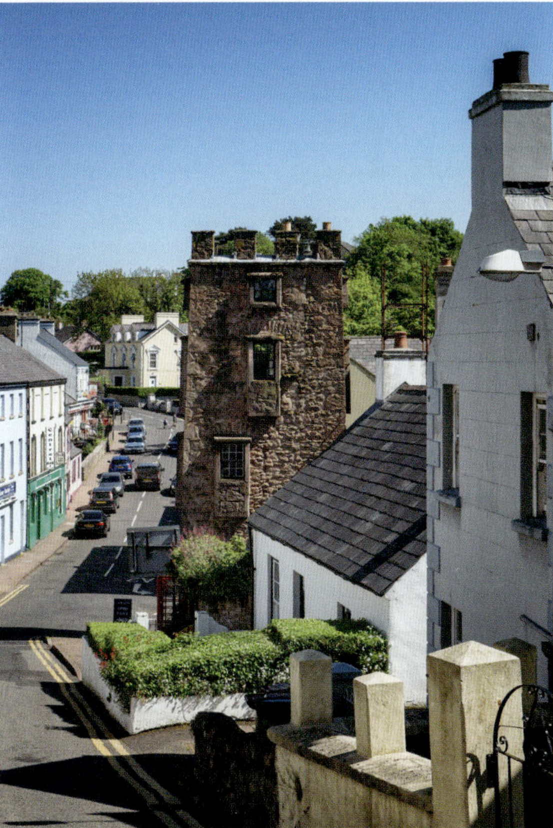

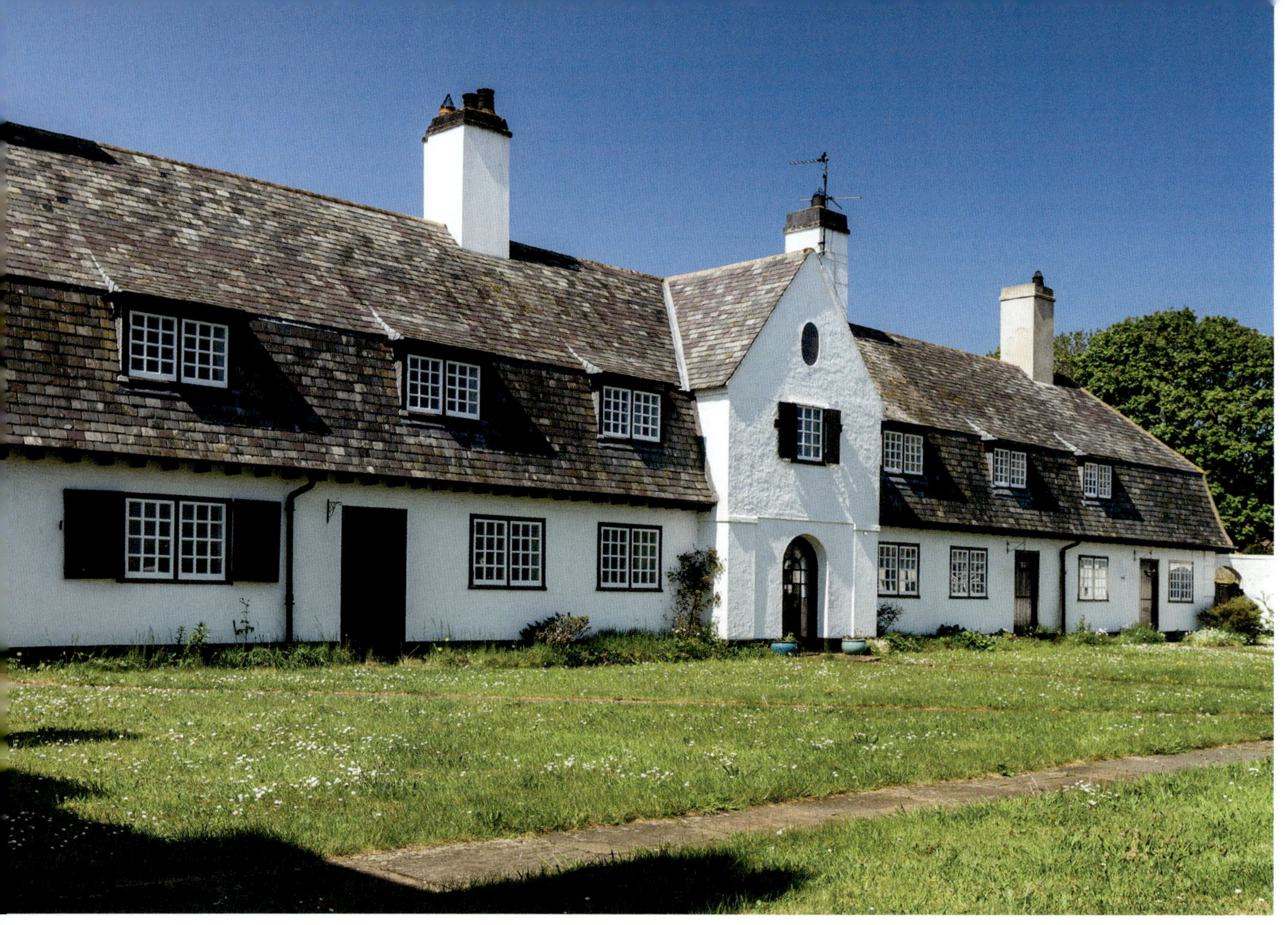

MAUD'S COTTAGES, CUSHENDUN

CUSHENDUN

The man who did more than anyone to create the beautiful village we see today was one Ronald John McNeill, Baron Cushendun, who came to live here in 1910.

A giant of a man, renowned for his fearsome temper, he once threw a book at Winston Churchill in the House of Commons while serving as an MP. Surprisingly, in view of his disposition, he became a successful diplomat and represented Britain at the League of Nations.

It was McNeill who commissioned Clough Williams-Ellis to rebuild Glenmona House, the village's grandest building, now open to visitors. He had previously asked the same architect, who was also responsible for the famous Portmeirion village in Wales, the location for the television series *The Prisoner*, to design the striking high-roofed cottages in the main square.

The Portmeirion connection is significant. Cushendun does feel slightly other-worldly, like its Welsh counterpart. Many of the buildings, including Glenmona House, have been owned by the National Trust since the 1950s and conservation is at the heart of its continuing appeal (it was designated as a Conservation Area in 1980). This includes the 18th-century warehouse that is now being run as the Corner House tearoom by the National Trust, and the

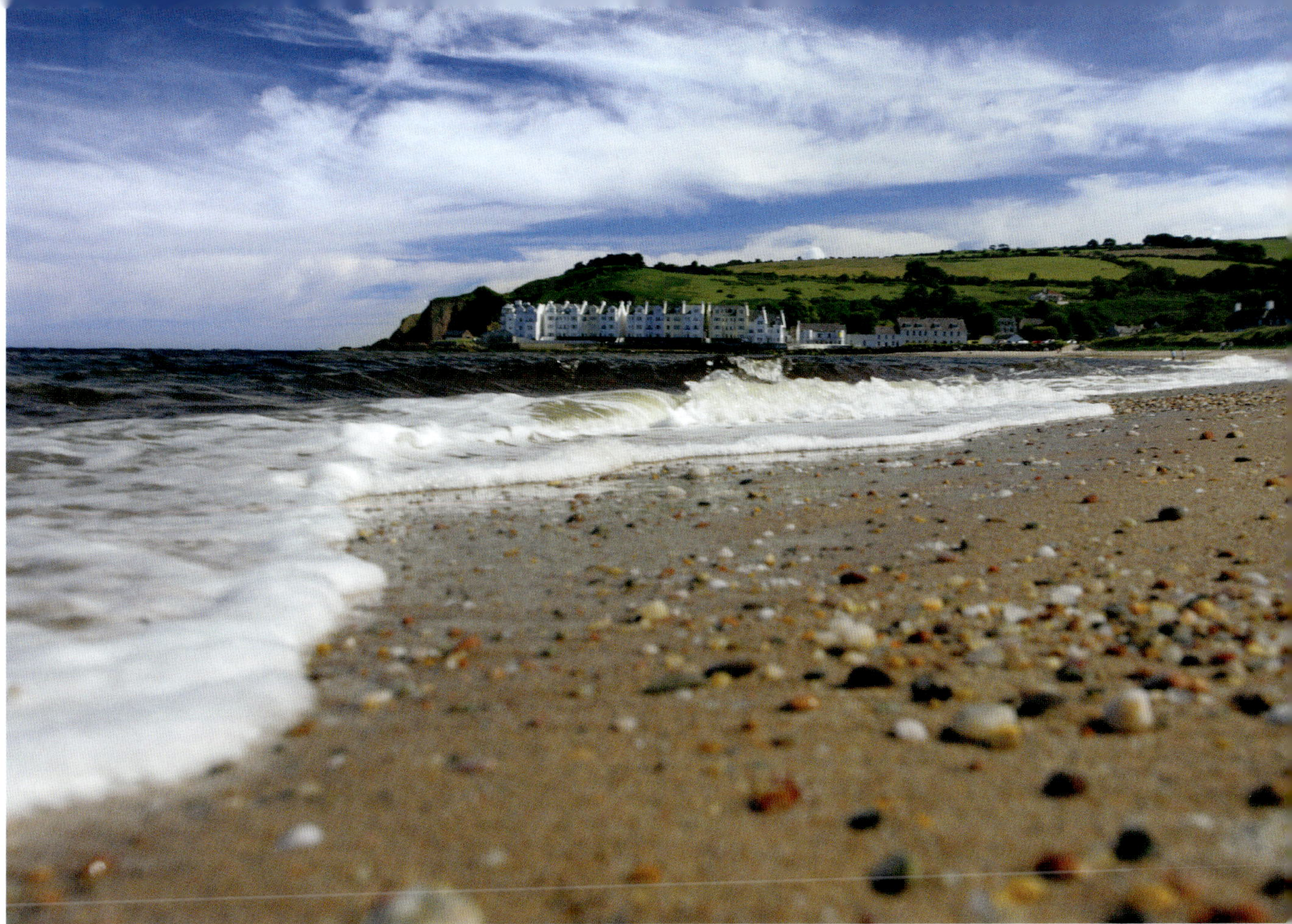

CUSHENDUN BEACH

famous Mary McBride's pub, once the smallest in Ireland.

The beautiful red sandstone church between the square and Glenmona House was built in 1840 so local Protestants didn't have to travel to Layde Church to worship. In its small graveyard, the Gaelic Revival enthusiast Ada McNeill and her fiercely unionist first cousin Ronald lie buried near each other.

Coming from Cushendall, follow the Knocknacarry Road into the heart of the old village. Turn left onto the bridge over the Dun River that flows to the sea nearby. You'll pass the Corner House tearoom on your right and Mary McBride's pub. The first of Clough Ellis's houses are on your left before you turn right and follow the road around with the beach on your right. Park at the car park you see soon on your left. You are in the grounds of Glenmona House, where you can visit their exhibition about the village.

Otherwise, walk back the way you drove, passing Maud's Cottages overlooking the water, and maybe enjoying a quick pint at Mary McBride's or a meal at the Corner House. Cross the bridge and turn left. Here you will meet *Johann*, a sculpture of a goat that was the last animal to be culled here in the foot and mouth outbreak of 2001. Continue past the apartments on your right as the little road ends in sight of the now world-famous Cushendun Caves.

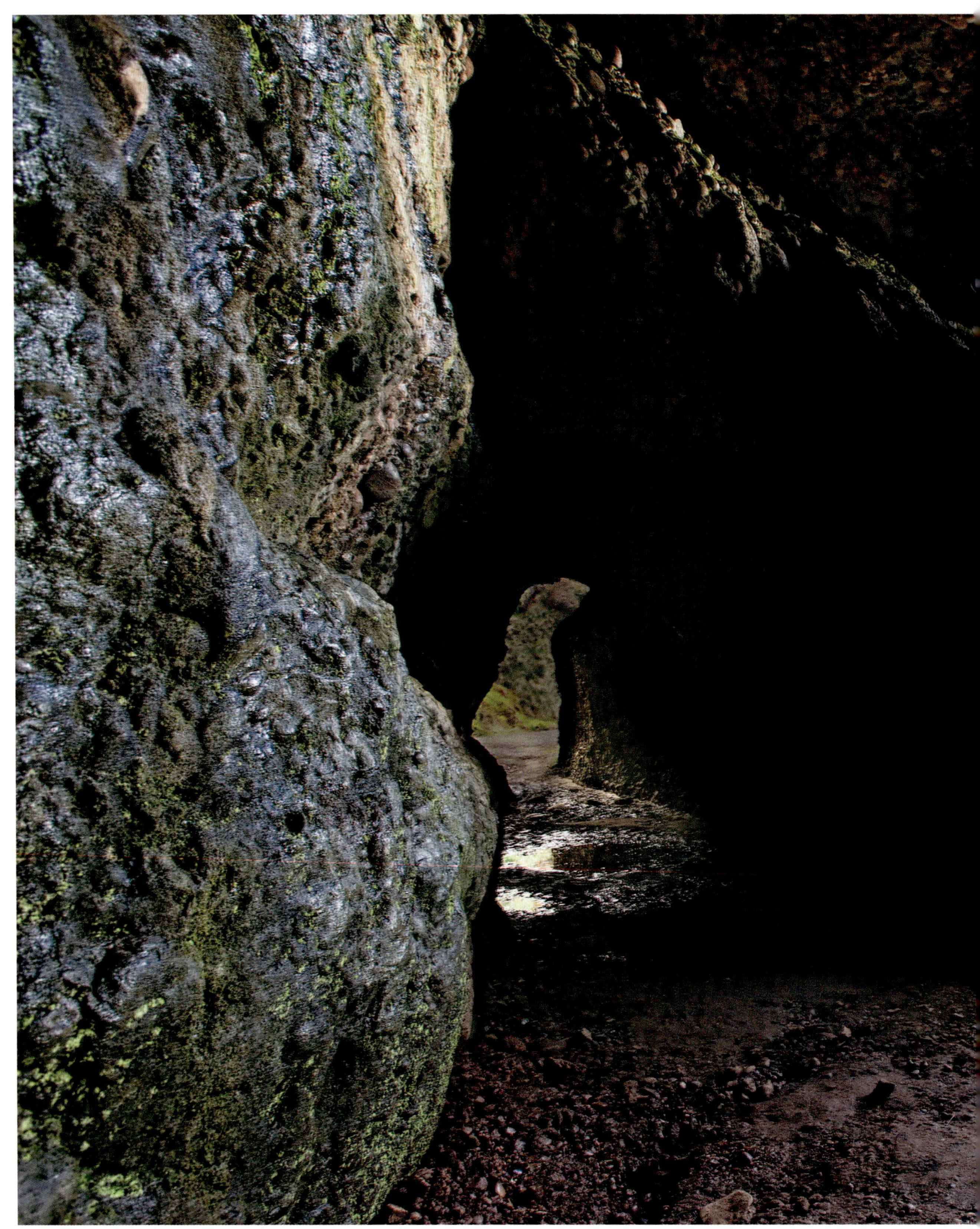

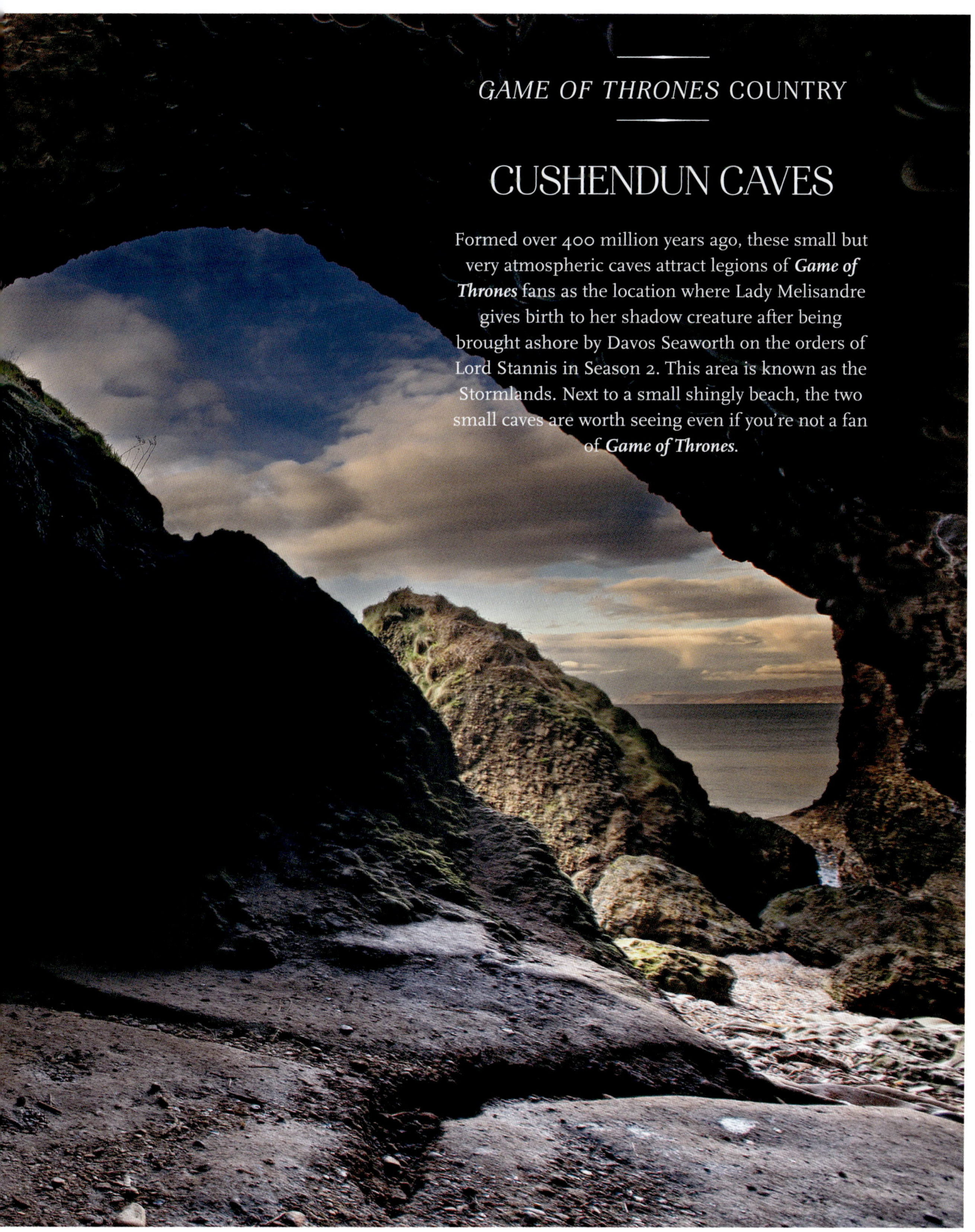

CUSHENDUN CAVES

Formed over 400 million years ago, these small but very atmospheric caves attract legions of *Game of Thrones* fans as the location where Lady Melisandre gives birth to her shadow creature after being brought ashore by Davos Seaworth on the orders of Lord Stannis in Season 2. This area is known as the Stormlands. Next to a small shingly beach, the two small caves are worth seeing even if you're not a fan of *Game of Thrones*.

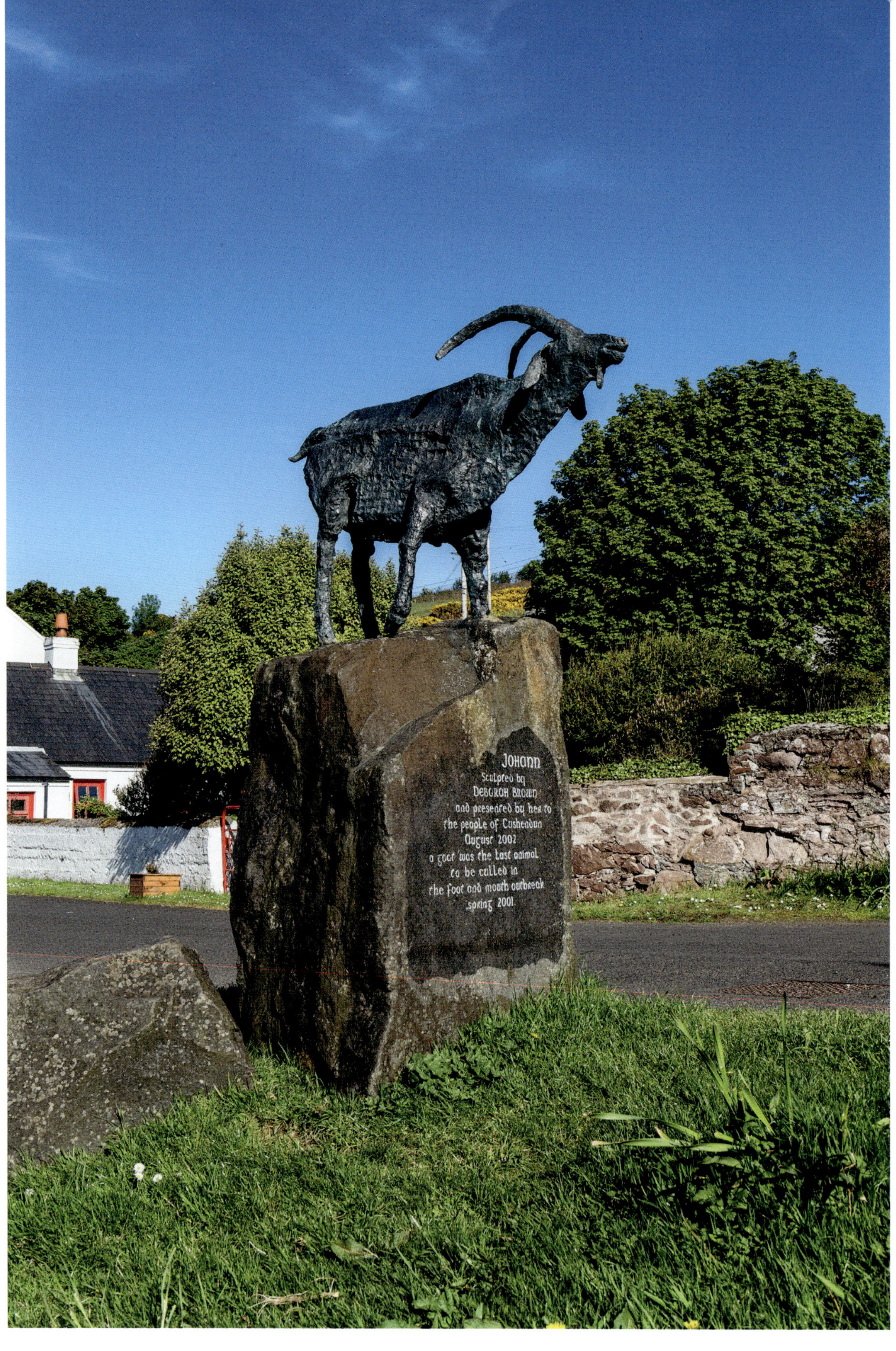

JOHANN, CUSHENDUN

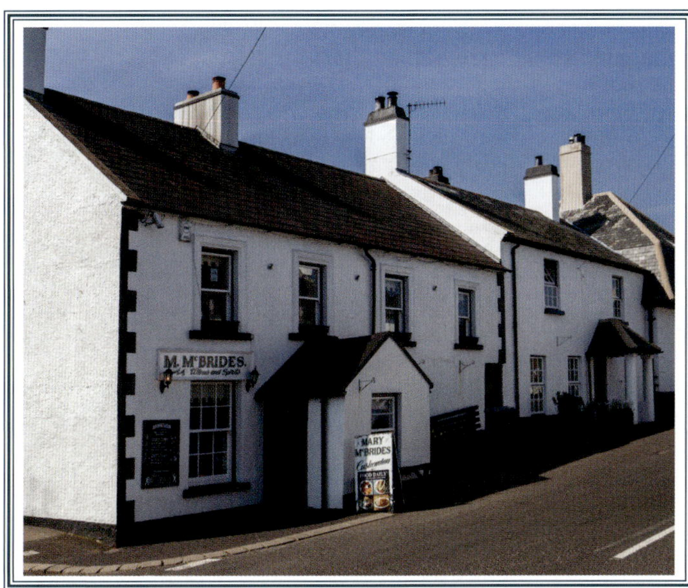

Door Nº. 8

Once known as the smallest bar in Ireland, the
atmospheric Mary McBride's pub in the heart of the
village, just around the corner from the Cushendun
Caves, proudly features the eighth door in the series.
Its main theme is the journey of Arya Stark.

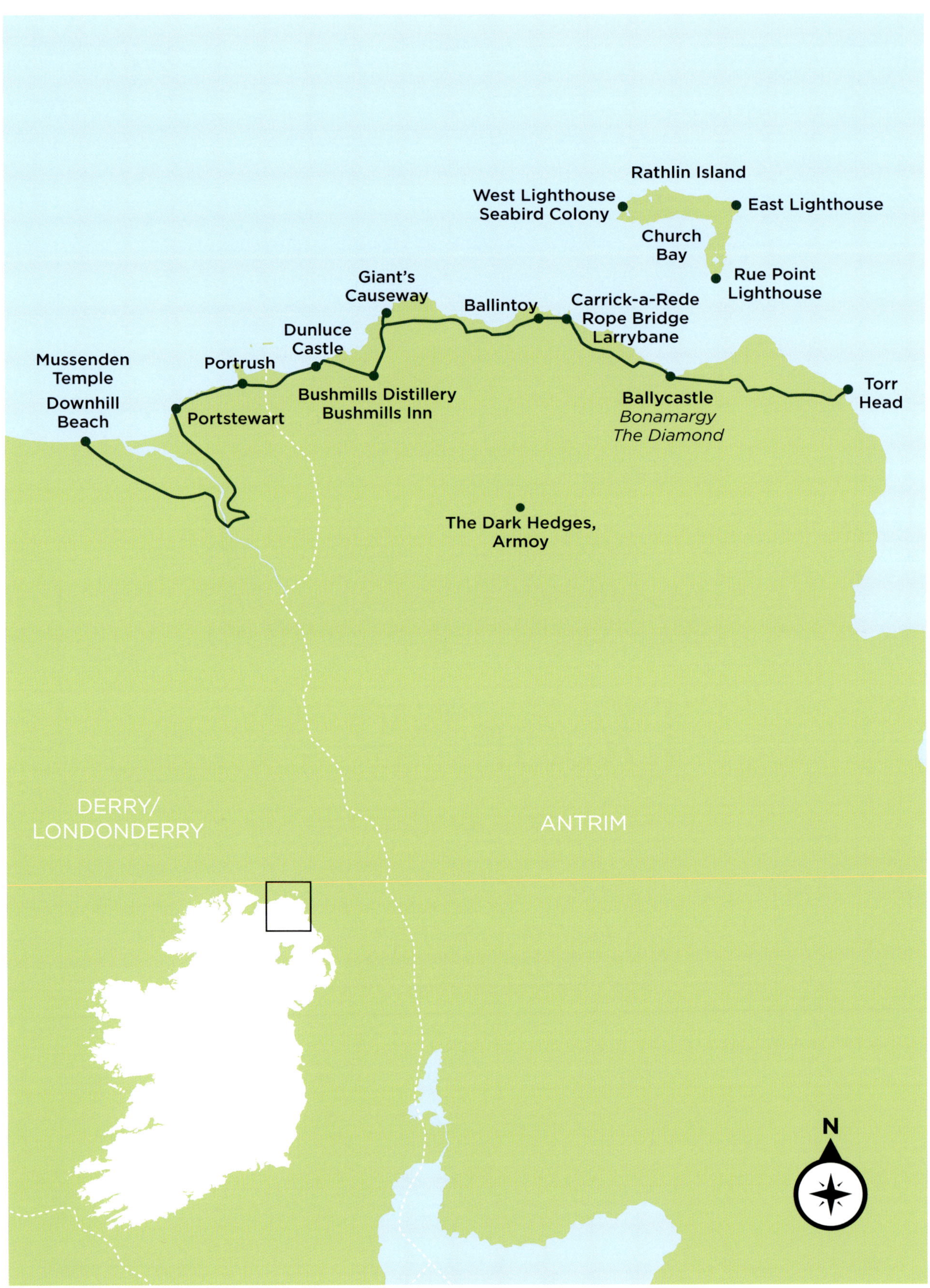

Rathlin Island
West Lighthouse
Seabird Colony
East Lighthouse
Church Bay
Rue Point Lighthouse
Giant's Causeway
Ballintoy
Carrick-a-Rede Rope Bridge
Larrybane
Dunluce Castle
Portrush
Mussenden Temple
Downhill Beach
Bushmills Distillery
Bushmills Inn
Portstewart
Ballycastle
Bonamargy
The Diamond
Torr Head
The Dark Hedges, Armoy
DERRY/ LONDONDERRY
ANTRIM
N

CAUSEWAY COAST

From the towering heights of Torr Head and Fair Head we travel to the home of the Ould Lammas Fair, Ballycastle. Then aboard the ferry to magical Rathlin Island and its world-famous seabird colony. Back on the mainland we cross the swinging Carrick-a-Rede Rope Bridge, high over the water, to an island brimming with birdlife.

Ballintoy's pretty harbour will be immediately recognisable to *Game of Thrones* fans. The most famous attraction of all, one of only three UNESCO World Heritage Sites on the island of Ireland, is next – the spectacular Giant's Causeway. Then we tour the world's oldest continuously licensed distillery in the charming village of Bushmills.

Home to the MacDonnells in medieval times, Dunluce Castle seems to defy gravity atop sheer cliffs over plunging Atlantic waves. Finally we explore two traditional seaside resorts: Portrush, with its famous golf course, and Portstewart, renowned for its beautiful strand and wonderful ice cream!

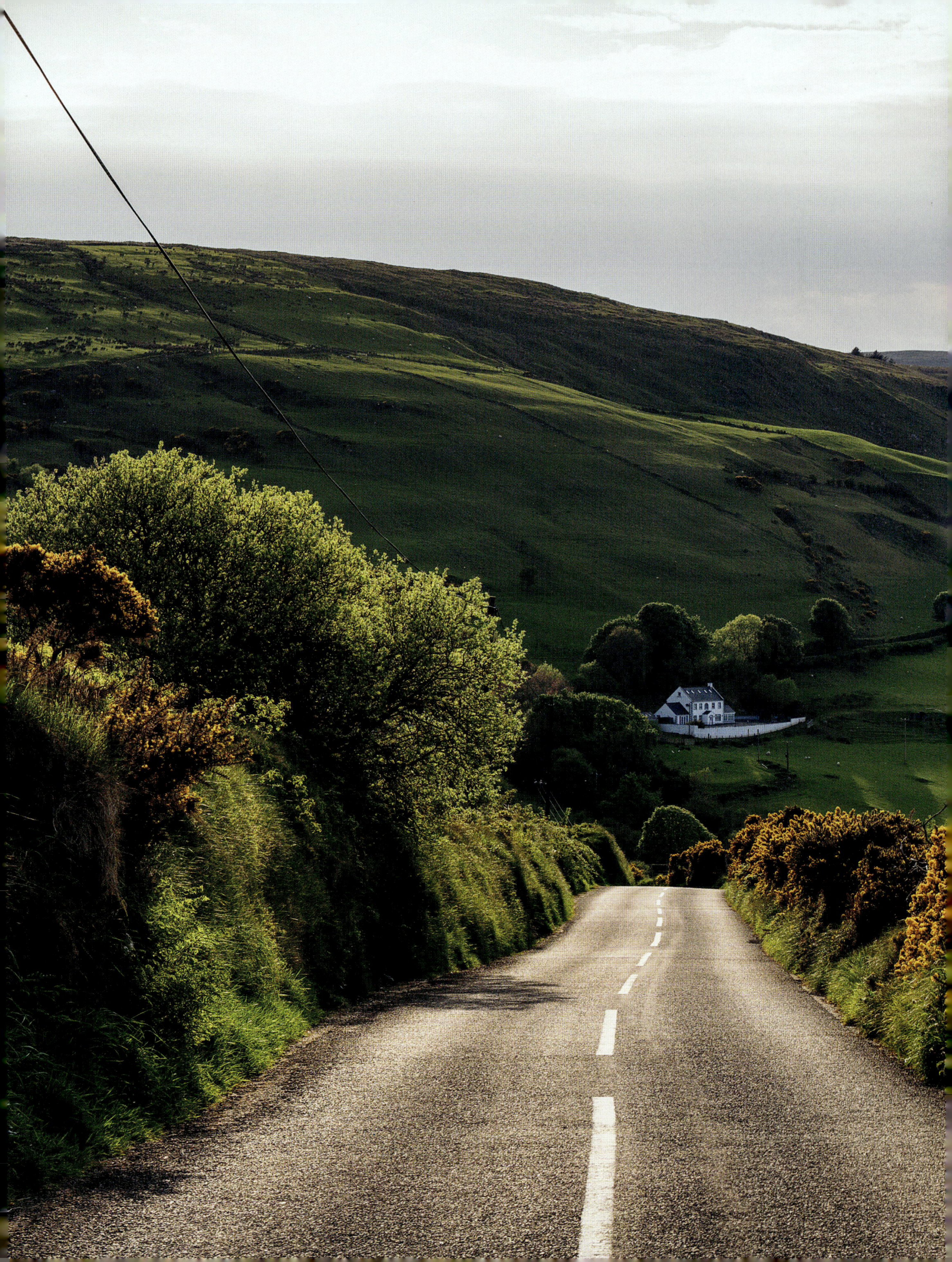

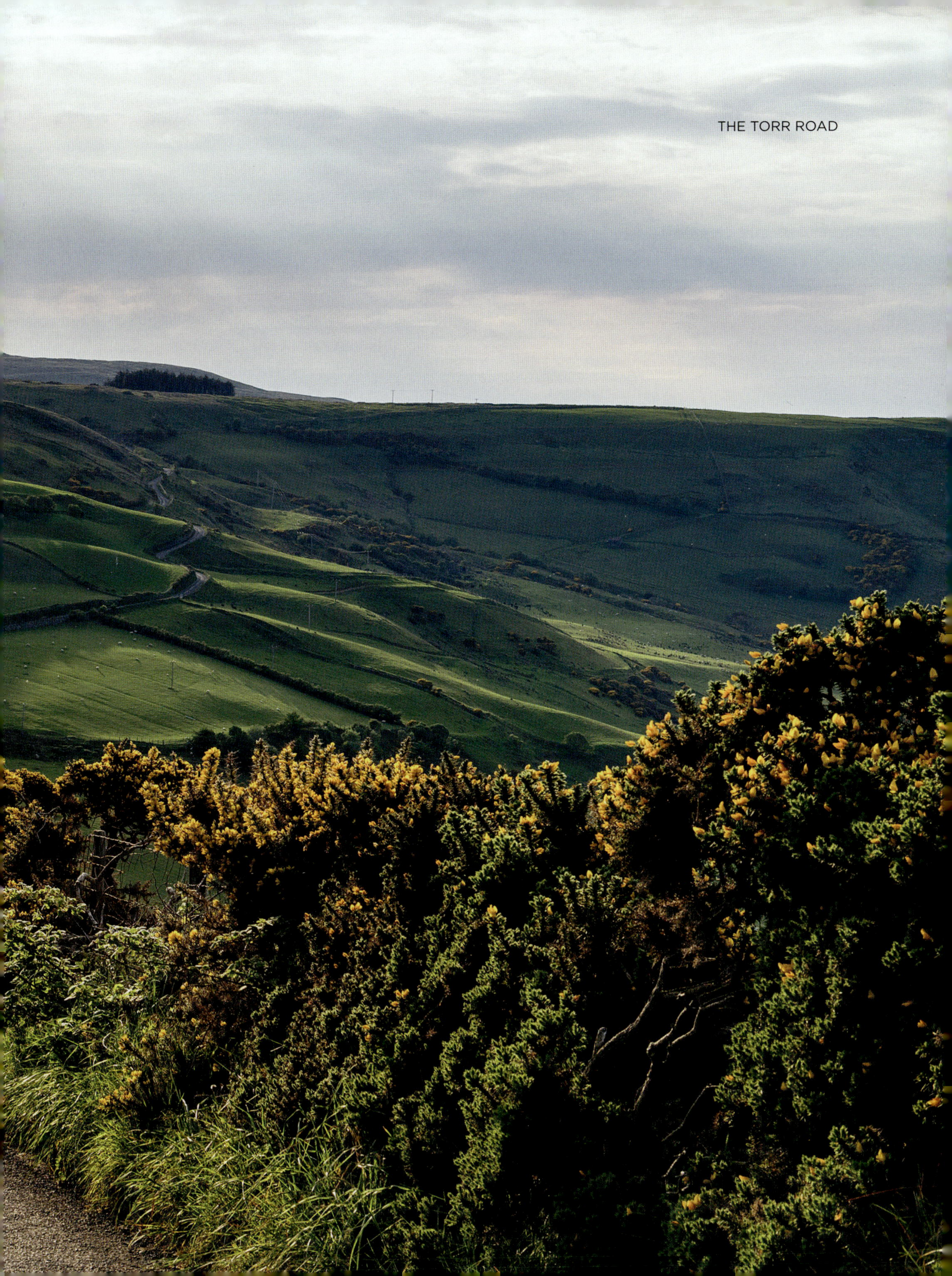
THE TORR ROAD

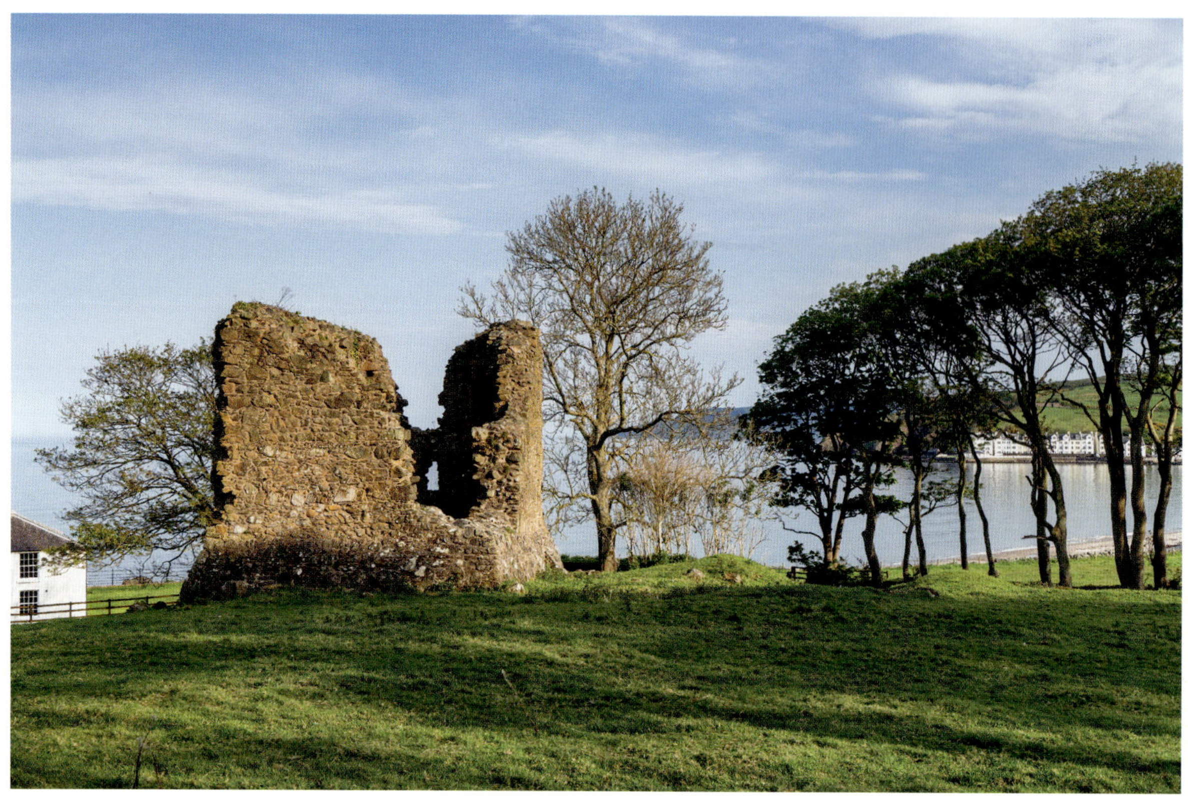

CASTLE CARRA

EN ROUTE TO TORR HEAD

Leaving Cushendun, turn left with the beach to your right. You now have a choice. You can rejoin the Causeway Coastal Route, a very pleasant drive to our next official stop at Ballycastle, or take the more scenic Torr Head scenic route on the Torr Road. We're taking the latter option.

Look out on your right for the ruins of 14th-century Castle Carra, once owned by Shane O'Neill, leader of the formidable O'Neill clan and self-proclaimed Earl of Ulster, who made the mistake of imprisoning Sorley Boy MacDonnell here in 1565. A couple of years later, the MacDonnells got their revenge. Entertaining O'Neill here, they stabbed him to death and sent his head to Queen Elizabeth's representative in Dublin to confirm the removal of one of her main Irish enemies.

Further up around the winding hilly road you will see a large cross above a cairn, erected in 1908. It marks the spot where Shane O'Neill's headless body is said to have been buried. It is believed that a stone from every county in Ireland was used in the cairn's construction.

You will see evidence as we leave Cushendun behind of the many dry-stone walls of the area and what are known locally as ladder farms – long, narrow strips of cultivated land rising steeply. The lower ground is generally more fertile and animals are usually grazed on the higher land – a practice locals call 'booleying' – in summer.

Though the driver needs to focus firmly ahead over these narrow, often winding and fast rising and falling roads, the views of the coast for passengers are spectacular, as the land occasionally plunges down steeply to the sea and headlands appear in the distance.

On this route we have three main stops before Ballycastle. Spectacular views and a world of breath-taking natural beauty can be seen for endless miles along the rugged rocks of Torr Head, Murlough Bay and Fair Head. They are all within easy reach of this road.

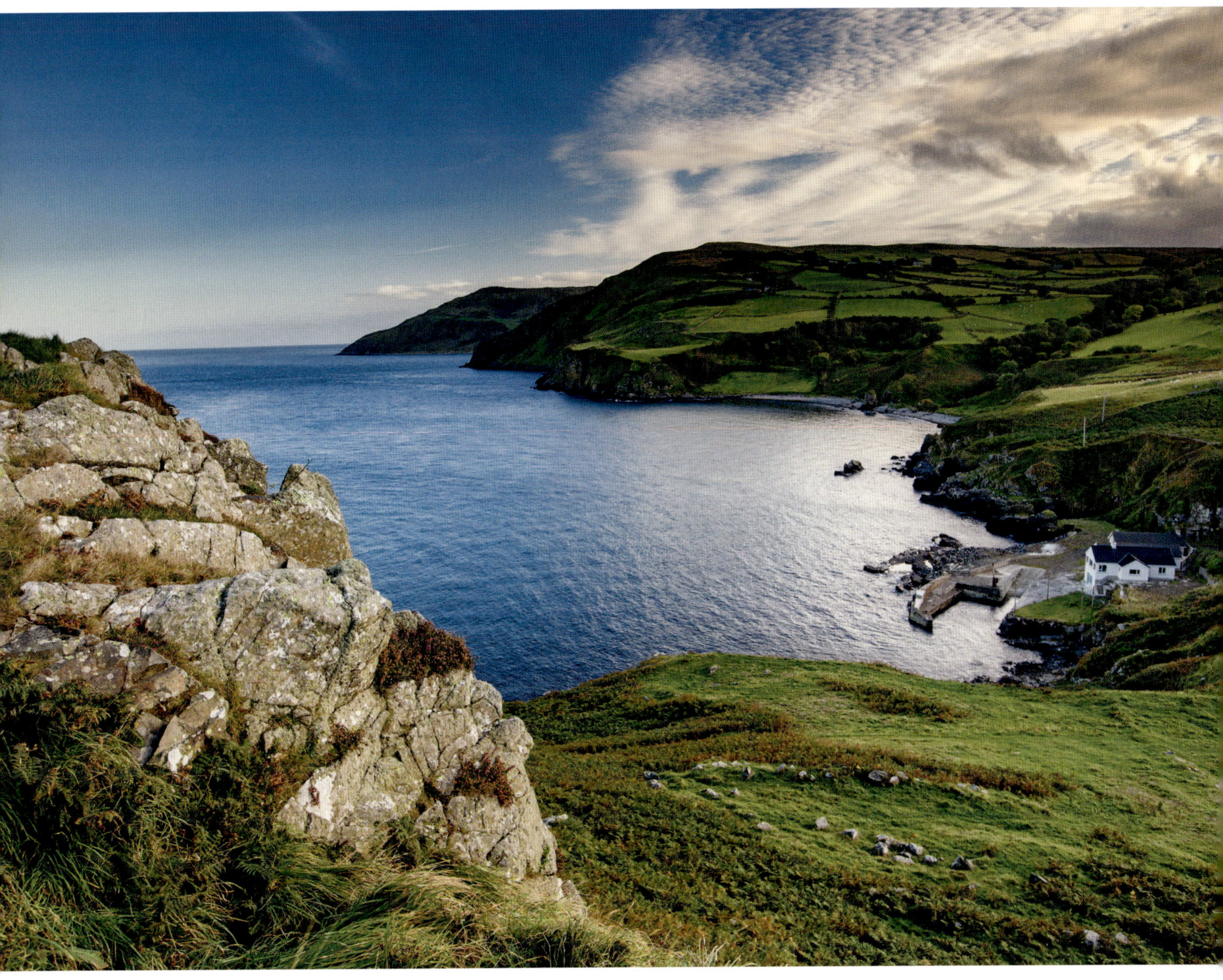

TORR HEAD

TORR HEAD

The road down to Torr Head is narrow, often little more than one car wide, but there are spaces to manoeuvre into to let oncoming cars pass. After dipping down, the road eventually leads to Torr Head itself. Put some time aside to walk around – you won't regret it.

From the head you can see the thundering waves crashing against the rocks and, easily visible on the horizon, the Mull of Kintyre. This is the closest Irish mainland location to Scotland. The ruined building at the top is an old coastguard signalling station. In the 1800s it recorded the passage of transatlantic ships, relaying the information to Lloyd's of London.

The ruin at the bottom by the car park is an old customs house, where the walls and ruins of sixth-century Altagore cashel can be seen too.

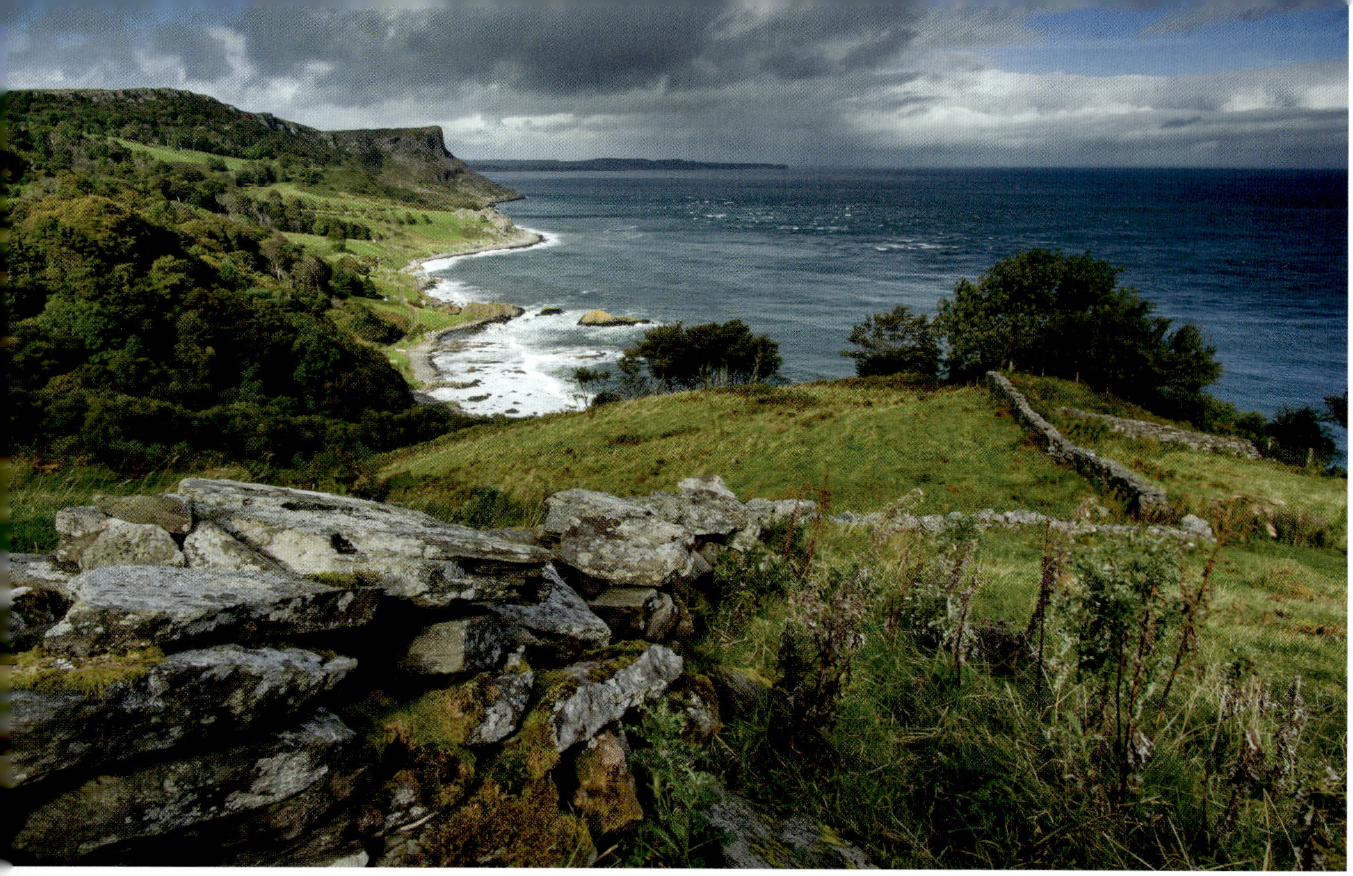

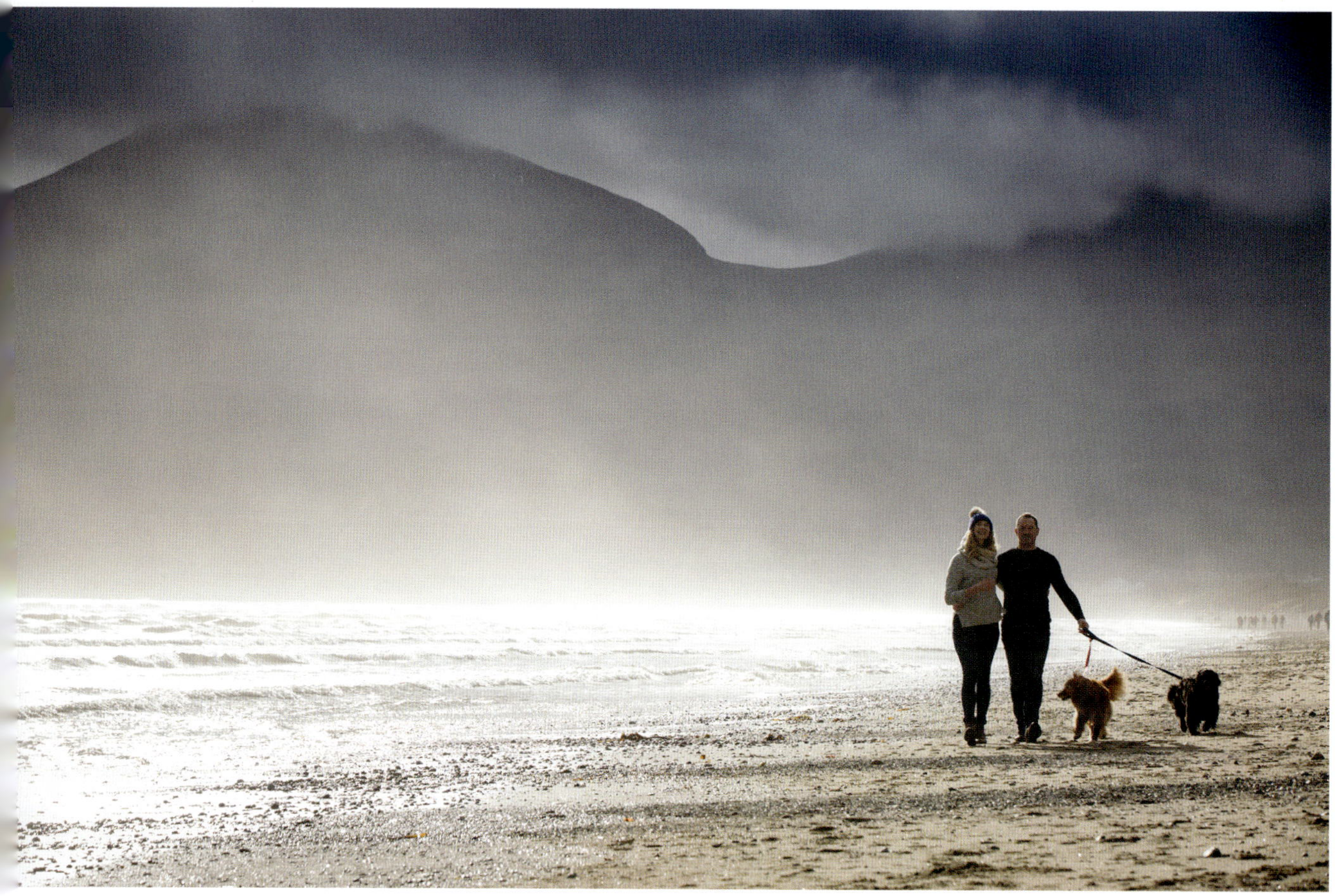

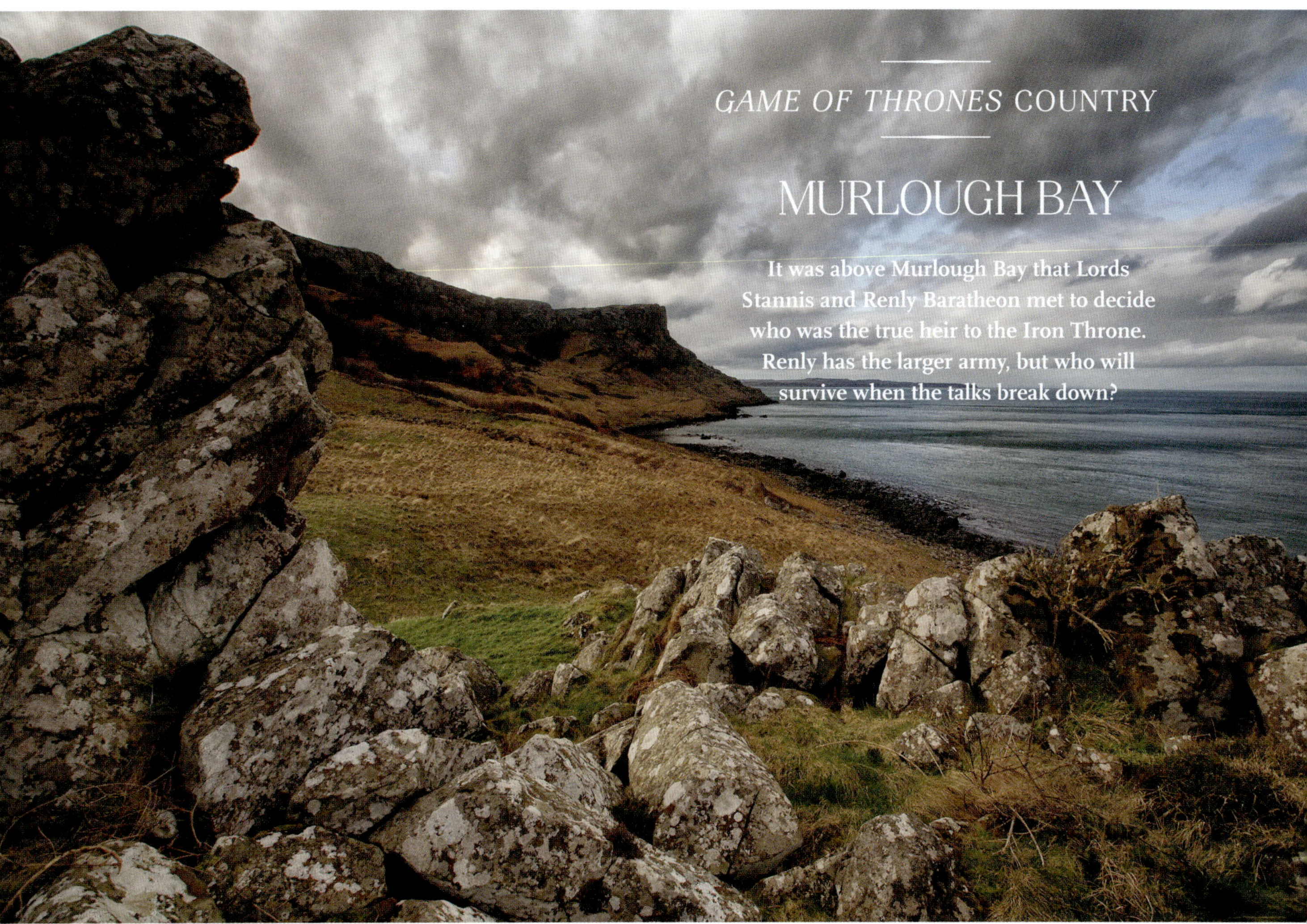

OPPOSITE AND ABOVE: VIEWS OF MURLOUGH BAY

MURLOUGH BAY

Again, it's a very narrow and sometimes steep road down to Murlough Bay. There are sheep on every side too, so be careful. But there are also some truly wonderful views as you descend to this delightful cove. Is it any wonder that a cross marks where Irish patriot Roger Casement had wanted to be buried?

(As he was arrested for arms smuggling just prior to the 1916 Easter Rising and tried and hanged for treason, this decision was taken out of his hands.)

From these wooded slopes you can see Fair Head to the north and out to Rathlin Island, the Mull of Kintyre and Western Scotland.

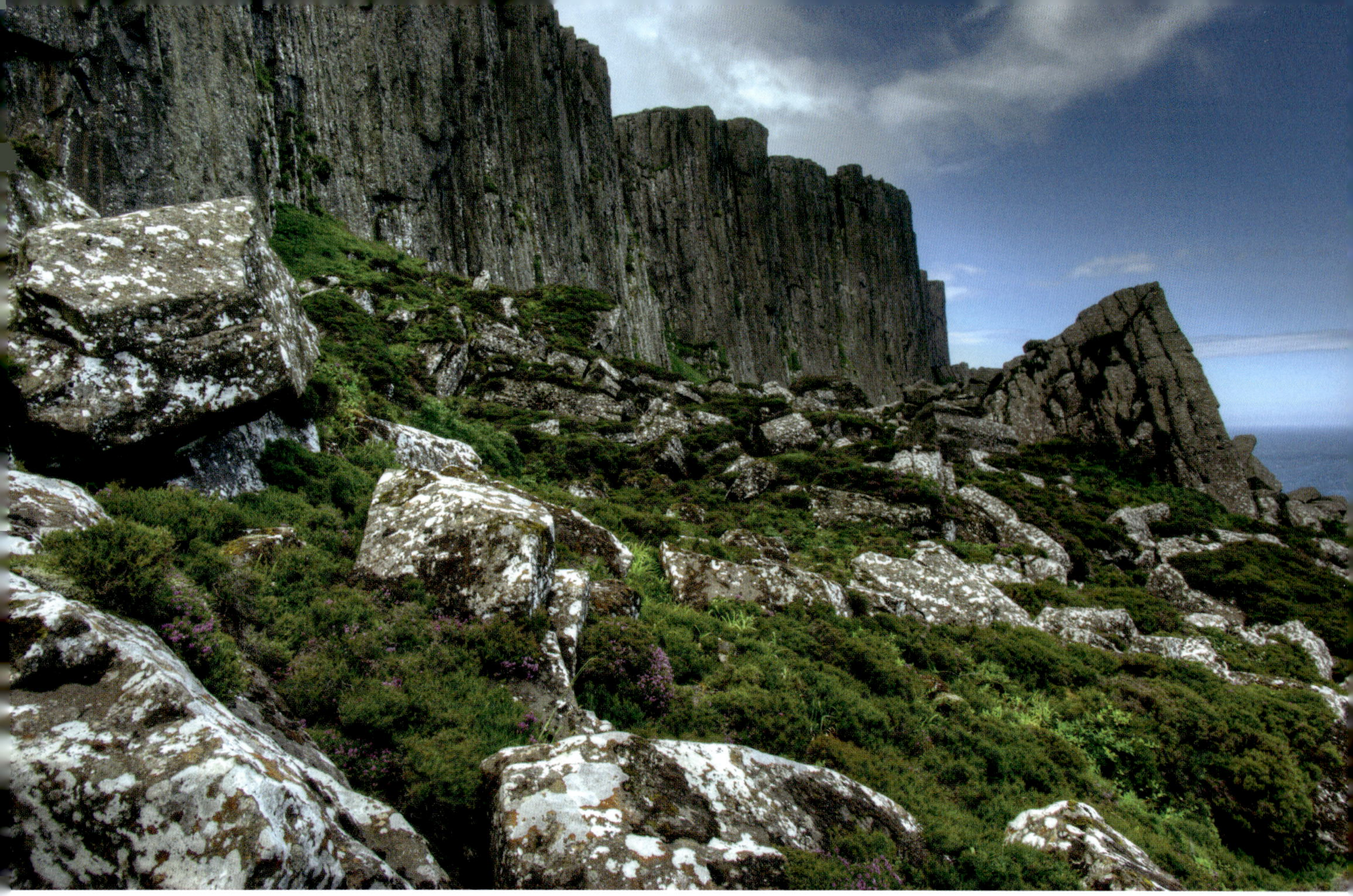

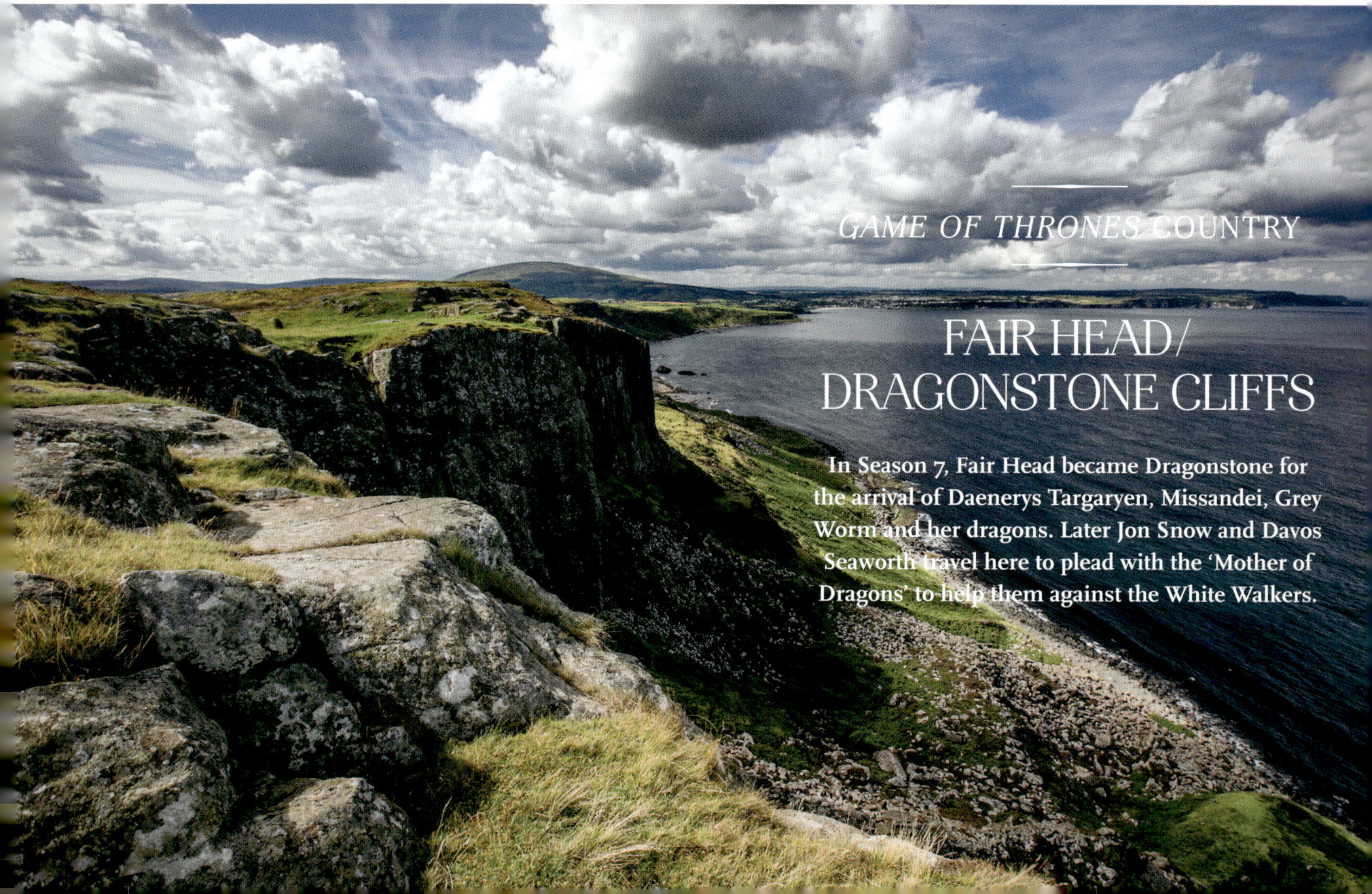

FAIR HEAD/ DRAGONSTONE CLIFFS

In Season 7, Fair Head became Dragonstone for the arrival of Daenerys Targaryen, Missandei, Grey Worm and her dragons. Later Jon Snow and Davos Seaworth travel here to plead with the 'Mother of Dragons' to help them against the White Walkers.

FAIR HEAD

The tallest cliff face in Northern Ireland, Fair Head rises 600 feet above sea level. It is beloved by rock climbers as it provides one of the largest expanses of climbable rock in either Ireland or Britain.

One of the first things you'll see as you approach the car park (fee) is a remarkable man-made Iron Age island or crannóg in the middle of Lough na Cranagh. You'll see sheep and some wild goats around the rocks beneath the cliffs, and the views are simply extraordinary.

A panel in the car park offers a choice of looped way-marked trails ranging from 1.5 miles to over three miles. These are worth it for the amazing views, including Ballycastle and Rathlin Island and its lighthouses, the Hebridean Islands and the Mull of Kintyre. Be careful along the cliff-top paths, especially in bad weather.

OFFICIAL CAUSEWAY COASTAL ROUTE BETWEEN CUSHENDUN AND BALLYCASTLE

The landscape won't be as spectacular, but it will be an easier drive than the route we have taken. Here you will pass the Glendun Viaduct, broad valleys and rolling hills, and several sites of interest. These include the famous vanishing lake of Loughareema, which can turn from a blue lake to a mud-cracked bed in a relatively short space of time. Apparently this is due to a chalk sinkhole becoming blocked. When the blockage is cleared, the water empties.

BALLYCASTLE

No historical character dominates this journey like Sorley Boy MacDonnell. Now we are entering the town where the notorious leader of the MacDonnell clan was born and where he is buried, near the site of one of his most crucial military victories.

Just outside Ballycastle, on the Cushendall Road to Fair Head, the atmospheric remains of an ancient Franciscan friary reveal much of the tumultuous history of this area. Bonamargy Friary was built around the end of the 1400s by Rory McQuillan of the clan that were then 'Lords of the Route'. The Route was a territory so vast it once stretched from the Glens of Antrim to Donegal, and was much contested by the Gaelic clans fighting for power following the demise of the Anglo-Normans in Ulster.

Bonamargy lies beneath Knocklayde Mountain at the foot of Glenshesk, one of the nine Glens of Antrim. In the 1580s a series of conflicts took place in this area that conclusively transferred power from the McQuillans to Sorley Boy's MacDonnell clan. A number of standing stones mark the burial places of soldiers killed during these savage battles.

The McQuillans and their allies, including two English companies, gathered in the vicinity of Ballycastle to make a last attempt to defeat the increasingly influential MacDonnells. Although outnumbering their opponents, the McQuillans' cavalry and heavily armed infantry were tricked into pursuing the MacDonnells over deep bog. Unable to move, they were soon routed, with any survivors pursued to their death around the countryside. Sorley Boy was now, very definitely, Lord of the Route.

Today, the relatively well-preserved friary – cloister, gatehouse, altar and church – is one of the most important stops for anyone wishing to get a sense of local history. Here lie buried several Earls of Ulster as well as the great man himself, Sorley Boy.

If you're of a nervous disposition, don't linger after dark. During the 1600s, a certain Julia McQuillan, aka the Black Nun, lived in the friary and her ghost is said to haunt it still – perhaps out of annoyance, as she asked to be buried near the entrance of the church so that worshippers would tread on her grave, thus ensuring her humility even in death.

The Black Nun was famous locally for several prophesies, though there is some dispute as to what exactly these are. Ask locally and you may get different answers. These could include the invention of horseless carriages

OPPOSITE: FAIR HEAD

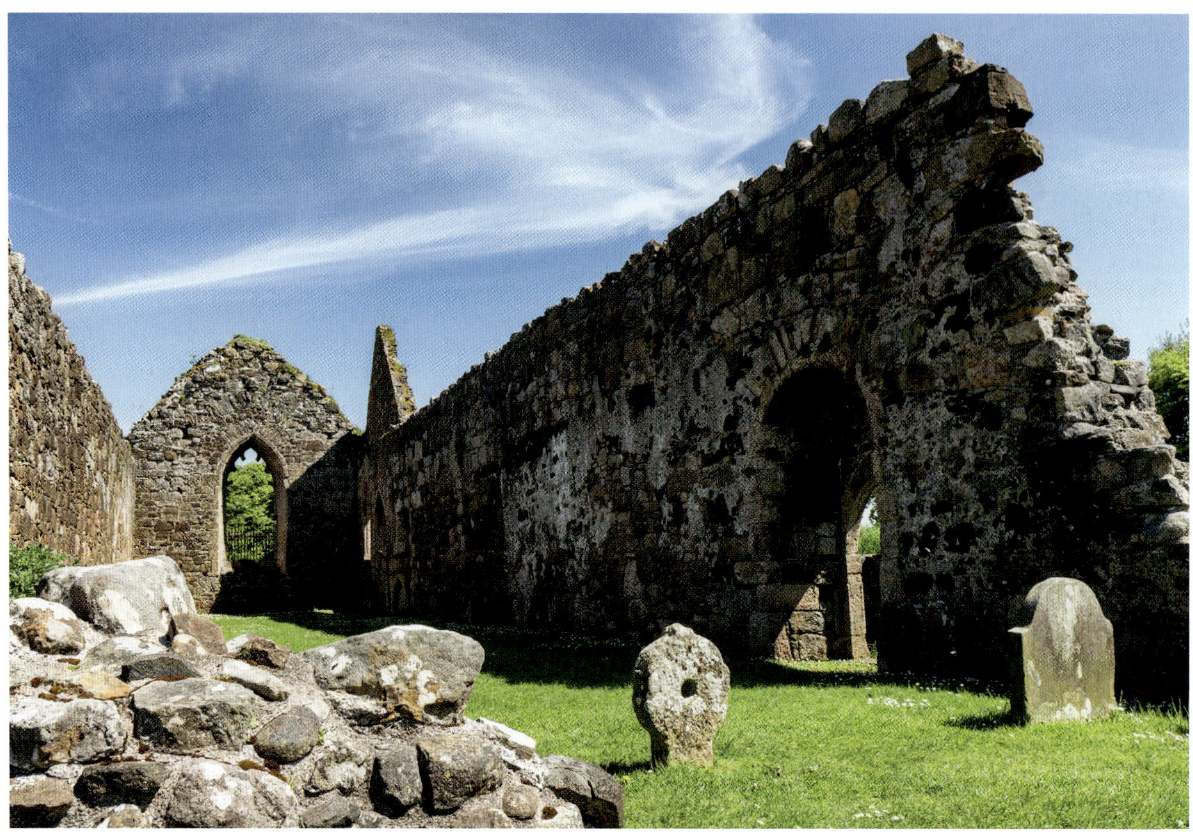

and, intriguingly, that Ireland would gain its independence with the arrival of a sailing ship with its sails on fire. She also predicted that two local standing stones would come together, which it is thought they did when they were used in the building of Ballycastle Harbour.

The building of this harbour, in the mid-1700s, briefly made Ballycastle one of the most important industrial towns in Ireland. This was thanks to a visionary called Hugh Boyd who had a lot to thank Sorley Boy for.

Sorely Boy was born in Dunineeny, 'Fort of the Fair', whose ruins are on the cliffs overlooking the ferry terminal. Ballycastle, 'town of the castle', is named for a castle built by his son Randolph, the first Lord of Antrim, in 1609. It was Randolph who granted lands here to the town's first constable, one Hugh McNeill, exactly a century before his great-great-grandson, Hugh Boyd, became landlord.

Financed by an initial grant of £10,000 from the Irish Parliament, Boyd built his harbour in the old bed of the River Margy with the East Pier on the Strand, where the Marina Pier and bowling green are now. Completed in 1748, it was the only harbour along the entire coast from Red Bay to the Foyle where ships could be sheltered.

Boyd built Ireland's first railway (of a sort) to transport coal from the colliery under Fair Head (coal mining actually continued to the 1960s). He also built a salt works and developed the local linen trade, which exported to the US, and a spectacular Glass House, where bottles were manufactured.

He lived in style in the old manor house near the sea front, where great parties were held with the likes of Ireland's most famous harpist, Arthur O'Neill, who played his first gig at 'Squire Boyd's' when he was a young man. The house, opposite the Marine Hotel, stands today.

Boyd's industrial renaissance didn't long survive him, but Ballycastle had another golden age when the railway arrived and the town's many Victorian houses were built.

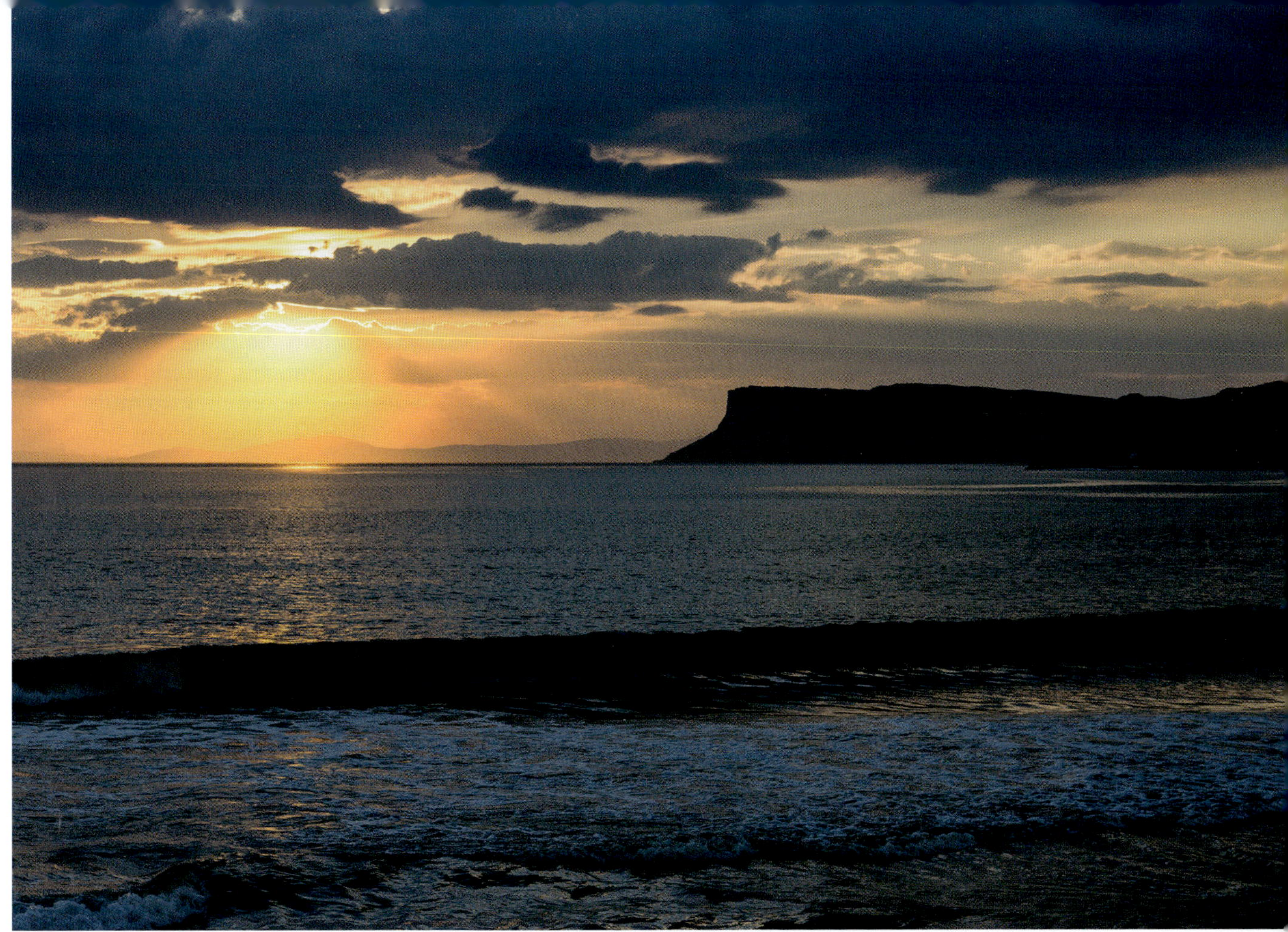

Mention Ballycastle to anyone from the north of Ireland and, inevitably, they will mention 'yellowman', dulse and the famous Ould Lammas Fair. The hub of this ancient fair is around the Diamond, where markets and fairs have been held since the late 1700s. This was where the hiring fairs took place, when men and women would line up in the hope of being picked by an employer for farm or domestic work.

Recent excavations beneath the Diamond revealed the vast walls of what some believe was a 16th-century castle, belonging to Sorley Boy himself. It is possible that Hugh Boyd took stone from that castle to build the lovely Holy Trinity Church that stands there now. Boyd himself is buried in a vault here, alongside members of his family.

Just up from the Diamond is the old courthouse, which now houses Ballycastle Museum. A centuries-old tower house forms the basis for the cells here. The Celtic Revivalists who founded the Feis na nGleann, the annual Glens festival celebrating Gaelic culture, were busy in Ballycastle too. The Irish Home Industries Workshop set up in a shop in Ann Street, employing the finest craftsmen of the time to pass on their skills to local boys to help them make wooden toys and models. You can see examples of their work in the Museum.

Have a look too at the beautiful banner featuring Princess Taisie, which was carried in the first Feis na nGleann in Cushendall. It is from Princess Taisie that Glentaisie, most northerly of the Glens, derives its name. Her great beauty attracted King Nabghodon of Norway to Rathlin Island, her home. Unfortunately for him, she was already betrothed to Congal, son of Rudhraith, King of Ireland. The two fought a mighty battle on Rathlin Island, ending only when Congal slew Nabghodon.

Having been granted land stretching from Ballycastle to Dunseverick Castle, the couple lived on the slopes of Knocklayde in a fort named Duntaisie.

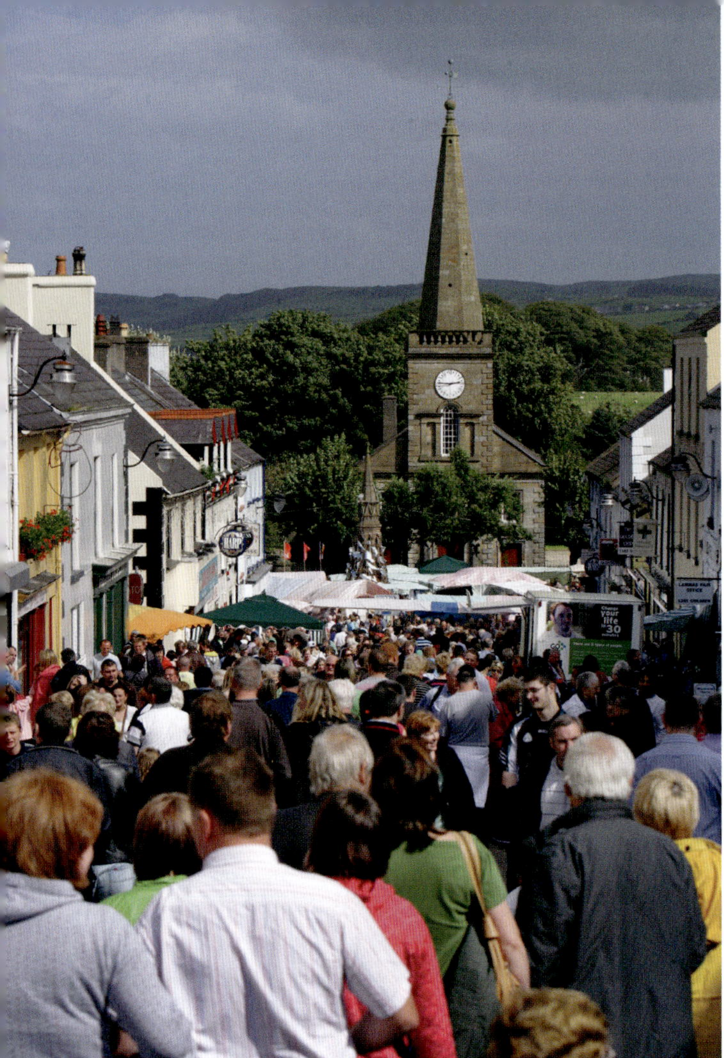

THE OULD LAMMAS FAIR

At the Ould Lammas Fair boys, were you ever there?
Were you ever at the fair in Ballycastle-O?

The famous song that celebrates this even more famous fair was written by a local bog-oak carver, John Henry Macaulay. It tells the story of a local lad who, while at the trenches in Flanders, recalls his love, Mary Ann, and the yellowman toffee she ate at the fair.

The fair itself, held on the last Monday and Tuesday of August, originated in the Celtic harvest festival of Lúnasa, and has much in common with the Puck Fair and Ballinasloe Horse Fair, Ireland's other most famous traditional festivals. Today, it still brings people from all around the world, including many returning exiles from Ballycastle, to keep alive the old traditions. Not least of these is the sale of dulse, the edible seaweed, collected locally on the shores all along the Glens and dried, and the honeycomb toffee-like yellowman.

Hundreds of stalls sells goods of all kinds while the horse-trading still goes on, as do the farming demonstrations, sheepdog trials and horse racing on the beach. Live music is everywhere and there's a spectacular fireworks display at the sea front.

It was during a wet Ould Lammas Fair in 1898 that Guglielmo Marconi arrived in Ballycastle to view progress on trials to establish one of the world's earliest commercial wireless signals.

Our next stop is Rathlin Island. There has been some kind of boat service between here and Rathlin for centuries, and today a popular ferry runs from Ballycastle to the island.

RATHLIN ISLAND

'A place that has space and a cleanness that lifts the heart', said Irish author Michael McLaverty of Rathlin Island, the only inhabited island in Northern Ireland.

It's less than seven miles on the ferry from Ballycastle, but a world away too. So distant from the routine and rhythm of ordinary life is Rathlin that even that sleepy town seems a cosmopolitan city by comparison. For an all too brief interlude you feel at one with the natural world, exposed to the elements, senses enveloped by chalk cliffs, sparkling bays, grasslands, lonely fields, heaving seas and the most amazing birdlife you are ever likely to encounter.

As you leave from Ballycastle on the ferry, the great headland of Fair Head emerges to your right and the famous white cliffs of Rathlin soon heave in sight. Seagulls dart over the waves, hovering as they near their prey. The distinct Scottish-tinged local accent fills the boat. It's just minutes (25 for the fast ferry, 45 for the car ferry – only limited availability for visitors, though) until the boat pulls into Church Bay, the tiny settlement that houses most of Rathlin's 100 or so population.

This journey to the first Irish island to be

populated by humans has been made regularly for centuries and for all kinds of reasons. By and large islanders have aimed to be as self-sufficient as possible, guarding the island's independence as fiercely as their environment. They have grown potatoes, barley and corn; caught crabs and lobsters; and kept cattle, pigs and sheep. They still do.

Every now and then a trip to the mainland would bring back flour and who knew what luxuries. Sheep and cattle have to be transported and family visited, for the ties between Rathlin and Ballycastle remain strong. The harvest would be gathered in after the Ould Lammas Fair, in which the islanders still play a part.

At times, just getting here has been a struggle. These waters, hosting the strongest tides anywhere around the island of Ireland, have witnessed more shipwrecks than any other Irish island. In Ireland's version of *Whisky Galore*, the barque *Girvan* ran aground near Bull Point in 1884 with 500 cases of the finest Scotch and Irish whisk(e)y. The seabed, it is said, is still littered with broken bottles. So awash was the island in whiskey, a rumour spread that even the pigs were allowed a few drams!

There really isn't a town to speak of on Rathlin – just a few houses overlooking Church Bay. The first thing you see as you alight from the fast ferry is the Manor House, part of the history of the island and a comfortable place to stay. There is just one, albeit rather large, pub, McCuaig's Bar. The centre of social life, it is crowded with visitors in summer, enjoying excellent fish and chips on the terrace overlooking the bay, while visiting musicians join the locals who keep the music scene going through winter.

Otherwise there's just a small co-op shop, a post office doubling as a souvenir shop, a tiny cafe and hostel and a handful of B&Bs, as well as the Boathouse Visitor Centre. But ultimately this is a place for rambling through beautiful scenery, appreciating spectacular views and what many believe is the finest birdlife in Europe.

Various features around the island mark its long history of occupation. It is believed that humans first came here from Scotland during the Stone Age. An archaeological dig in the north-west of the island found large amounts of porcellanite, a rare form of crystallised basalt which was used to make axe heads. The only other place in Ireland where it is found is outside Cushendun. These axes were traded to Scotland, England and Wales, and possibly further afield.

Nor was Rathlin left untouched by the early Christian missionaries who followed St Patrick. St Columba, en route to Iona in Scotland, was one such visitor, but St Comgall, who founded a monastery in Bangor, made the most significant contribution. It was under the auspices of Bangor that Comgall established a monastic settlement here in the sixth century, on the site of today's St Thomas's Church, not far from the Manor House. This early church was attacked a couple of centuries later in the first Viking raid on Ireland. The Vikings returned twice to plunder and destroy the settlement.

While we can't be too specific about times – keeping records was not a preoccupation of the MacDonnells – Rathlin was for some time under the ownership of the one-time Lords of the Route, who based themselves at Rathlin Castle. At this point readers would feel a little cheated if there wasn't a Sorley Boy connection. This time, though, he or those belonging to him were on the wrong end of the savagery.

During dangerous times, Sorley Boy and his comrades would send their wives, children, elderly, and sick to Rathlin Island for safety. During one of his regular altercations with the English Crown, Sorley Boy did just this, little knowing that the notorious English adventurer Sir Francis Drake, under the instructions of the Earl of Essex, had his sights set on the island. Drake stormed the castle and demanded its surrender. A few were given safe passage but, in one of the most terrible massacres in Irish history, the English forces hunted down and slaughtered hundreds of women, children and elderly, having already killed the defenders of the castle.

It is said that Sorley Boy, who had to follow events from the mainland, lost many relatives of his own that day. Little wonder that he would later burn Carrickfergus to the ground in revenge. This was not the last massacre on the island. We will come to an equally terrible event later.

The modern story of Rathlin begins with the Reverend John Gage – descended from a

Norman knight called de Gaga, an associate of William the Conqueror – who bought Rathlin Island in 1746. His son Robert built the first section of the Manor House a few years later. It was home to the family until the 1970s.

Its first restoration owes much to one Richard Branson and a spot of bother he got into back in 1987. His transatlantic hot-air balloon journey ended unexpectedly early in waters off Rathlin, and so grateful was he for his prompt rescue and welcome from the ever-hospitable islanders that he donated £25,000 to them. Some of this was used to restore the lovely Georgian Manor House, which was later turned into a hotel. It was refurbished again in 2017 at significantly greater cost, and a stay here gives you a great insight into the island's history.

RAMBLING AROUND RATHLIN

There are several walks around Rathlin. As there is only one main road, it's very hard to get lost, but essentially it's a tale of three lighthouses!

It is advisable to begin at the Boathouse Visitor Centre in Church Bay. Built of chalk and basalt as a base for the Waterguard, whose unenviable task it was to deter the highly efficient smugglers of the island, it is just a short walk from the ferry stop. While you're there you can find out all about the smugglers as well as getting a unique insight into the island's heritage and history. This includes Robert the Bruce's famous encounter with the spider, which we will soon come to. Self-guided walks are also available here.

On these walks you could visit the island's three lighthouses, smugglers' coves, seals sunning themselves in delightful Mill Bay or, nearest to the Boathouse, the 18th-century kelp house in Church Bay. Kelp – seaweed collected on rocks or the seashore after storms – was a major export from these parts. The seaweed was burned in one of the 150 kilns that that existed here, eventually forming a molten mass that hardened when cooled. It was used in glass making, bleaching linen, photography, medicine and the drug industry.

THE WEST LIGHTHOUSE AND SEABIRD COLONY

The one walk you should not miss is the longest – just over four miles, up and down hills, through fields and grasslands to the West Lighthouse and its fabulous views. About a mile before you reach your destination, you'll encounter first Kinramer and then Kebble nature reserves with their extensive areas of grassland, dry heath and marshes and lakes. You can take the Kebble cliff walk along a dramatically rising route with views of sea stacks emerging from the Atlantic.

Known as the 'upside-down lighthouse', as its light is at the bottom, the West Lighthouse was built between 1912 and 1916, and has the only red light used in Ireland. To understand life in Rathlin and enjoy its spectacular views as far afield as Donegal and Islay in Scotland, a visit to the West Lighthouse should be mandatory for anyone coming to the island.

If you have binoculars, bring them! From the observation point at the top you can look to the waters below, maybe picking out whales, dolphins and porpoises and occasionally basking sharks.

But it is the view of the cliffs that offers one of the nature lover's greatest experiences. Each spring and summer thousands of birds congregate here, making it one of the world's largest seabird colonies. Squabbling for nesting sites amid the cliffs and the stacks that rise from the waters below are fulmars, guillemots, kittiwakes and dozens of other bird species. But the stars of the show are undoubtedly the puffins, which dig their nesting burrows on earthy banks or in the cliffs themselves. These brightly billed sea-parrots arrive in their thousands in May and leave by mid-August, returning each year to lay a single egg.

An exhibition at the lighthouse reveals the island's story and, just as importantly, the nature of the birdlife that can be found.

The other two lighthouse walks can be adapted on your return from the west of the island or can begin at Church Bay, the hub of Rathlin.

OPPOSITE: VIEWS OF RATHLIN AND THE RATHLIN FERRY

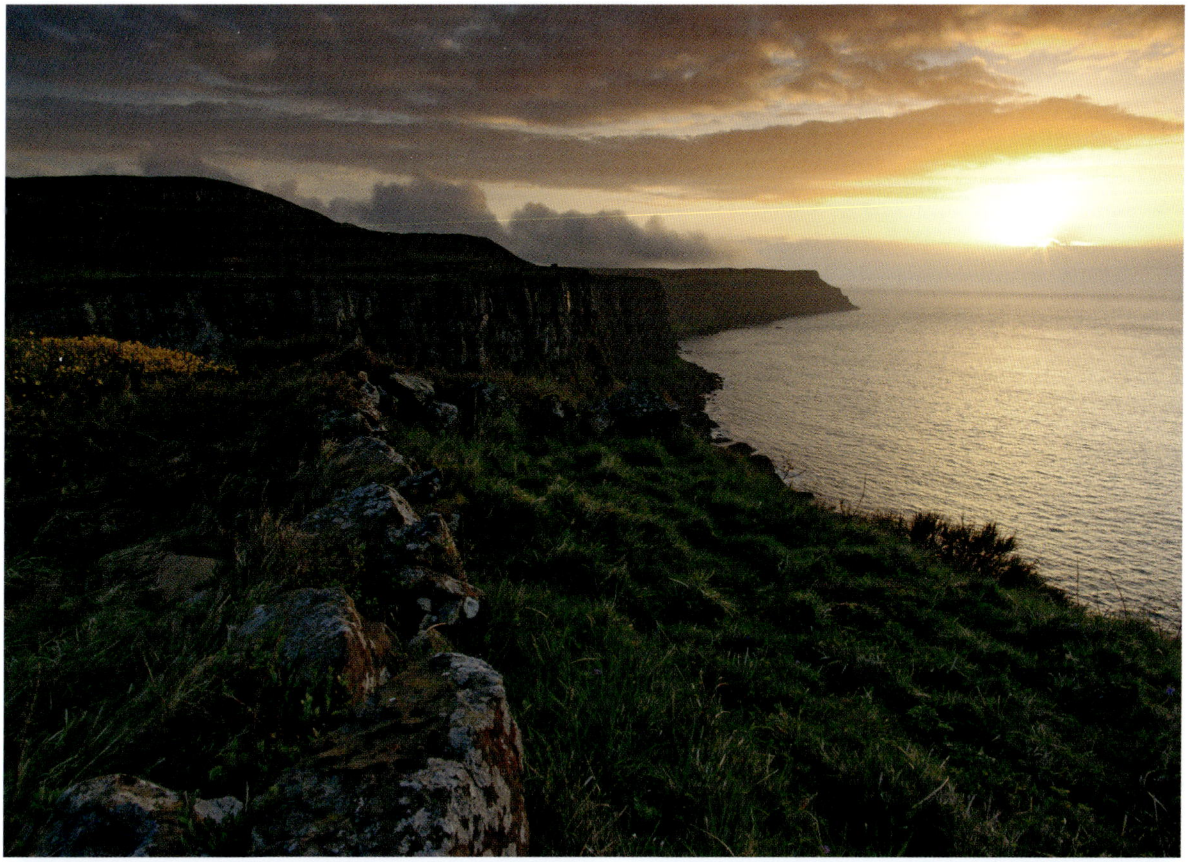

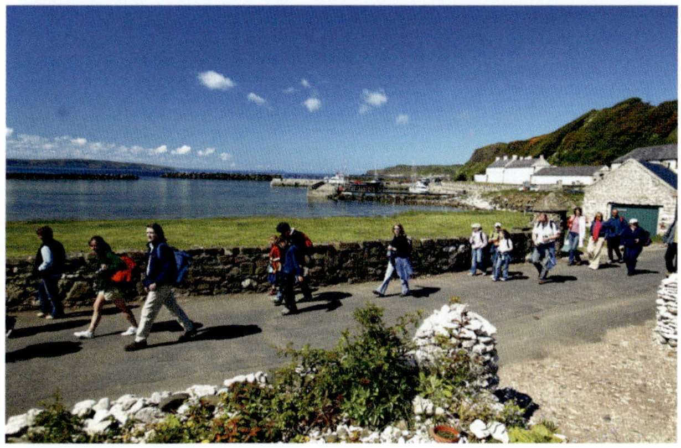

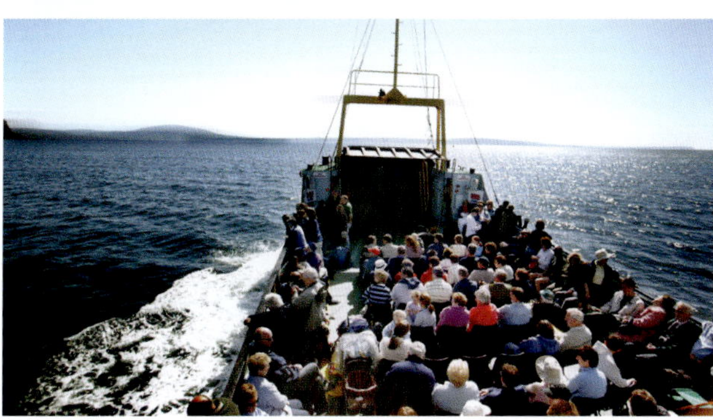

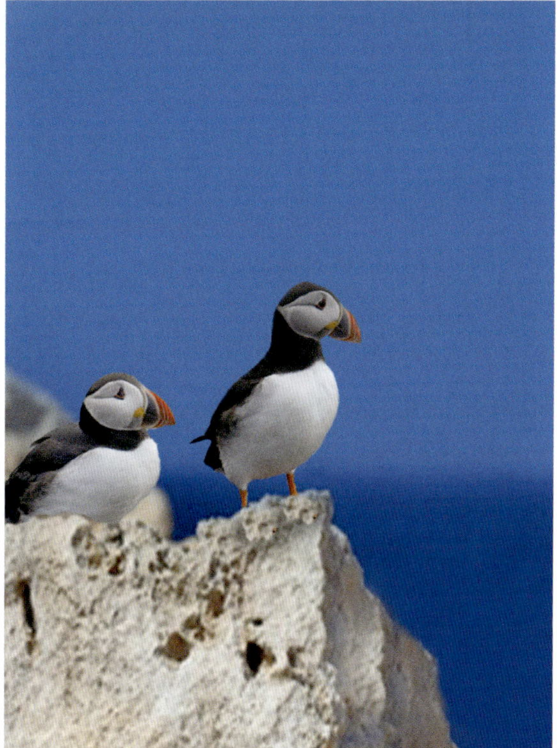

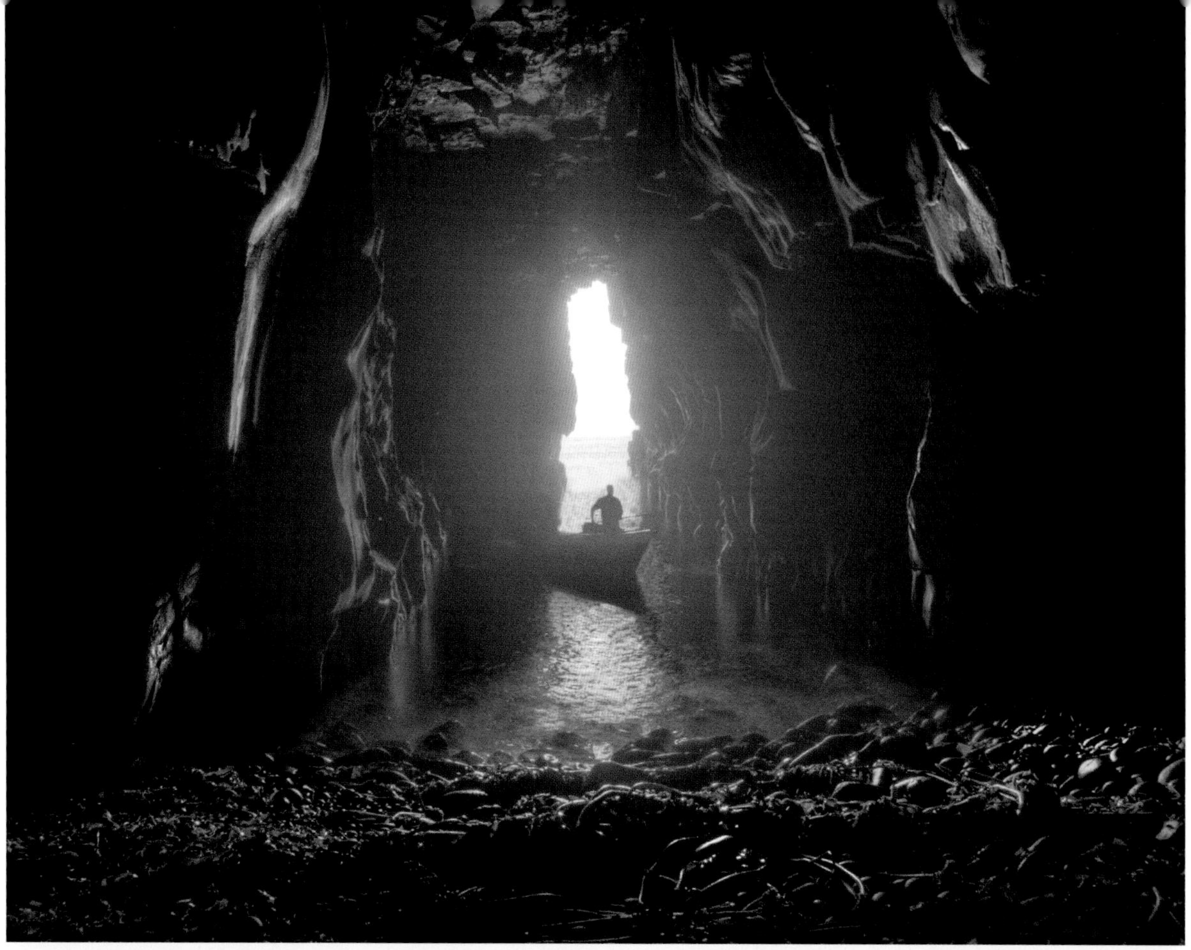

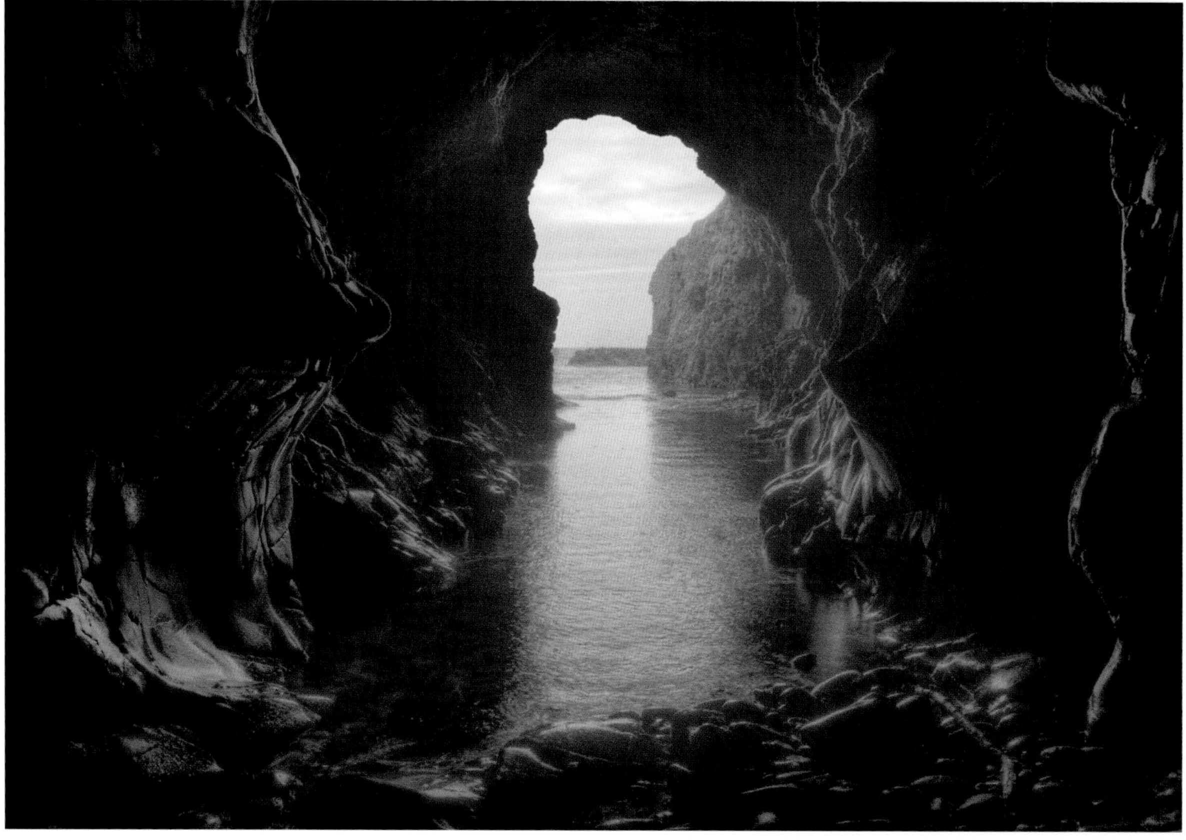

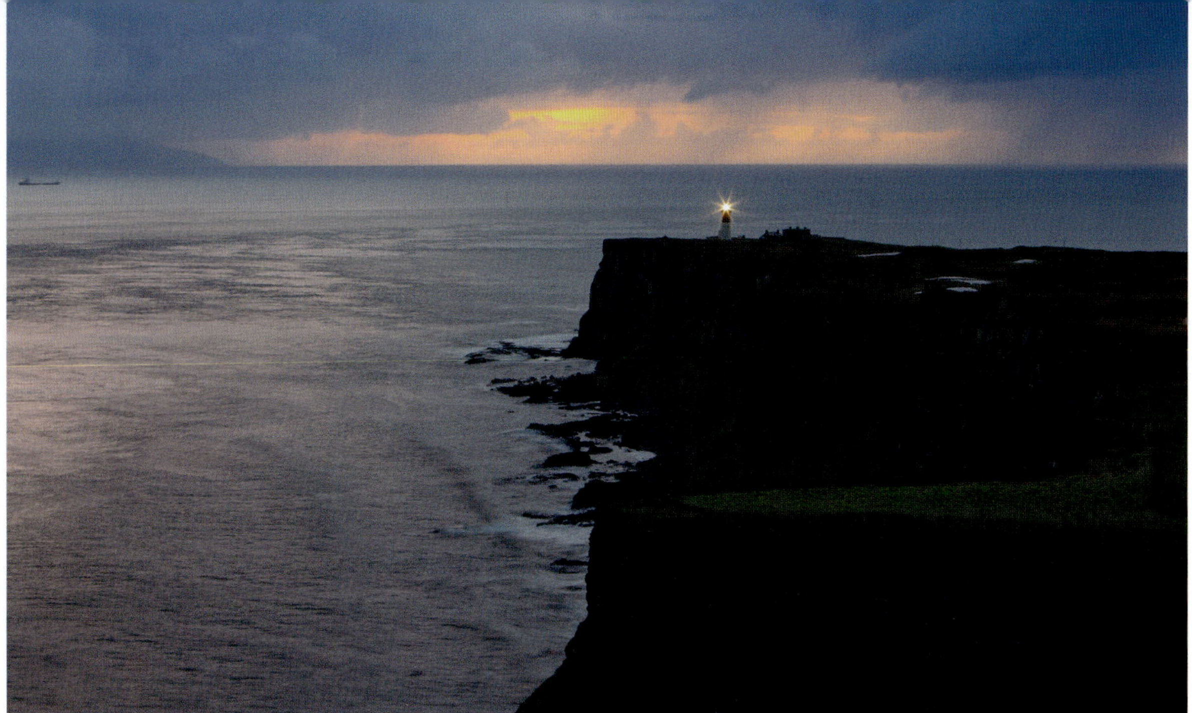

OPPOSITE TOP: BRUCE'S CAVE, RATHLIN. OPPOSITE BOTTOM: OWEYNAGOLMAN CAVE, RATHLIN. ABOVE: RATHLIN'S EAST LIGHTHOUSE

THE EAST LIGHTHOUSE

The first built of Rathlin's three lighthouses, the East Lighthouse has been guiding ships to safety since 1856. To its left, concrete slabs used to support an aerial built by Guglielmo Marconi can still be seen. The Italian electrical engineer who invented a radio signalling system known as wireless telegraphy established a pioneering radio link with Ballycastle here, to speed up transmission of local shipping information to the ship-owners in Liverpool.

If you walk along the coast southwards from this lighthouse you will soon see a small wall on the cliff edge, the remains of what is known locally as Bruce's Castle, originally built by the Normans. Beneath the lighthouse is Bruce's Cave, where future Scottish king Robert the Bruce is said to have taken refuge after fleeing his native Scotland and the army of Edward I in 1306.

Although the famous legend of Bruce and the spider was more likely an invention of Walter Scott, some think it is possible that Bruce did take refuge in a cave here.

These photos are from local expert in cave photography Andy McInroy, who has spent years photographing the caves of Rathlin. He believes it is more likely that Bruce visited the magnificent Oweynagolman cave, 150 yards from Bruce's Castle, known locally as Avaragh. The Bruce connection was rekindled in 1968 when Lord Bruce, a descendant of the Scottish king, visited Rathlin bringing Robert the Bruce's sword, its leather hilt and, believe it or not, his set of teeth!

RUE POINT LIGHTHOUSE

The third lighthouse is at Rue Point, near the southern tip of Rathlin. Near here another terrible massacre took place in 1642, when over 1600 Campbell soldiers invaded the island, overwhelming the few hundred island men and MacDonnells at the 'Hollow of the Great Defeat'.

This massacre was partly due to settling old scores but also had a religious dimension, coming as it did after the 1641 uprising, when Gaelic forces made a last desperate attempt to drive out the Protestant settlers that had been planted on their land. The powerless wives and children of the Catholic MacDonnells watched from the high ground of the Hill of the Screaming as their hugely outnumbered men were killed before them. Then they themselves were put to the sword or driven over the cliffs at the Chasm of the Women near Rue Point.

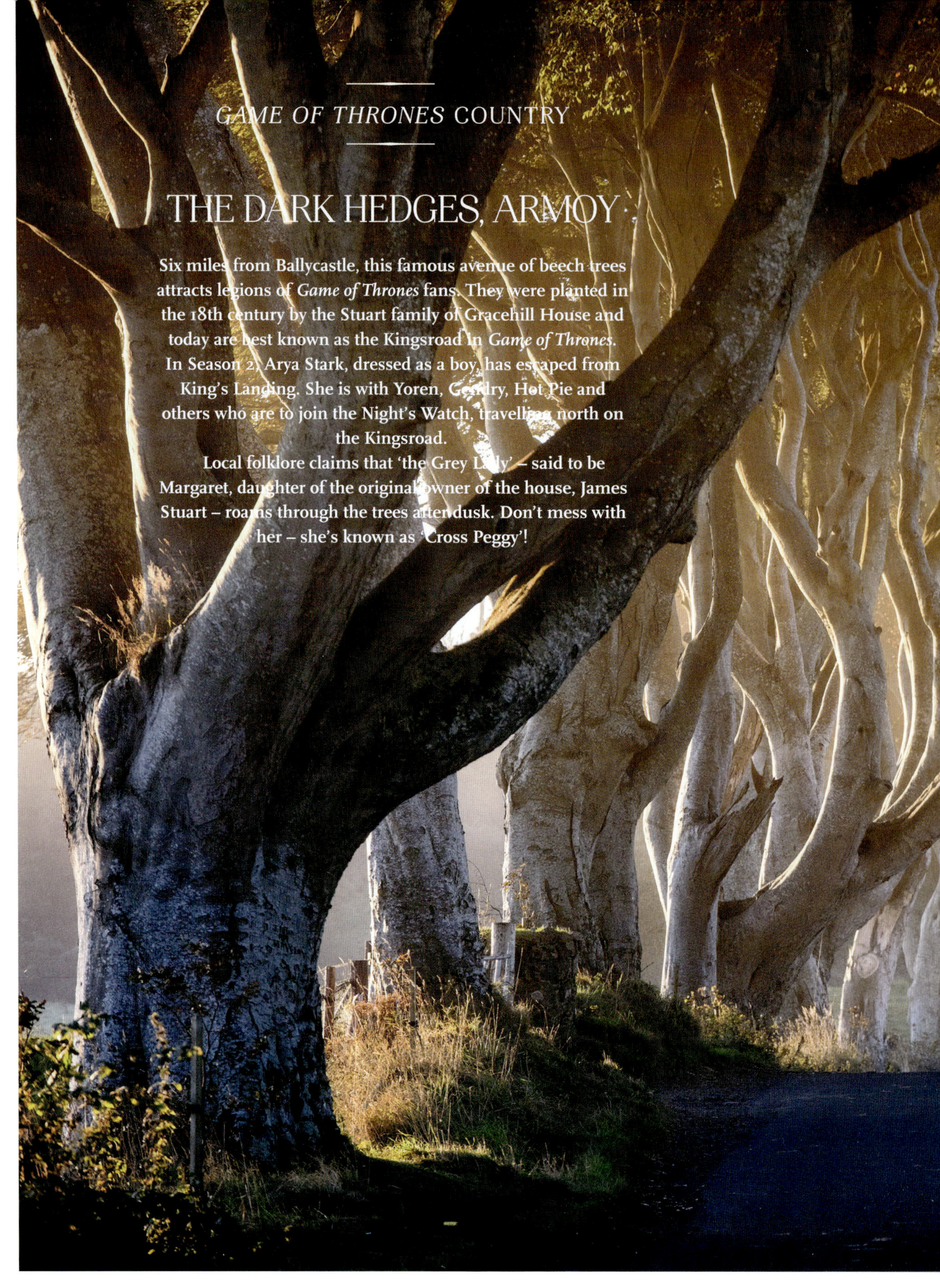

GAME OF THRONES COUNTRY

THE DARK HEDGES, ARMOY

Six miles from Ballycastle, this famous avenue of beech trees attracts legions of Game of Thrones fans. They were planted in the 18th century by the Stuart family of Gracehill House and today are best known as the Kingsroad in Game of Thrones. In Season 2, Arya Stark, dressed as a boy, has escaped from King's Landing. She is with Yoren, Gendry, Hot Pie and others who are to join the Night's Watch, travelling north on the Kingsroad.

Local folklore claims that 'the Grey Lady' – said to be Margaret, daughter of the original owner of the house, James Stuart – roams through the trees after dusk. Don't mess with her – she's known as 'Cross Peggy'!

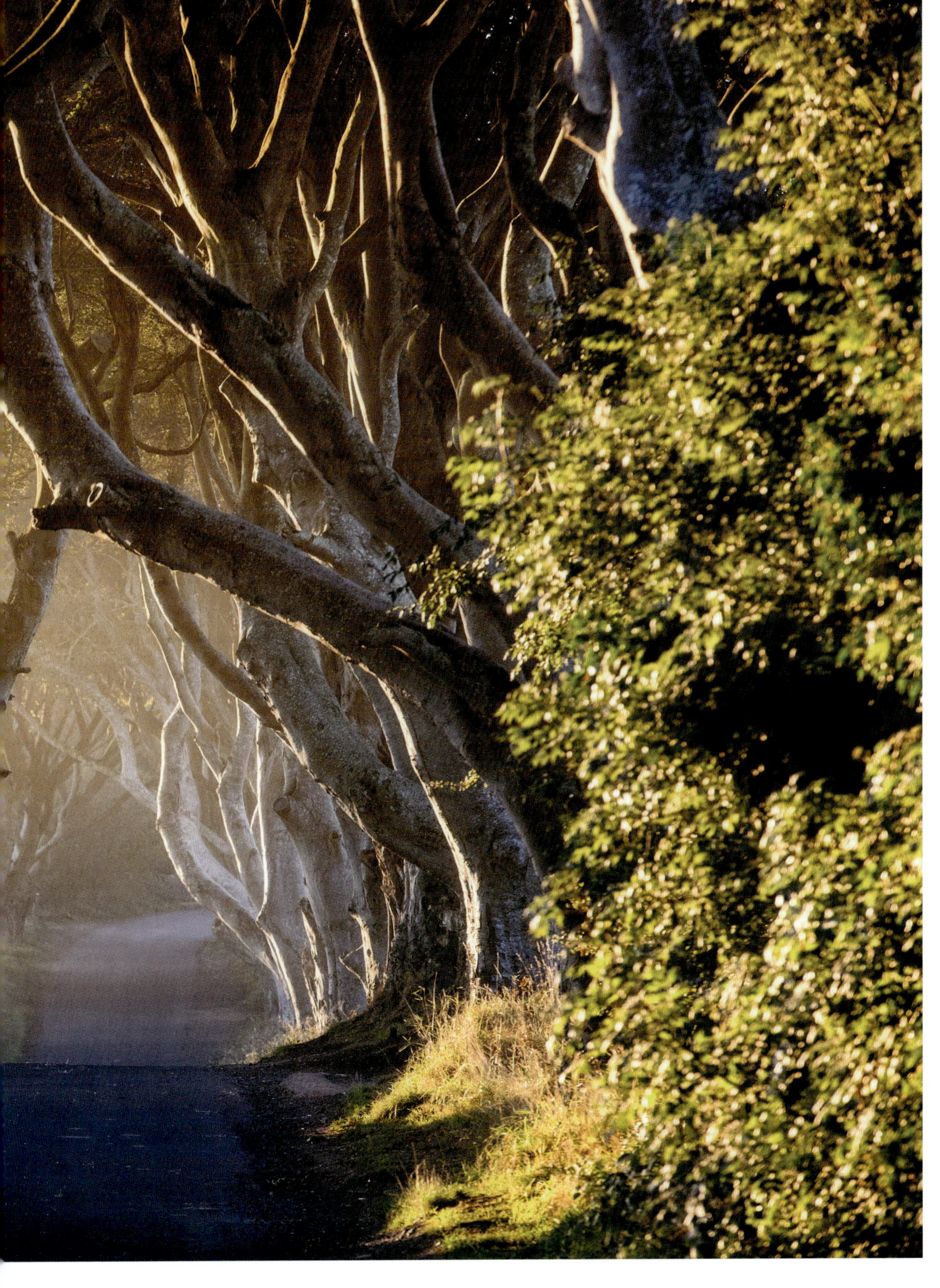

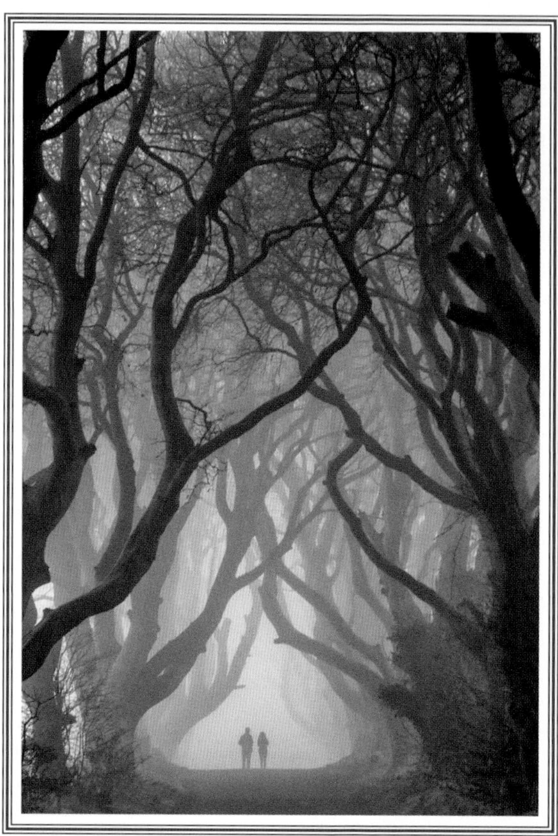

Door N°. 7

Today the avenue of trees no longer belongs to
Gracehill House, but the beautiful house is still there
and the estate now hosts a bar and restaurant, as well
as an 18-hole championship golf course. It also has
the seventh door in the *Game of Thrones* series, which
depicts the three-eyed raven and several sigils. At the
bottom of the door, a beech leaf within a crown refers
to the beech trees of the Dark Hedges.

KINBANE HEAD

From Ballycastle onwards we start to encounter the most famous attractions of the Causeway Coastal Route, in surprisingly quick succession. Most of these spectacular landmarks involve dizzying views to the waters below. Clearly the MacDonnell clan didn't suffer from vertigo, as they built several castles on dramatic cliffs.

About three miles (five kilometres) outside Ballycastle, we find the first of these. Located on the wild Kinbane Head, all that remains of Kinbane Castle is the ruins of a small tower and wall, but if you have the nerve to walk around the nearby cliff-top paths (please take care: they can be narrow and steep as the cliffs fall away to the sea), the views of Rathlin Island across the bay and Scotland beyond it are stupendous.

Kinbane Castle was built by Sorley Boy's older brother, Colla, in the 1540s but didn't long withstand attacks from the English, being demolished within a decade or so. Colla had been appointed Captain of the Route (much of the Causeway Coast and Glens of Antrim) as his elder brother James focused on the MacDonnells' interests in Scotland. These were considerable, as they were constantly involved in the power battles of that country.

Colla was greatly respected and gave the English forces trying to unseat the clan in Antrim a real run for their money. However, he died of battle wounds at Kinbane Castle in 1558 and the captaincy of the Route passed to Sorley Boy.

It is said that during his tenure here, a group of besieging English soldiers were massacred in a cave nearby, later evocatively known as the 'Hollow of the English'. The castle was built up again, but was finally destroyed in the 1700s.

PORTANEEVY VIEWPOINT

Not far from here you can pull into Portaneevy Viewpoint for an unusual perspective on the world-famous Carrick-a-Rede Rope Bridge, and also enjoy views of Rathlin Island ahead and nearby Sheep Island.

CARRICK-A-REDE ROPE BRIDGE

If walking on a slightly swaying rope bridge 30 metres above swirling waters is your idea of fun, then join your fellow daredevils here. The name means 'rock in the road', the rock (actually a volcanic plug) being the island you're taking the bridge to, and the road being the path taken by Atlantic salmon as they return to their place of birth to spawn in the Bann and Bush rivers. Sadly, fewer and fewer have done so since the 1960s, hence the demise of the salmon industry here.

A working fishery was located here from the 1700s until recent times, and this perilous-looking bridge is actually a much safer modern version of the original bridges made by salmon fishermen. The deep waters around here are ideal for netting fish and the fishermen made the very rough rope bridges so they could check their nets on the island. They even used to haul their fishing boats up here for safety, using a crane.

Evidence of the fishermen's lives can be seen on the island courtesy of a restored bothy and old ropes, as well as remains of the gear for lifting the boats and nets.

From the car park the walk is magnificent, with wonderful views beyond Rathlin Island to the Mull of Kintyre and great cliff views as you wind down past coastal farmland.

If you have the nerve to look down and around as you make your way across the bridge, you might spot a porpoise or seal in the water. Even the steep walk down to the bridge is an enthralling experience, with the sound of guillemots, oystercatchers, razorbills, kittiwakes and fulmars increasing to a crescendo as they swoop around the cliffs.

The island is listed as an Area of Special Scientific Interest. The views and birdlife somehow seem even more impressive here.

There's a great walk on the other side of the car park too. From here you can walk to Larrybane Head, where puffins breed in the cliffs and you get the closest view of Sheep Island, to which sheep were ferried by boat to graze.

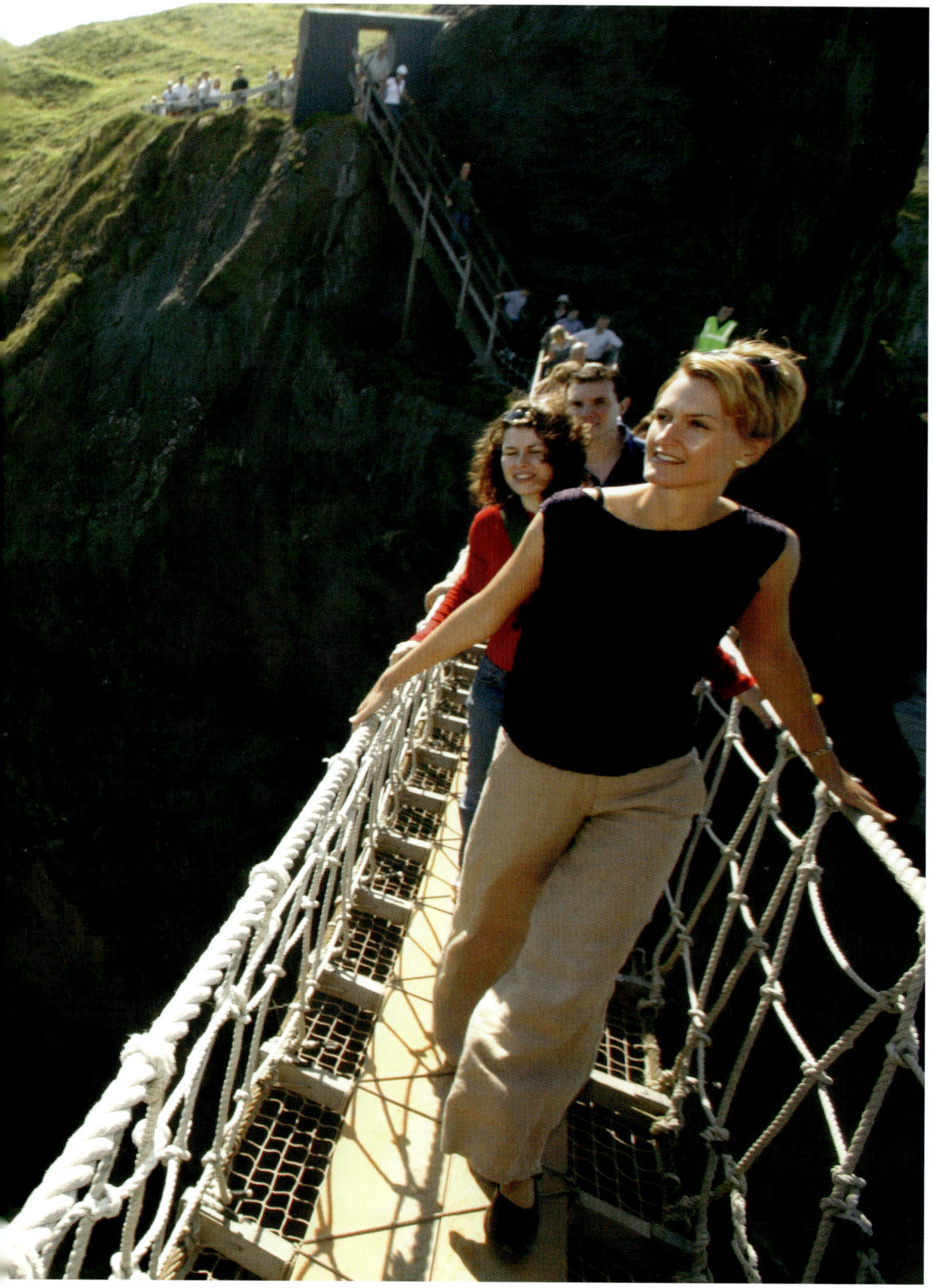

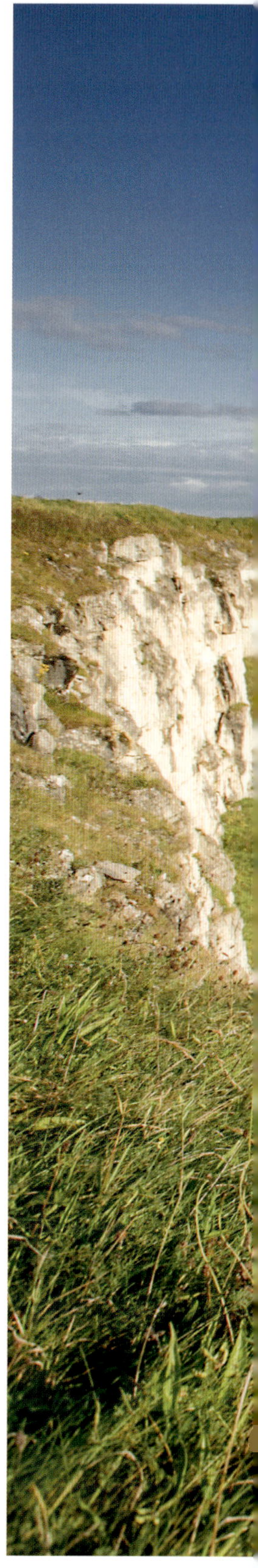

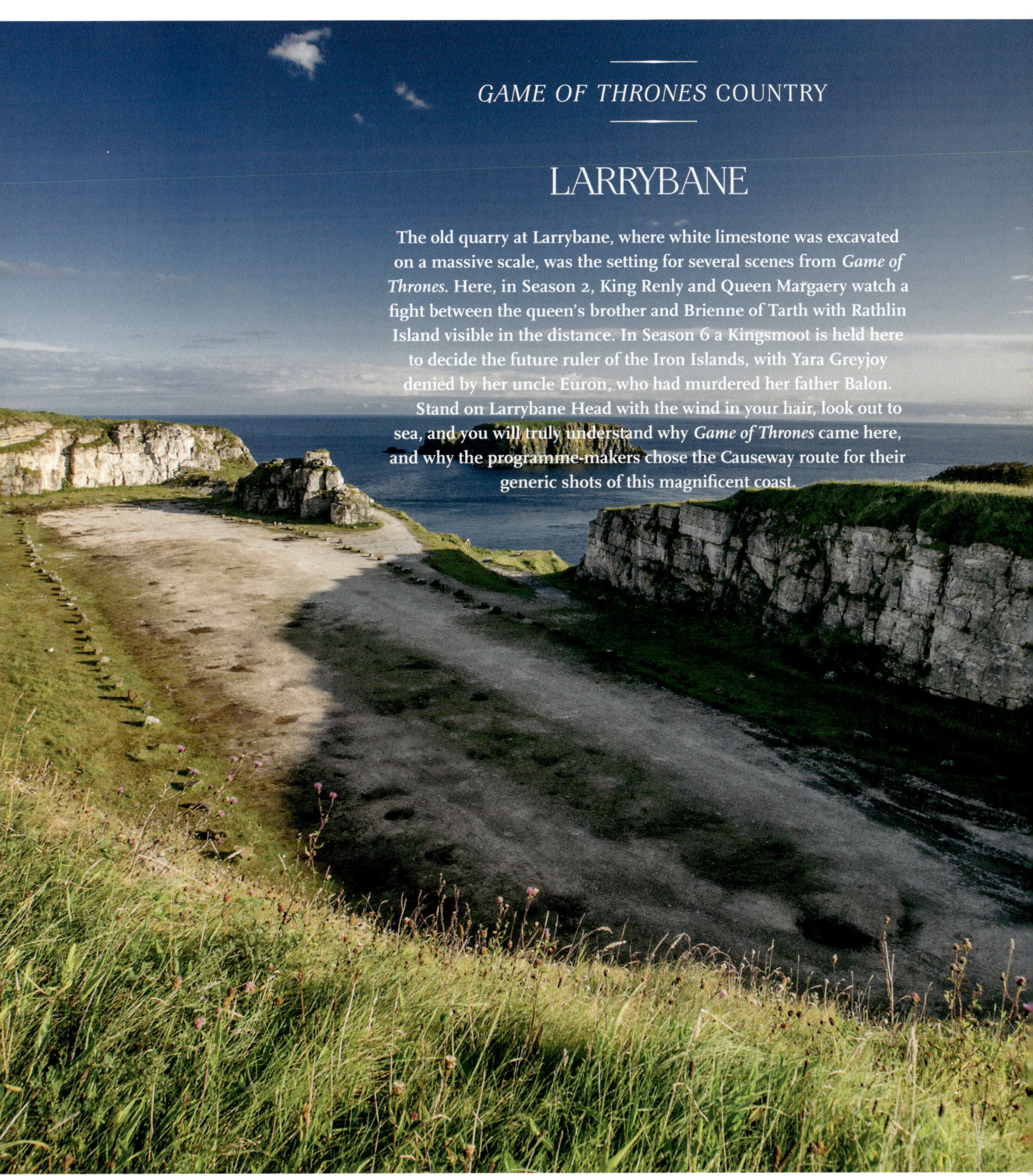

OPPOSITE: CARRICK-A-REDE ROPE BRIDGE. ABOVE: LARRYBANE QUARRY

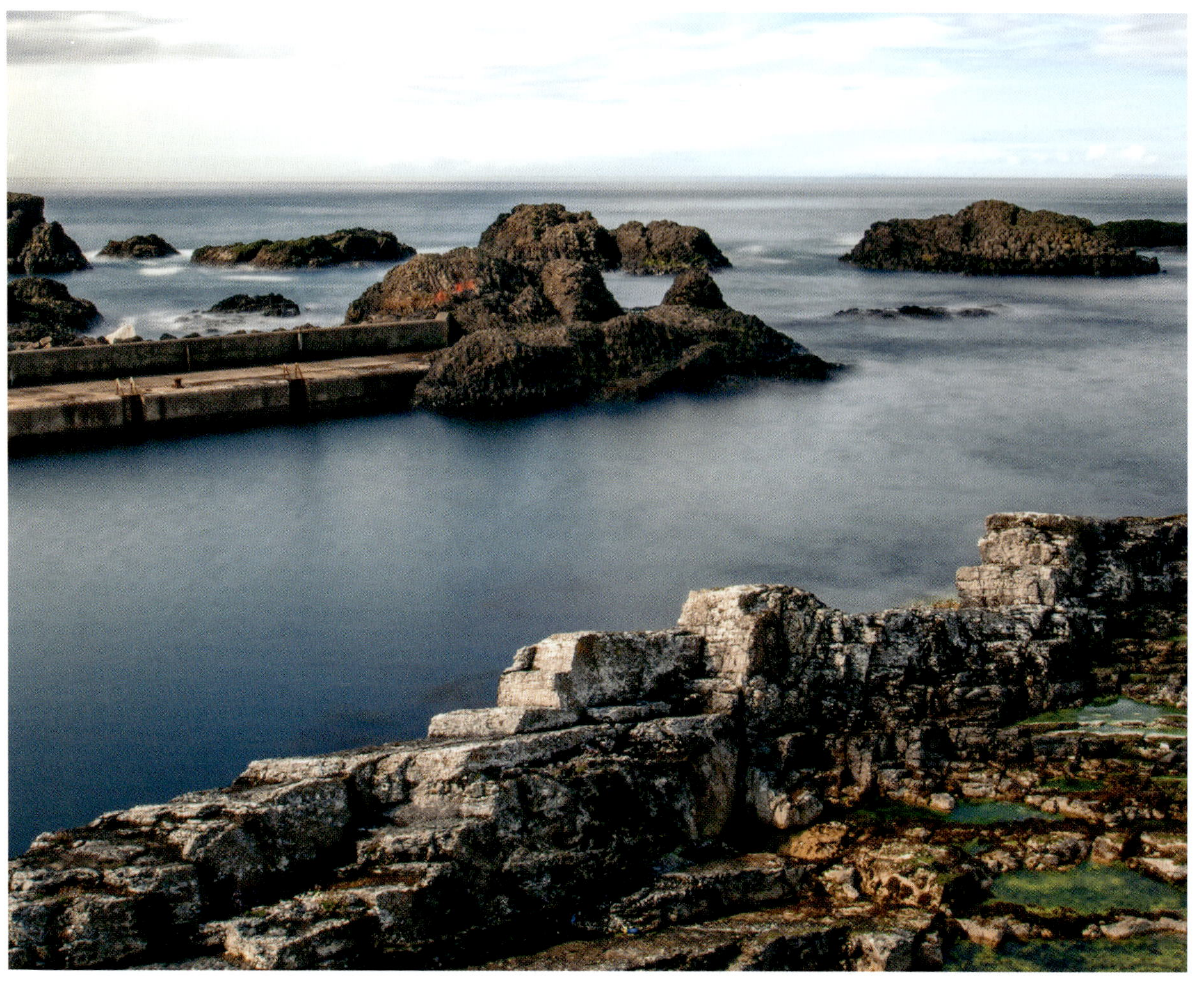

BALLINTOY AND BEYOND

BALLINTOY

You can see the distinctive white tower of lovely Ballintoy Church as you sweep down Knocksoghey Brae. Standing out against the blue of the water, it looks almost Mediterranean from this perspective.

But it's the idyllic little harbour as you descend to the sea that attracts the visitors. Beyond it, amazing rock formations lead the eye to Rathlin, Sheep Island and even Scotland, and along a dramatic line of cliffs with their ancient caves. Basalt rocks and islets are everywhere, and this acts as a modest but intriguing eye-opener for the forthcoming heavyweight attraction, the Giant's Causeway.

On your way down look out for the distinctive-looking Bendhu House, built with bare concrete in a cubist style by a Cornish artist.

This harbour, built from local limestone blocks, was packed in the 1800s (well, it wouldn't take much) with ships taking burned lime products and setts (stones) for the pavements of burgeoning industrial cities in England and Scotland. Fishing boats have used its shelter for centuries, but today its fame comes from another source.

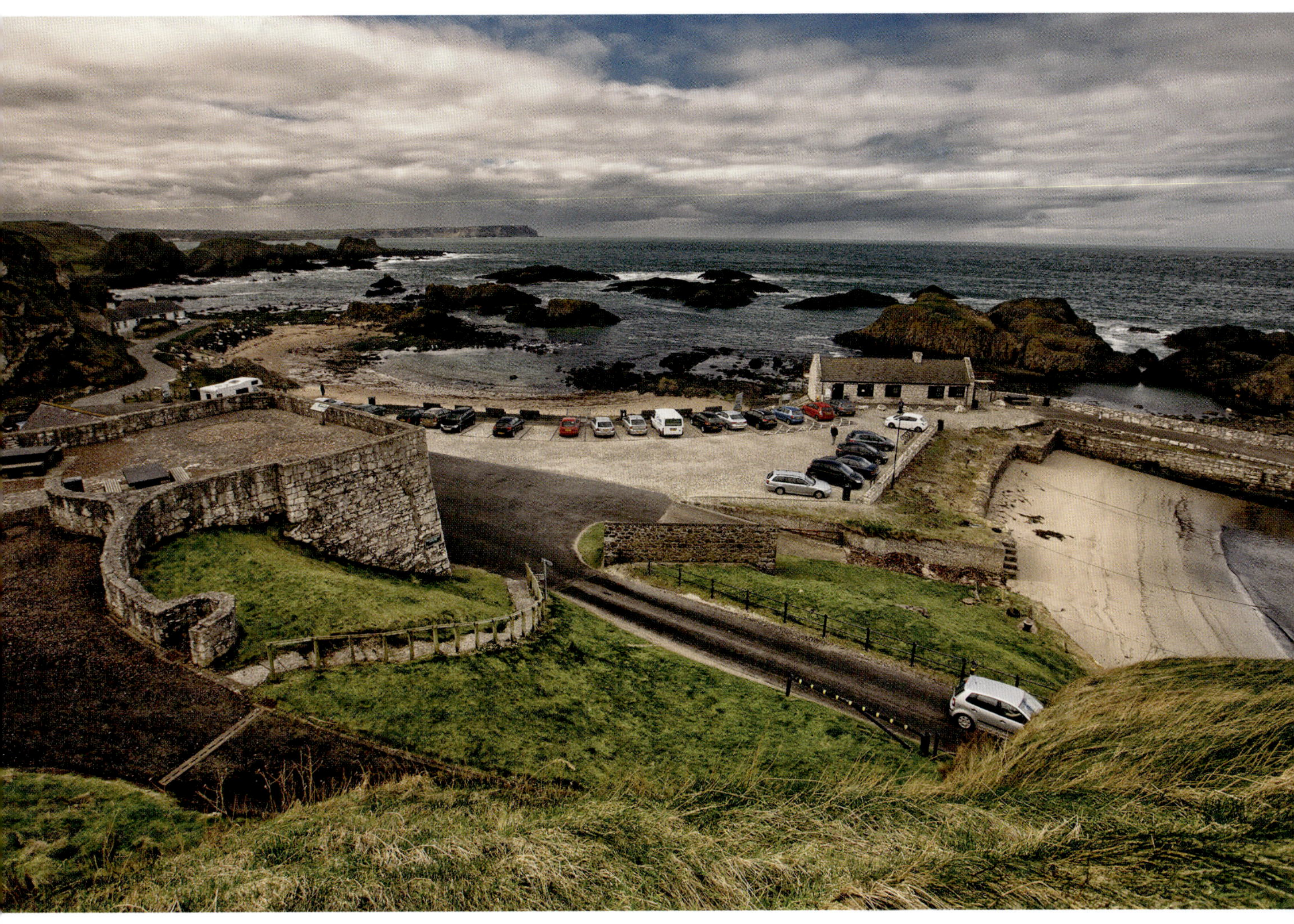

BALLINTOY HARBOUR/LORDSPORT HARBOUR, IRON ISLANDS

Ballintoy Harbour and the nearby beach were used several times as locations in *Game of Thrones*, including as Lordsport Harbour in the Iron Islands. In Season 2, Theon Greyjoy arrives back at Lordsport Harbour to try to convince his father Balon, ruler of the Iron Islands, to back Robb Stark in an attack on King's Landing. He is later baptised on the nearby beach in the faith of the Drowned God to symbolise his return to the family. The beach also became Dragonstone in Season 4 when Melisandre oversaw the burning of some of Stannis's bannermen.

In Season 6 parts of the beach were used when the priests of the Iron Islands and Aeron Greyjoy reminded Yara that the new ruler of the Ironborn would be decided at a Kingsmoot following the death of her father, Balon. In a later episode the beach is used as the setting for Balon's funeral, the drowning and rebirth of his successor Euron and the escape of Balon's children, Yara and Theon.

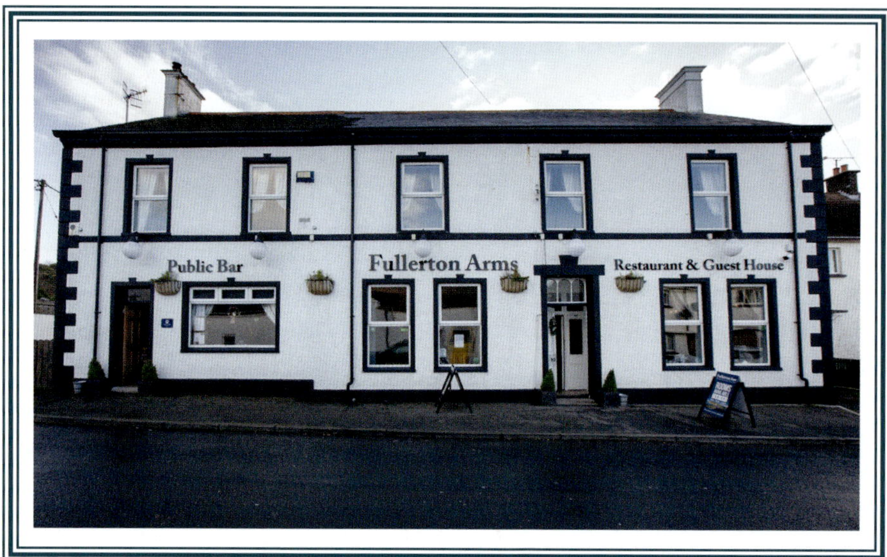

Door Nº. 6

Ballintoy's main street is home to the Fullerton Arms,
which hosts the sixth door in the series with a carving of the
largest of Daenerys Targaryen's dragons, Drogon, gripping
Dothraki stallions in his claws.

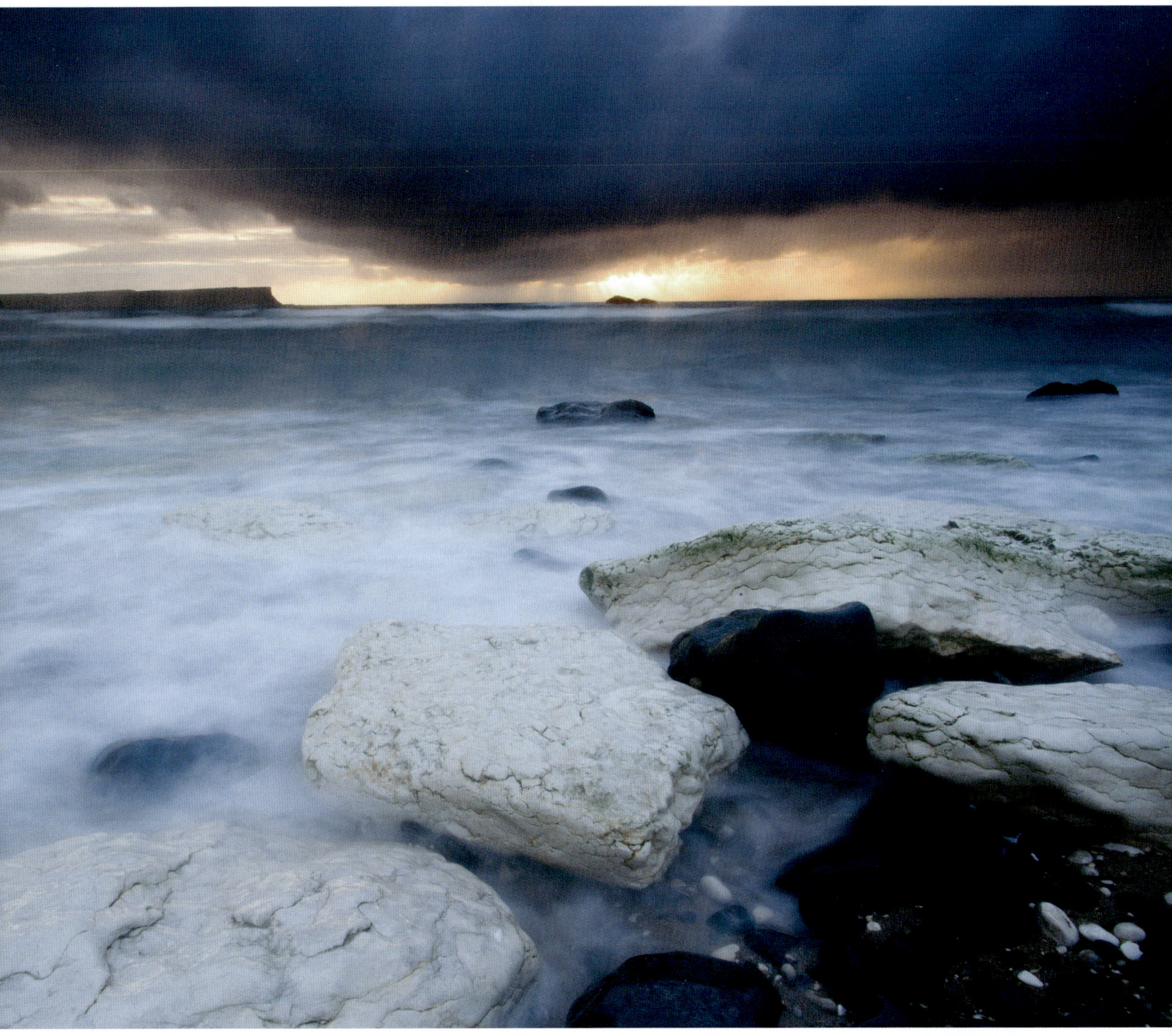

WHITEPARK BAY

Whitepark Bay is not just one of the most beautiful stretches of coastline in Ireland, it was one of the first human settlements on the island. Archaeological discoveries have revealed that axes and arrowheads were made and probably exported from here, thanks to the abundance of flint in the limestone cliffs.

On the highest point on the hills overlooking the bay is a dolmen, one of three passage tombs in the vicinity, known as the Druid's Altar.

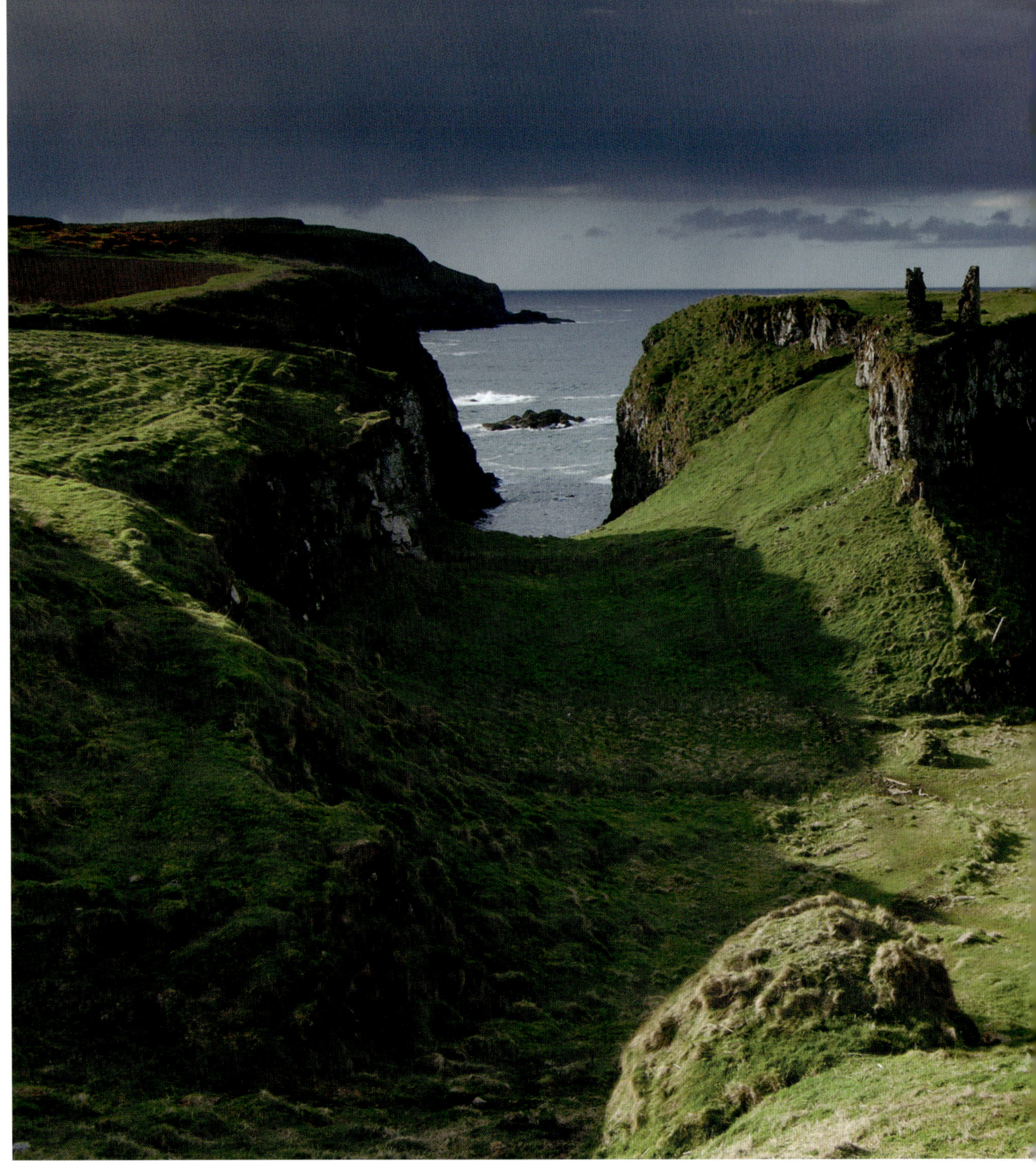

DUNSEVERICK CASTLE

Just three miles from the Giant's Causeway is another example of a ruined castle in a crazy clifftop location. In truth there is very little of it left, just the remnants of the gate lodge. But pull into the lay-by, look across, and take in 16 centuries of Irish history with the amazing views. The brave can actually walk up to the ruins from sea level.

It's believed that Saint Patrick baptised Olcán, a future Bishop of Ireland, here in the fifth century. Not long after, this became the seat of Fergus the Great, King of Dalriada

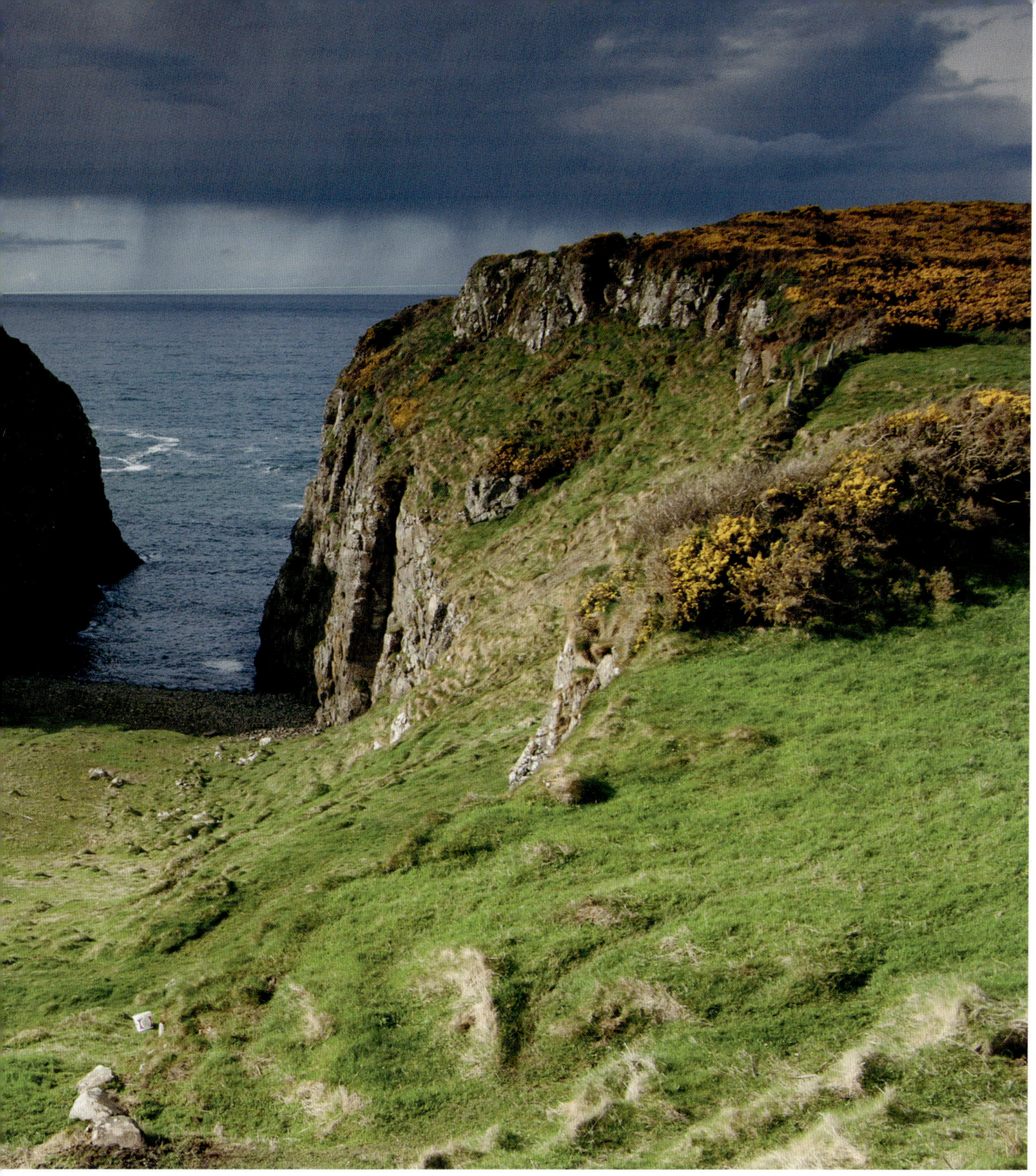

RUINS OF DUNSEVERICK CASTLE

(the kingdom that straddled western Scotland and north-eastern Ireland) and it is said that the sixth-century coronation stone used by Scottish kings originated here.

From the 11th century the O'Cahan clan occupied a castle here, God help them, though they lost it in the early 1300s, only to recapture it in the 1500s. It was finally destroyed by the troops of Oliver Cromwell, Lord Protector of the Commonwealth of England, Scotland and Ireland, in the 1650s.

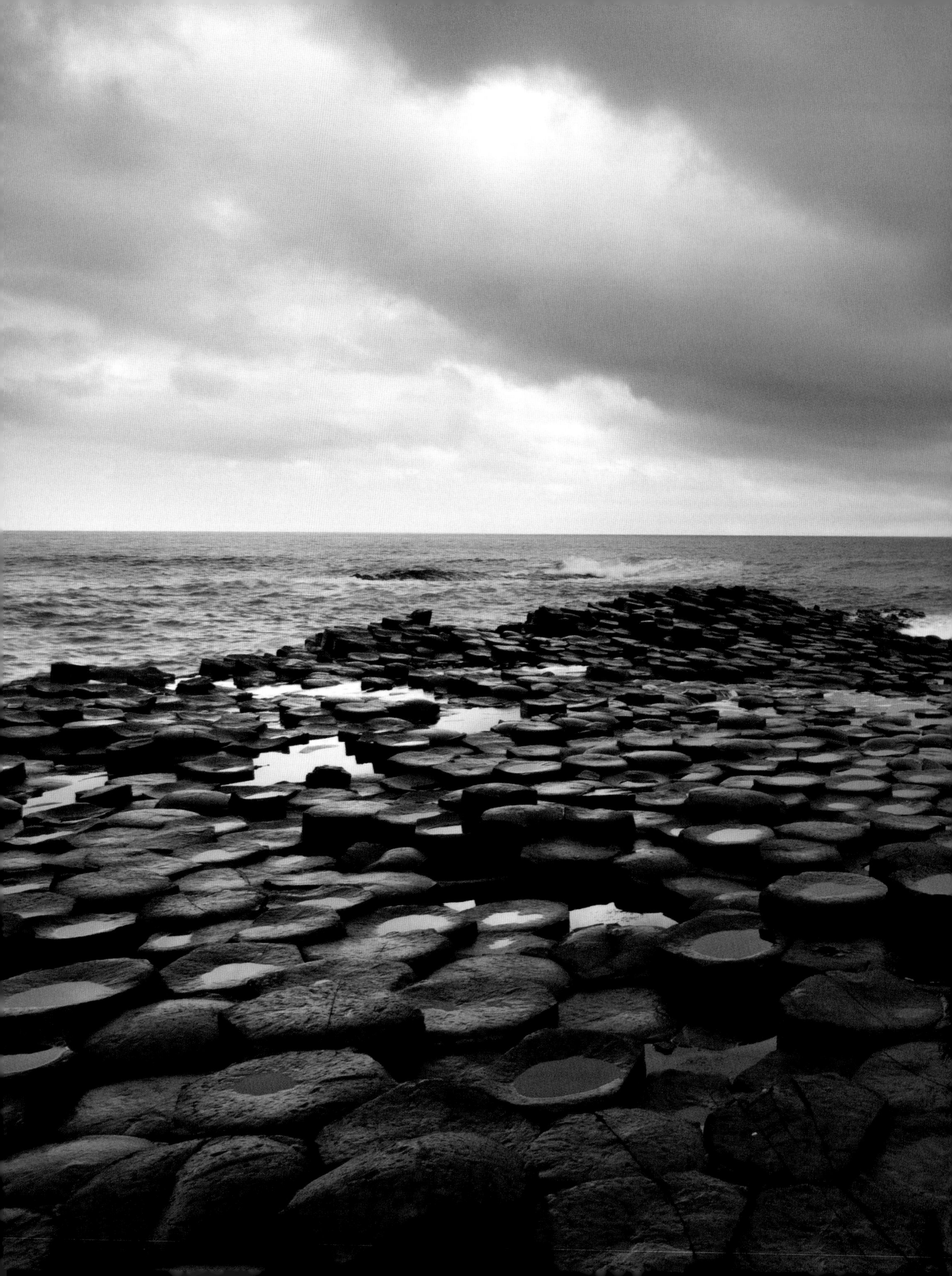

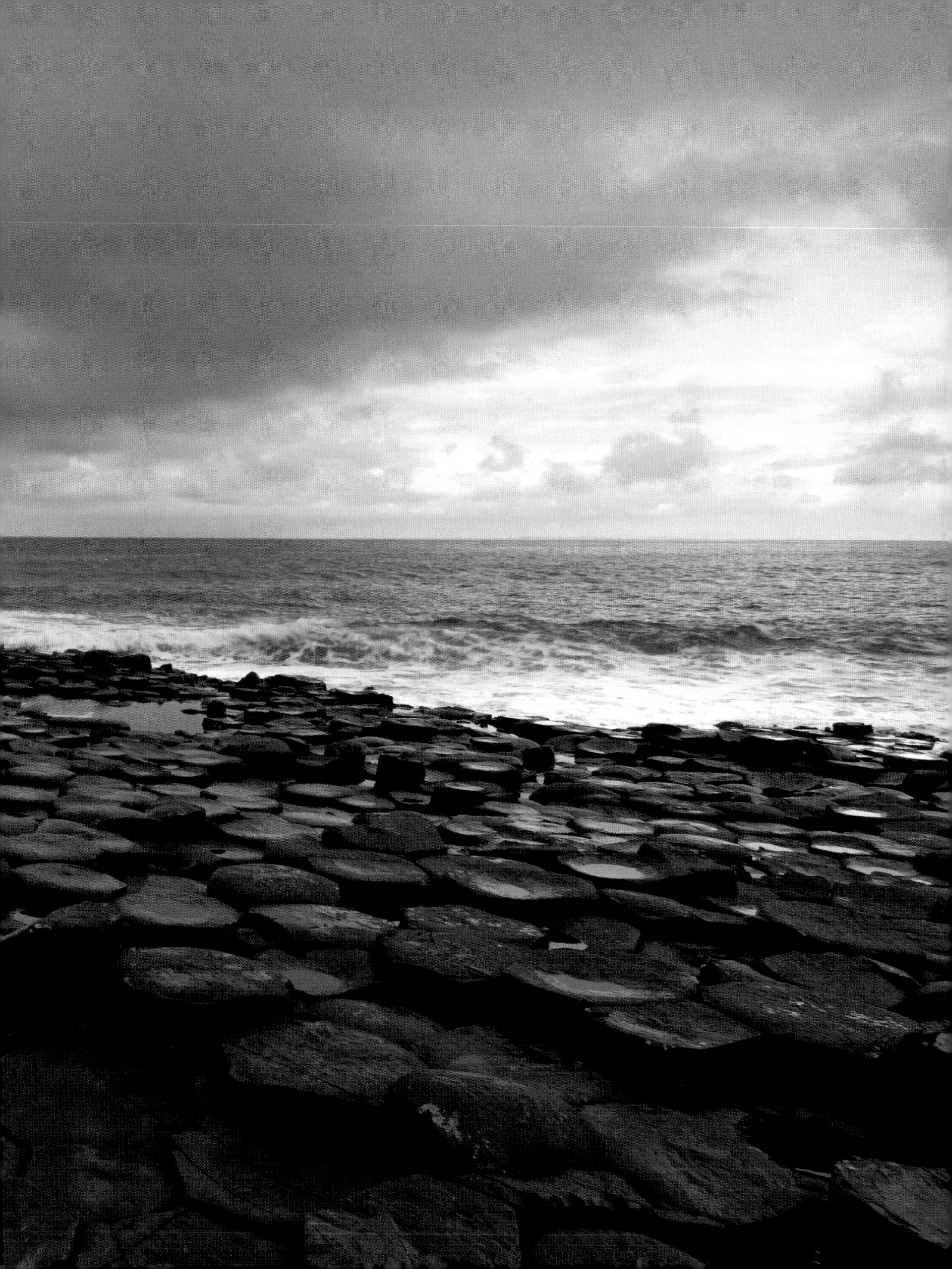

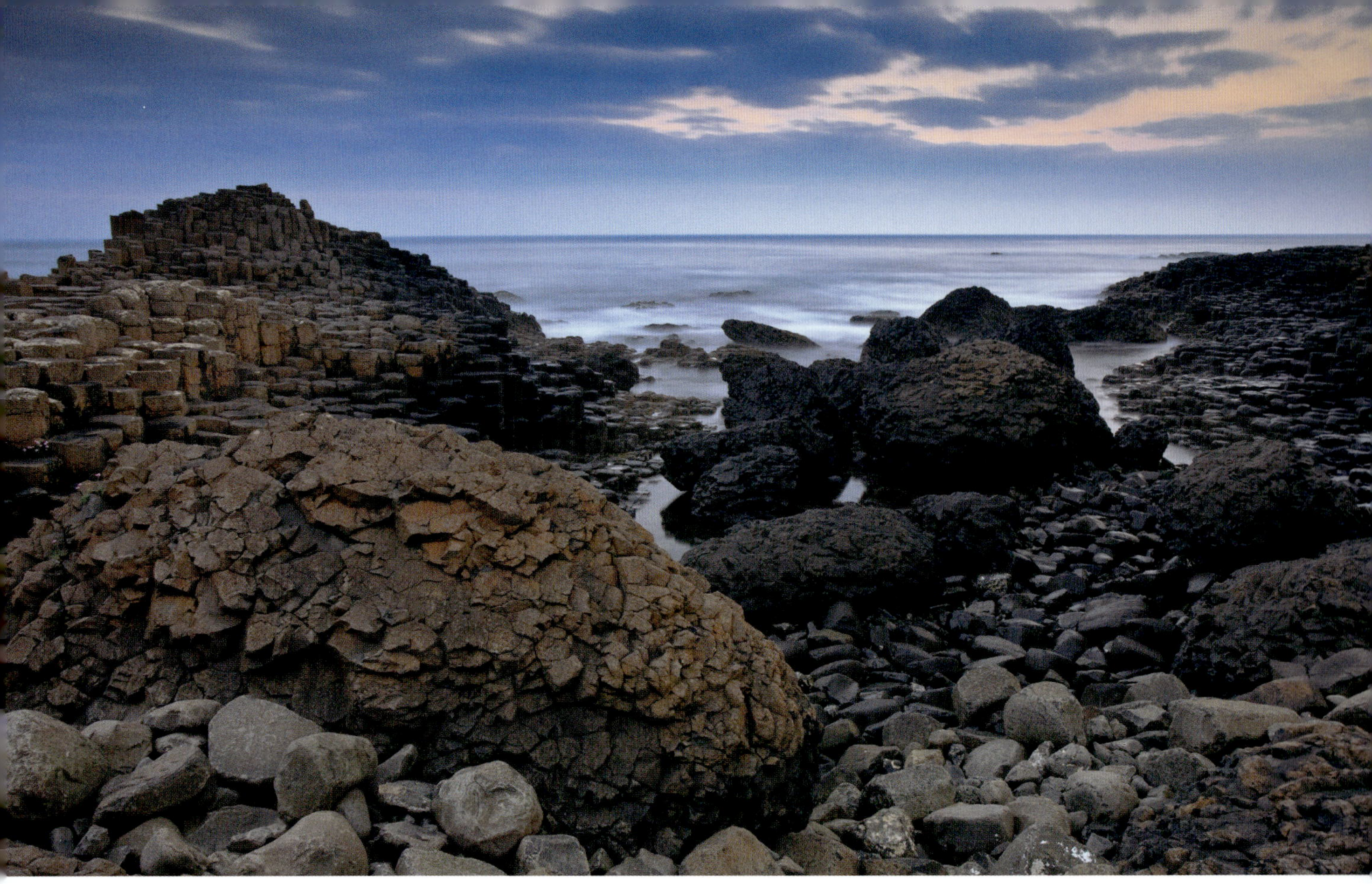

THE GIANT'S CAUSEWAY

It looks like the beginning of the world, somehow: the sea looks older than in other places, the hills and rocks strange, and formed differently from other rocks and hills – as those vast dubious monsters were formed who possessed the earth before man.
(William Makepeace Thackeray)

The Giant's Causeway does indeed feel like we are witness to a divine, bizarrely beautiful, but not universally successful attempt to form order from chaos.

It was created by powerful elemental forces over 60 million years ago when eruptions of molten lava rearranged the landscape, cooled and then were battered into shape by wind, water and ice: cycles of creation and erosion repeated over millions of years.

Today it is simply wondrous. 40,000 hexagonal basalt columns of various sizes leading to the sea: one of the world's most remarkable vistas.

Thanks to its creation myth, derived from Irish legend, this remarkable landscape acquired a name that's the perfect hook on which this spectacular coastline can hang its globally renowned identity. This is a place where giants stride.

The legendary explanation, apparently preferred by most visitors, is that Irish giant Finn McCool formed a vast pathway of local rock grabbed from the coastline to enable him to reach Scotland, barely 20 miles from here, to fight the local giant Benandonner. On arriving at the other end Finn discovered that his opponent was far bigger than he had imagined and raced home, followed by a furious Benandonner.

Fortunately for Finn, he had married above his intellect, and his wife disguised the not-so-giant warrior as his own baby son. Terrified by the prospect of fighting the father of such a large baby, Benandonner hurtled back to Scotland, tearing up the pathway as he went and leaving only the coastal columns we see today.

There are three parts to the Giant's

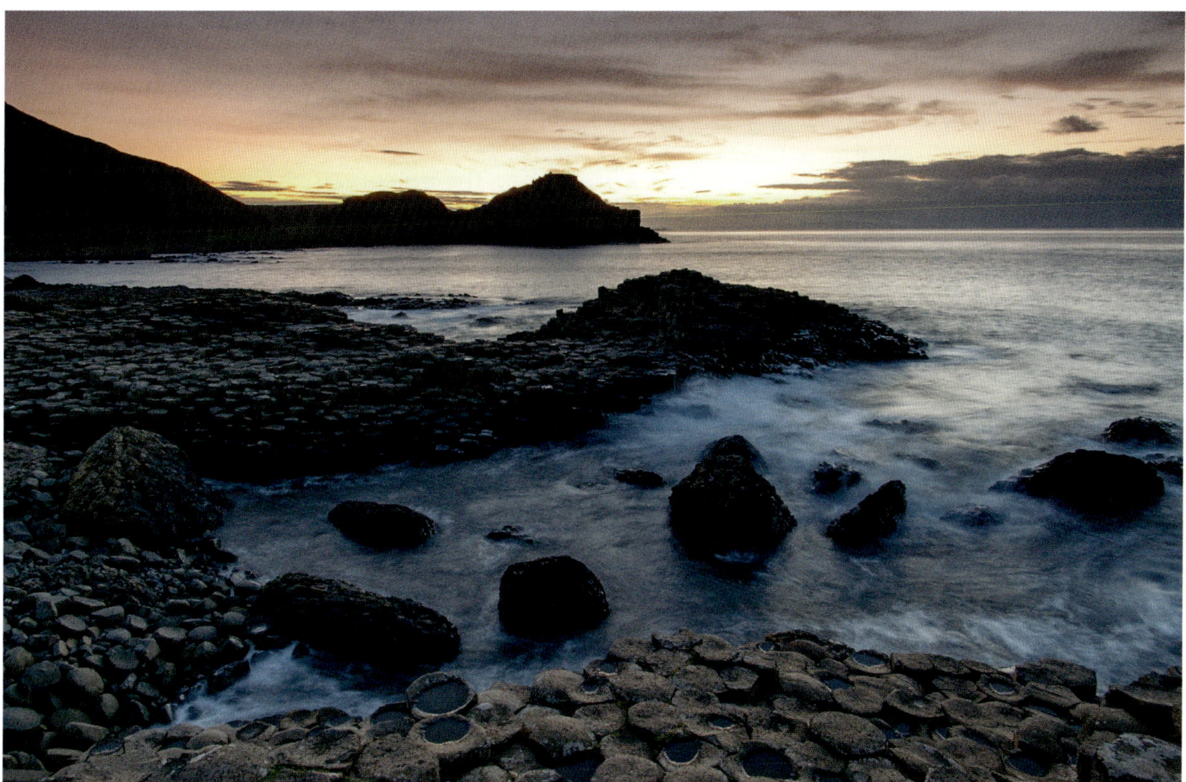

Causeway, and the audio guide you receive as you leave the Visitor Centre to take the path down will give you all the detail you need.

Some of the most recognisable views of the columns can be found in the Middle Causeway, home to the Wishing Chair, where columns have been aligned like a natural throne. There are various stipulations for those making a wish, not least wiggling your bottom three times afterwards!

The Giant's Marbles and the Giant's Well can be found in the Little Causeway, hardest to reach of the three.

The Grand Causeway is the largest of the three, with the most columns, and is home to the Giant's Fan, the Giant's Cannons and, above all, the Giant's Gate.

Just past the Grand Causeway is Port Noffer (the Giant's Bay), which should not be missed. Here you'll find the huge Giant's Boot, lost by Finn as he fled home. You will also have good views of the Giant's Organ and the Giant's Chimneys.

If you want to get the full experience, away from the tourist trail, you can take a guided tour, or a self-guided five-mile walk, along the cliff-top path from Dunseverick Castle to the Giant's Causeway over dizzying heights and narrow rugged paths. The views are stupendous – perhaps rather scary at times – as you get higher and higher, looking down at basalt rock islets and across to Rathlin Island before coming down to the Giant's Causeway. This miracle of geology has been attracting visitors for hundreds of years, but the real tourist mania began in the 1800s.

Enjoy a pint or a bowl of chowder in the charmingly old-fashioned Causeway Hotel, adjacent to the Visitor Centre, and you'll be part of this history.

Established by Elizabeth Henry in 1836, the hotel earned a steady business from the growing crowds, but had a battle on its hands when Kane's Refreshment Rooms entered the fray, especially in later years after Mary Jane Kane persuaded the Prince of Wales to drop in for tea and the establishment became known as Kane's Royal Hotel.

In those days many locals made a living as guides, some taking visitors to the causeway by boat, and competition was fierce. It grew fiercer when William and Anthony Trail took over the lease of the Causeway Hotel in 1887. Four years earlier they had opened the world's first hydroelectric tram, between Portrush (where the railway stopped) and Bushmills. Now they extended it to the Giant's Causeway and large numbers of visitors began to disembark from the terminus, which the Trails artfully built just by their hotel, leading to warfare between the independent guides and their own.

The Giant's Causeway was now well and truly on the tourist map and by the 1920s, when the Causeway Hotel and Kane's Royal Hotel were under the same ownership, tourism was thriving. Sadly, dwindling numbers in the post-war years saw the closure of the tramway and, in the 1960s, the demolition of Kane's Royal Hotel itself.

But the decision in 1986 to apply for UNESCO World Heritage status for the Giant's Causeway (the only such site in Northern Ireland) helped bring a new generation of visitors. In 2012 the multi-award-winning Visitor Centre was opened at a cost of over £18 million. The same year, the Giant's Causeway and Bushmills Railway was opened on the original two-mile tramway track, taking visitors into Bushmills and back.

Since 1961 the Giant's Causeway has been run by the National Trust, which also bought the Causeway Hotel in 2001. The number of visitors has never been greater – over a million a year – making it Northern Ireland's most popular attraction.

BUSHMILLS

The two-mile journey, on a train that once served at Shane's Castle on the shores of Lough Neagh, passes by the lovely beach after leaving the Giant's Causeway. It takes about 20 minutes (it's quicker by road). You can walk from the destination stop to Bushmills Distillery and Bushmills Inn, the two main attractions of this charming village.

No town in Northern Ireland has as many listed buildings as Bushmills and it's no wonder it has a conservation area at its heart. The village developed in the early 1800s, with its water mills at the centre of local industry. Among the preserved historic buildings is the Old School, which was designed by Clough William-Ellis, also responsible for Portmeirion village in Wales and several buildings in Cushendun.

The village grew as a tourism resort when the railway was developed from Portrush to the Giant's Causeway, stopping at Bushmills. Many people visited because of the whiskey that was winning awards right through the 1800s. The distillery is generally regarded as the world's oldest continuously licensed whiskey distillery.

BUSHMILLS DISTILLERY

It was back in 1608 that King James I granted Sir Thomas Phillips a licence to distil *uisce beatha* within the Rowte, or Route as we know it. *Uisce beatha*, the Gaelic for 'water of life', was eventually adulterated to 'whiskey' by English speakers. No doubt the MacDonnells of Dunluce Castle enjoyed more than a few drops of the local elixir, distilled within staggering distance.

In 1784 the name 'Old Bushmills' was first registered and the familiar pot still trademark was introduced by owner Hugh Anderson. Like most Irish whiskey, Bushmills is triple distilled (Scotch is distilled twice), and Bushmills earned a reputation as one of the country's finest. It shared double billing with a temporary exhibit, the Eiffel Tower, at the Paris Exposition of 1889. Both enjoyed success: Bushmills got a gold medal and the tower became permanent.

It wasn't until the twin threat of Prohibition in the US in 1920 and the success of blended whisky from Scotland that Irish was surpassed as the world's favourite whiskey. There were many dozens of Irish distilleries then. Those that survived can be counted on the fingers of one hand.

When Prohibition ended in 1933, Bushmills was ready to fight back. It sent to Chicago 'the biggest shipment of bottled whiskey that has ever left an Irish port'. One in the eye for the bootleggers.

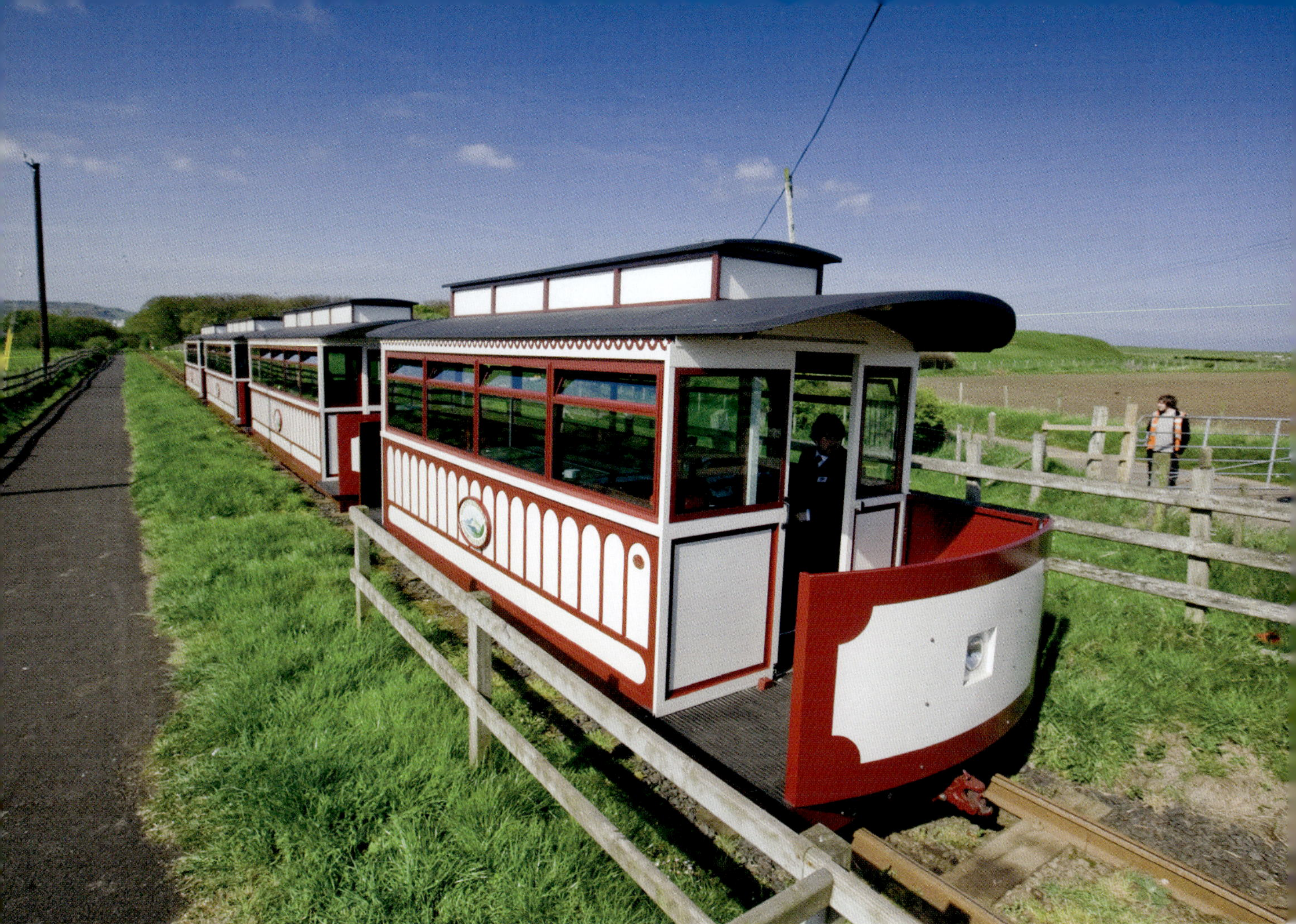

THE BUSHMILLS RAILWAY

You can discover the history of Bushmills whiskey and the secret of its success on a tour of the distillery, and see the little-changed distilling process, from the transformation of malted barley to wort to the barrels – sherry, port, bourbon and Madeira – used to mature the whiskey for periods of up to 21 years.

The distillery is the only place where you can buy Bushmills' 12-year-old reserve, and if you take a tour you can sample this for free at the bar at the end. A fine selection of the local whiskey can be enjoyed at the town's other great institution, the Bushmills Inn.

THE BUSHMILLS INN

Around the time that what is now Bushmills whiskey was first granted its licence, a coaching inn was built in the village that would also become world famous. Its destiny would be linked not just to the distillery but to the Giant's Causeway too.

Indeed, today the acclaimed restaurant at the Bushmills Inn is housed in the original coach house and stables, although the hotel itself dates only from the 1820s. It was at the inn, then known as Kane's Commercial & Family Hotel, that visitors stopped to try the famous local whiskey, staying over en route to the Giant's Causeway.

The inn ceased trading for several decades and the building was used, among other things, as a bicycle factory and a chicken coop! Since sensitive restorations in 1987 and 2009 it has become again a major stopping point for visitors, who can relax in front of a peat fire in the bar or, in summer, sit outside sampling one of the fine Bushmills whiskeys.

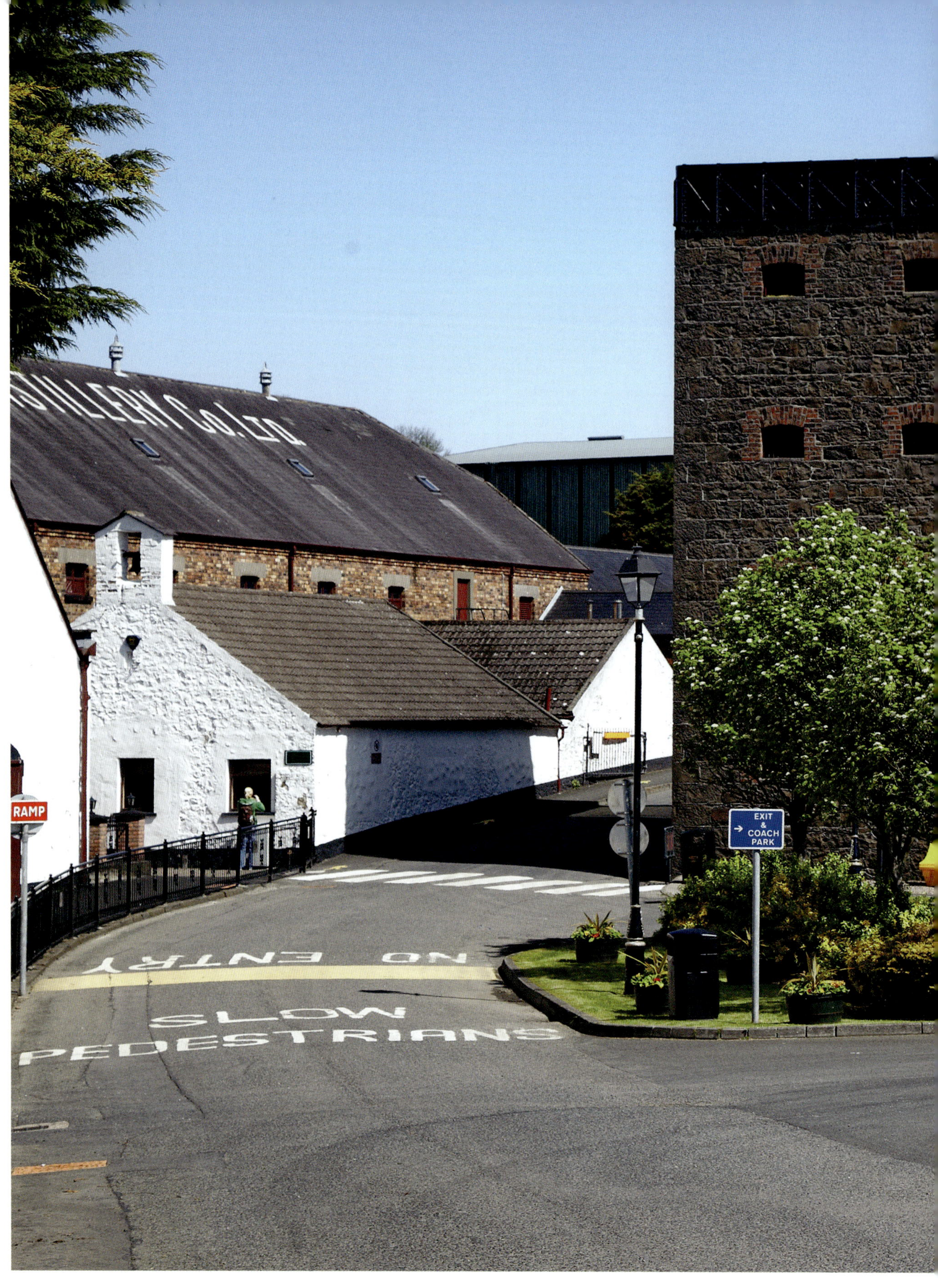

RAMP
EXIT & COACH PARK
NO ENTRY
SLOW PEDESTRIANS

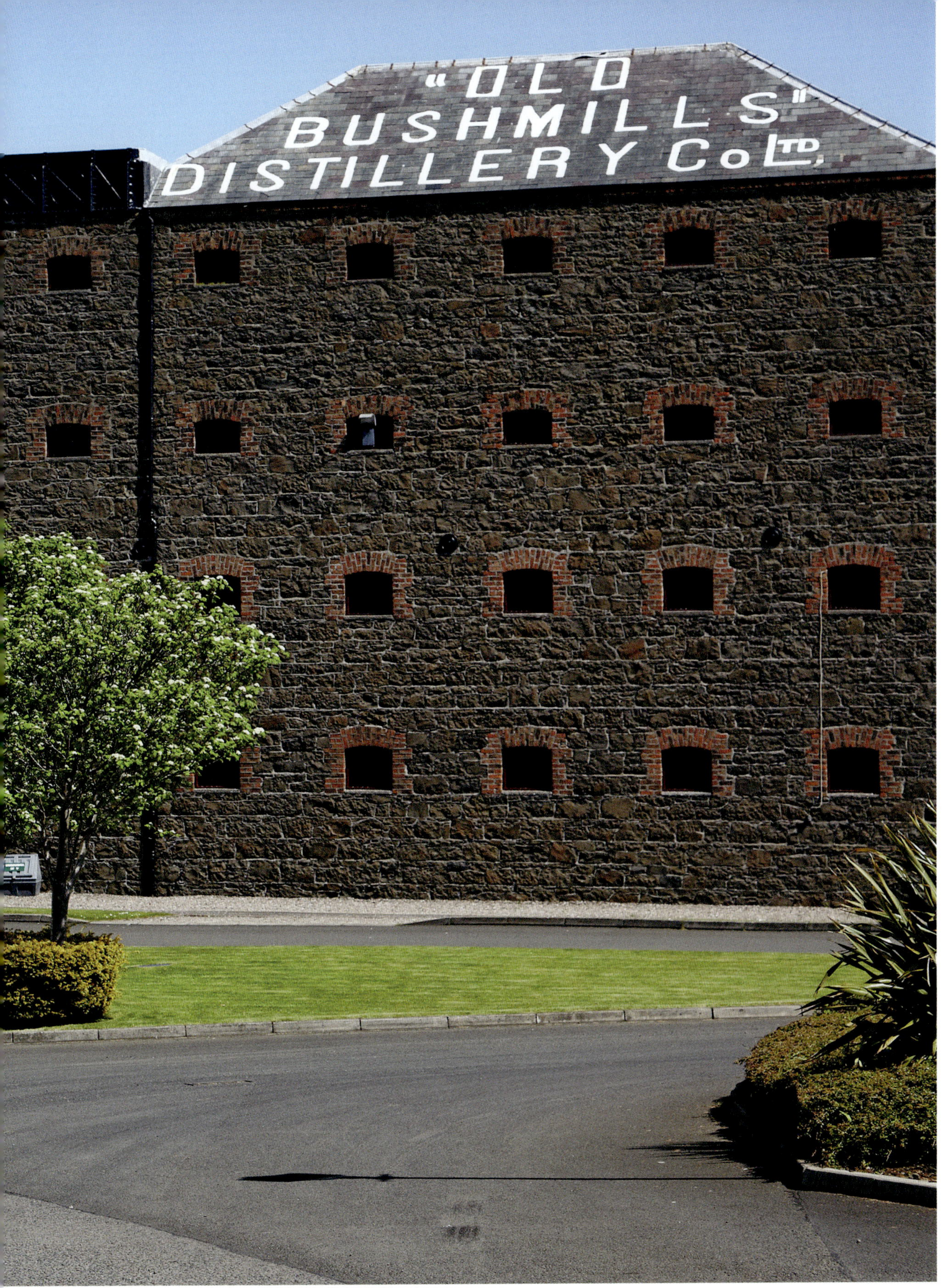

THE BUSHMILLS DISTILLERY

DUNLUCE CASTLE

Standing high above sheer basalt cliffs that plunge down to crashing Atlantic waves, Dunluce Castle in its pomp would have rivalled anything *Game of Thrones* could create. But it was a castle in another famous fictional world it is believed to have inspired – Cair Paravel, where the High Kings and Queens of Narnia ruled in Belfast-born C.S. Lewis' *Chronicles of Narnia*. And although it was first built by another clan, the now ruined Dunluce Castle is as much a part of the MacDonnell story of this journey as the 17th-century Glenarm Castle where the family still live.

The first defences built here were probably the underground passages and chambers, tunnelled beneath what is now the site of the northern tower, which provided a hiding place from marauding Vikings. It was during the ascendancy of the Anglo-Normans in the 13th century that this area became an estate, and it was after their power waned and they intermarried into the leading families of the Gaelic clans that the first castle was built.

This was around 1500 and the clan responsible was the McQuillans, probably of Scottish origin. Then Lords of the Route, they managed to hold on to Dunluce for a little over 50 years, until they were dispossessed by the more powerful MacDonnells, their sometime allies in the clan wars that raged in this part of Ulster.

James MacDonnell, leader of the Islay-based clan (the island can be seen from Dunluce on a clear day) and busy with Scottish power struggles at home, appointed his younger brother Sorley Boy to command the castle and, eventually, the Route itself. It was a shrewd move. When deposed after a siege of the castle by English troops, Sorley Boy achieved the seemingly impossible by winning it back.

Enter Dunluce Castle and make your way over the bridge to the site of the southern tower. Look down, if you dare! Then imagine the fearless Sorley Boy and his intrepid followers scaling those sheer cliffs from the waters far below with nothing more than a few ropes to help them. If you're English, you might now feel the inclination to flee! For, needless to say, once safely inside, the MacDonnells slew its defenders and reclaimed the castle.

Sorley Boy the warrior we know, but the secret of his longevity lay not so much in his courage as in a remarkable facility for knowing when to bend the knee. Following his victory he journeyed to Dublin, where he begged forgiveness from the Lord Deputy of Ireland for his actions. Aware of the numbers of expensive English troops it would take to dislodge the MacDonnells, the Lord Deputy agreed to renew the grant on their lands.

The story of Dunluce's golden age, however, really began not with Sorley Boy but with his son, Randal Arranagh. It was he, succeeding his elder brother James, who managed to navigate the clan through the last hurrah of the Gaelic chieftains' resistance to English rule, the Nine Years War, and, despite being on the losing side, received forgiveness from the now quite broke English Crown. The MacDonnells, not for the first time, changed sides, though it would be a little while before the Catholic clan embraced the Protestant religion.

In 1603, the new king of England, James I, agreed that Randal Arranagh could stay at Dunluce and continue to own his other manors in the area, provided he 'build a castle or mansion house upon each within seven years'. Randal, who would become the first earl of Antrim, not only began the rebuilding of Dunluce Castle but also constructed a new town outside the castle walls (only recently rediscovered) for Protestant Scottish settlers.

As you wander the atmospheric ruins of Dunluce, try to imagine what the castle would have looked like in the years following Randal Arranagh's death in 1636. You might be surprised. Here in this windy, isolated spot, far from Europe's high society, his son, Randal Og, reinvented Dunluce as a highly fashionable palatial home. He refurbished Dunluce, now boasting a magnificent Mansion House, with the finest furniture from Europe, including curtains donated by Lord Wolsey. Randal Og could afford it: his wife, Lady Catherine Manners, widow of the Earl of Buckingham, was one of the richest women in England.

But the MacDonnells had little time to enjoy

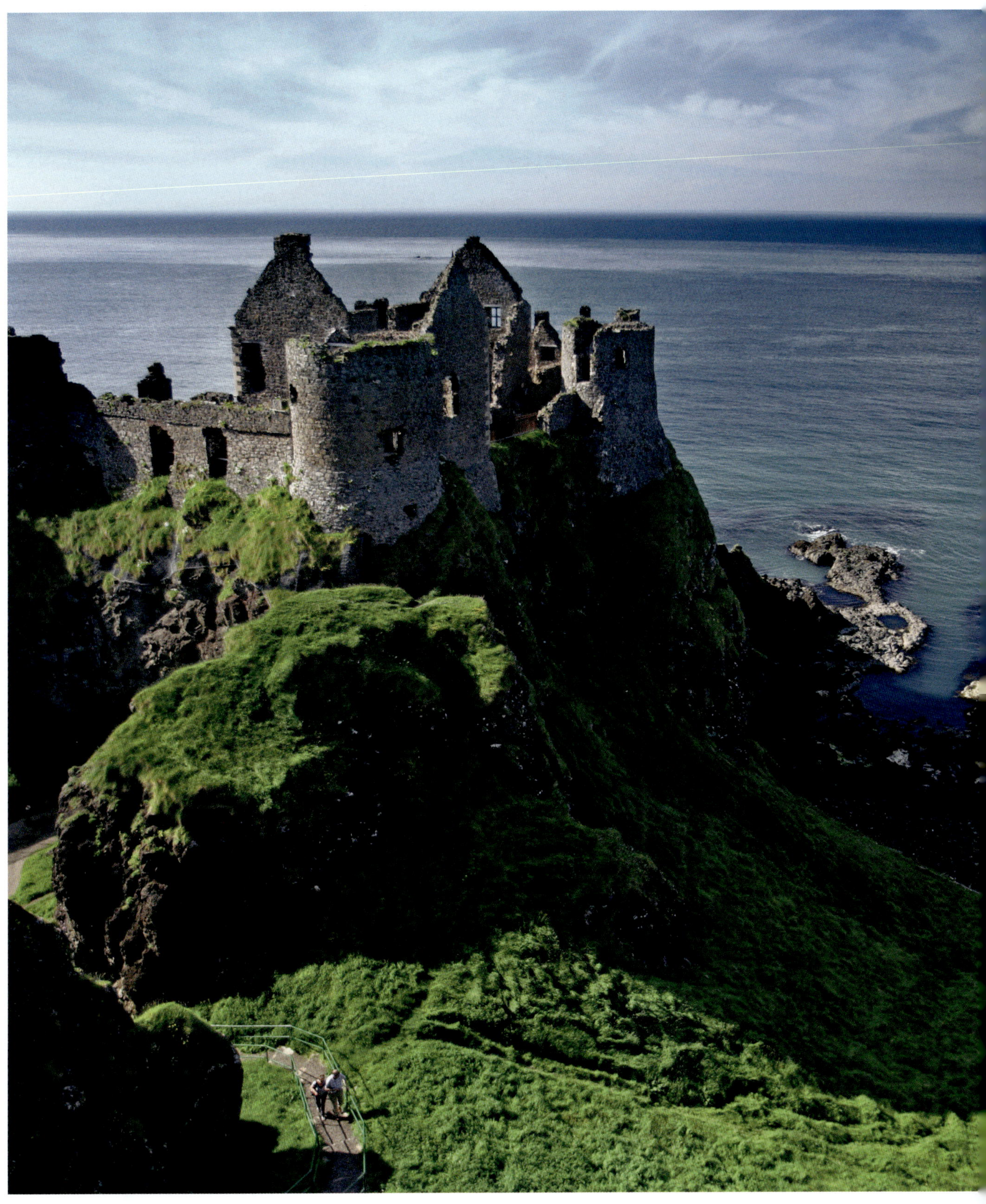

DUNLUCE CASTLE

their beautiful home. General Munro, at the head of an army of Scottish Covenanters, imprisoned Randal Og, a Royalist and friend of King Charles I, in 1642, plundering the castle. Inevitably, Randal Og switched his allegiance to the Parliamentarian side during the English Civil War and then back to the Royal side, when Charles II regained the throne. Now Earls of Antrim, the MacDonnells continued to exert power, but the great days of Dunluce Castle were over.

Local folklore has it that the MacDonnells decided to move from Dunluce when their kitchen collapsed into the sea during a storm, dragging several staff members with it. The truth is that the clan hit troubled times after, yet again, backing the wrong horse: this time in the Irish-based battle for the English throne between William III and James II. With finances tight they decided to abandon Dunluce, eventually making Glenarm Castle their family seat. It remains so today.

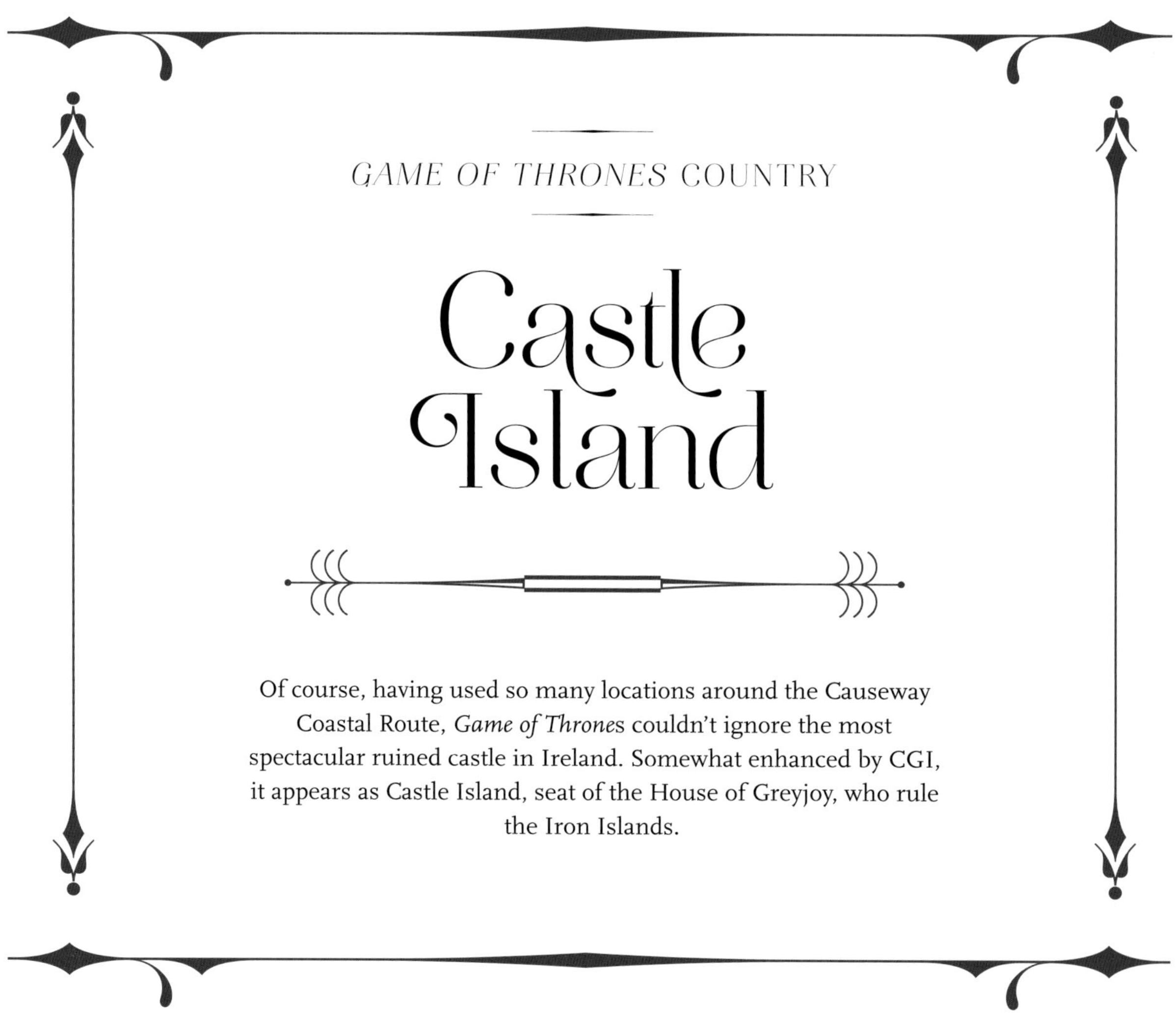

Castle Island

Of course, having used so many locations around the Causeway Coastal Route, *Game of Thrones* couldn't ignore the most spectacular ruined castle in Ireland. Somewhat enhanced by CGI, it appears as Castle Island, seat of the House of Greyjoy, who rule the Iron Islands.

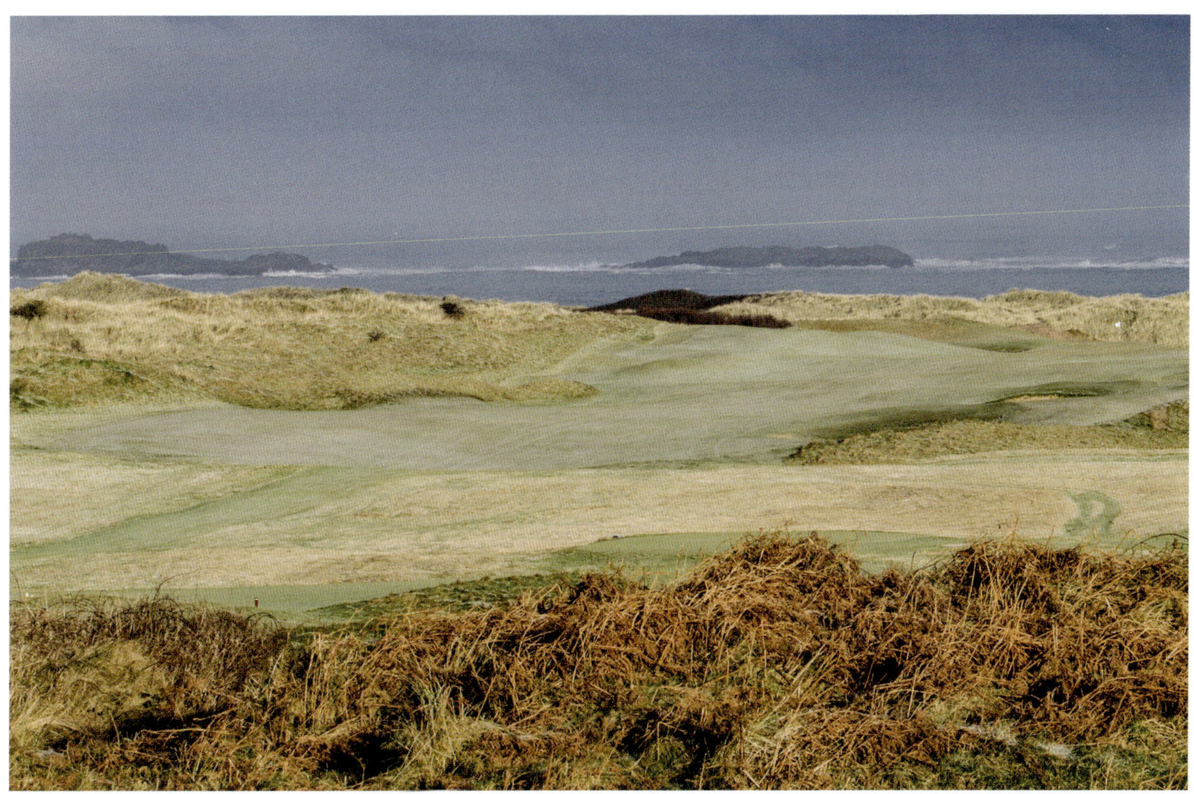

PORTRUSH GOLF CLUB

PORTRUSH

From Dunluce Castle, looking westward you can easily spot Portrush and its famous golf club. That is why one of the world's finest links courses is named the Dunluce Links.

If Whitehead is the epitome of the refined Victorian seaside resort, Portrush is its cheerful bigger cousin, abounding with popular bars, restaurants, amusement arcades, ice-cream parlours and all kinds of water sports and water amusements to complement its ample beaches.

Given an impetus by the arrival of the railway which brought fun-seeking visitors from all parts of Ireland, Portrush really gained its renown from the presence of one of the world's favourite golf clubs, Royal Portrush. It is also famous as one stage of the thrilling North West 200 motorcycle race, which also takes in Portstewart and Coleraine, every May.

Formed in 1888 as Portrush County Club, it gained the 'royal' appendage after the Duke of York and then the Prince of Wales (later King Edward VII) became patrons. The club, a pioneer of Irish and British golf, enjoyed various firsts, including the first professional tournament held in Ireland, in 1895.

It has taken time to perfect. It wasn't until 1929 that the course was moved deep into the abundant sand dunes, and only in very recent times were the finishing holes – always regarded as the club's Achilles heel – replaced.

Needless to say, the course has hosted the world's best golfers of their eras, including Gary Player, Arnold Palmer, Jack Nicklaus and Tom Watson. The success of a trio of Northern Irish golfers – Rory McIlroy (who holds the course record) and Graeme McDowell and Darren Clarke (who are members) – helped bring the club the ultimate honour, hosting the 148th Open in July 2019. The only other time the Open has been held outside Scotland or England was also at Portrush, in 1951, when the flamboyant Max Faulkner triumphed.

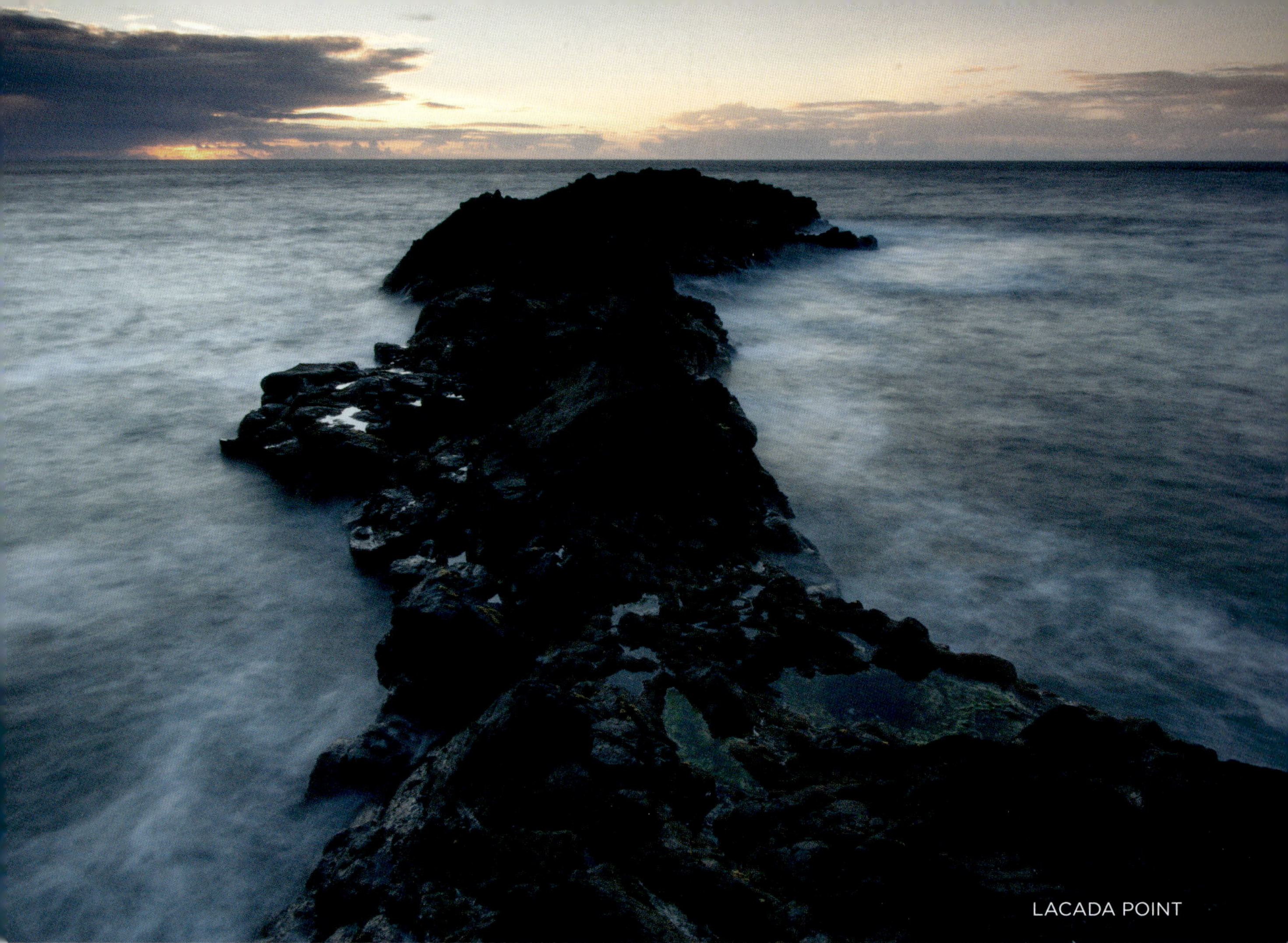

PORTSTEWART

Less than four miles from Portrush, Portstewart is virtually its extension, creating a seemingly endless seaside resort. Its beach, the Strand, has few equals even along this glorious stretch of coastline. Managed by the National Trust, this vast and broad expanse of sand is loved by all kinds of water sports enthusiasts, including the surfers who come in droves to ride the waves here. Anywhere else in Europe this beach would be packed solid with visitors throughout the summer but here, as elsewhere along the route, there is space to breathe in its beauty.

The National Trust also owns Harry's Shack, a wonderfully atmospheric fish and seafood restaurant with an outdoor area overlooking the beach. Enjoy a plate of locally caught fish with a pint of IPA from the Portrush brewery Lacada (named after a rocky area near the

Giant's Causeway where the Spanish Armada galleon *Girona* was wrecked) on a warm summer's evening and you'll feel you're in paradise.

The town has another famous culinary story, which reflects the strong Italian influence on Northern Irish cuisine. On the promenade, with views of the vast Dominican College that dominates Portstewart Harbour, is the main outlet of one of Ireland's most famous ice-cream makers: Morelli's. The family come from (and still regularly return to) the tiny hamlet of San Andrea in the Liri Valley, not far from Monte Cassino and its famous Benedictine abbey. It was in this area that many of the Italians who came to Ireland in the early years of the 20th century originated.

As with their one-time neighbours, the Fuscos, who settled in Belfast, the Morellis

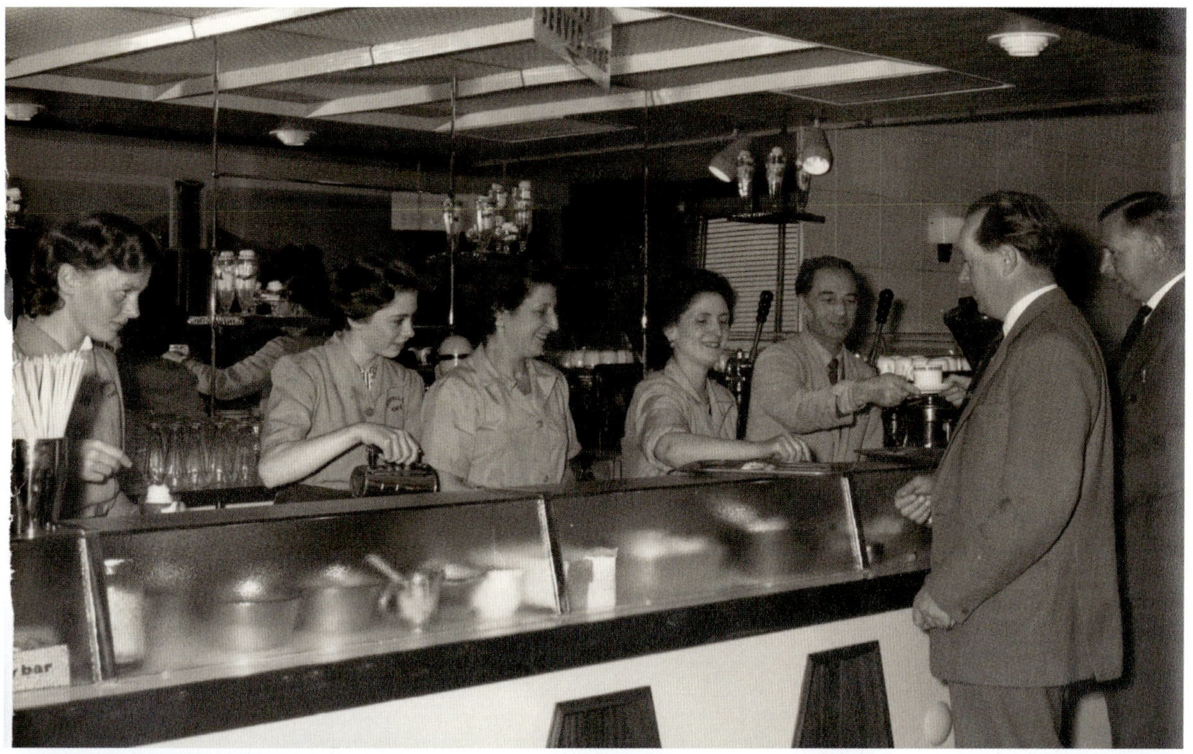

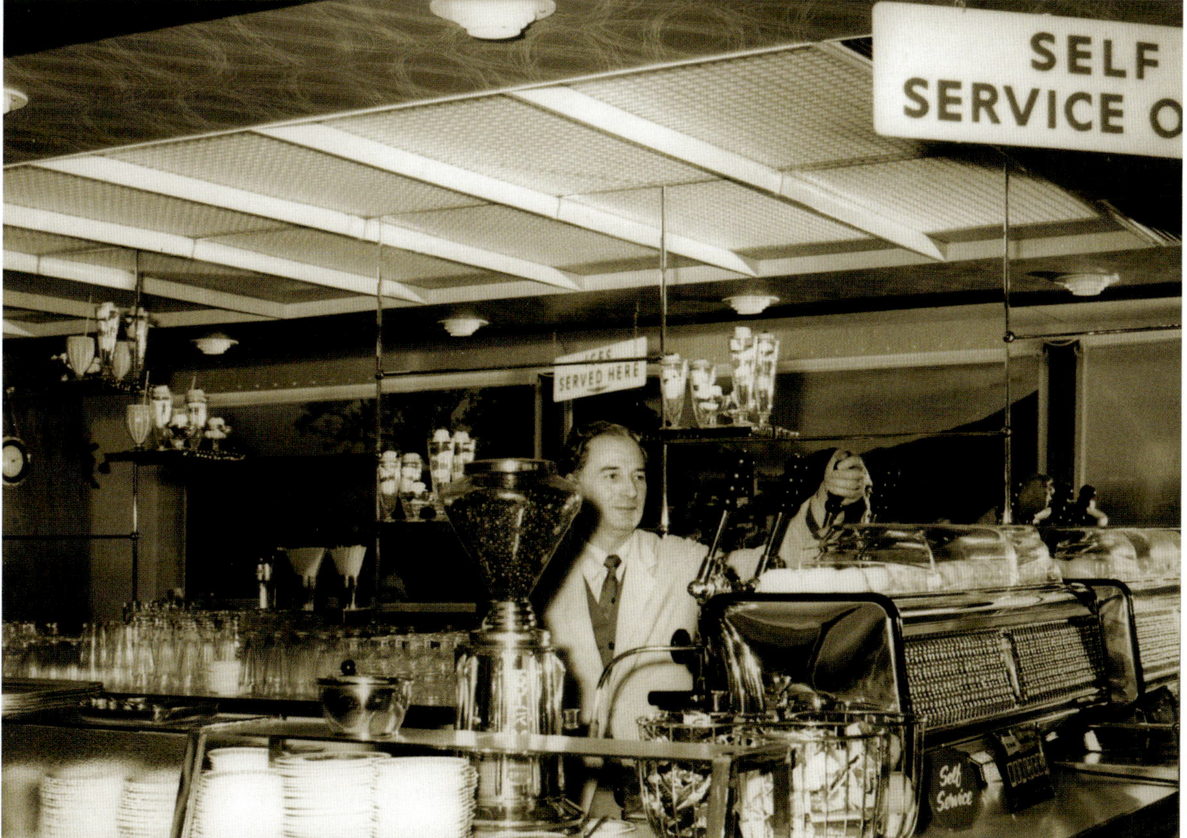

TOP: ANGELO MORELLI WITH FAMILY, STAFF AND CUSTOMERS; AND BOTTOM: IN THE ORIGINAL
MORELLI'S ICE PALACE

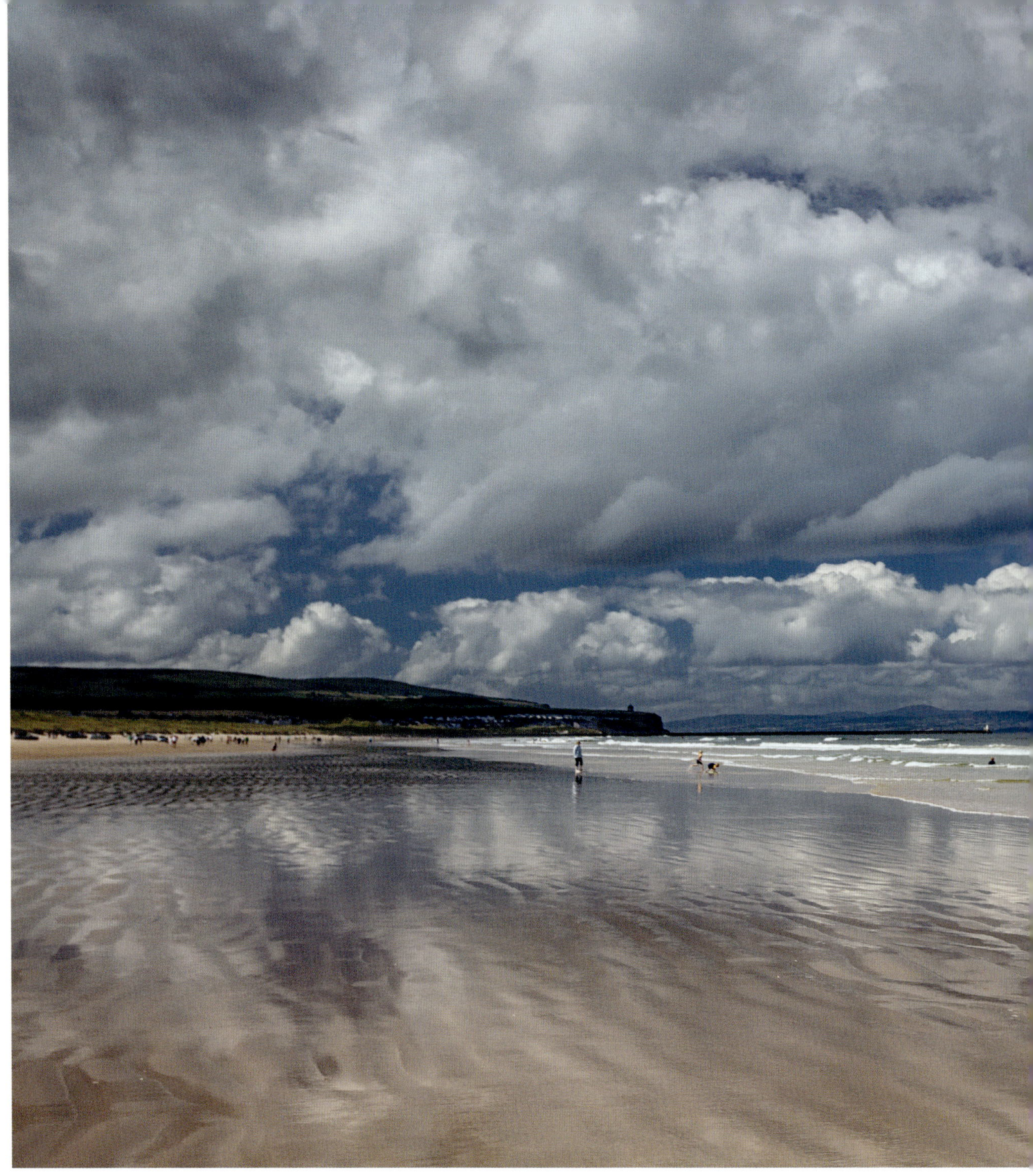

brought their love of food – particularly fish and chips and ice cream – to a grateful Ireland. The first Morelli to arrive in this part of Ireland was Joseph, who opened a cafe in Ballymena in 1911. He was followed by his brother Dominic, who opened a fish and chip shop in Coleraine. When Dominic returned to Italy, his business was taken over by a third brother, Peter, who quickly added an ice-cream parlour and taxi service to the emerging empire. In 1927, Peter opened the Ice Palace in Portstewart, which he later sold to his nephew Angelo. It would later be taken over by Angelo's son Nino.

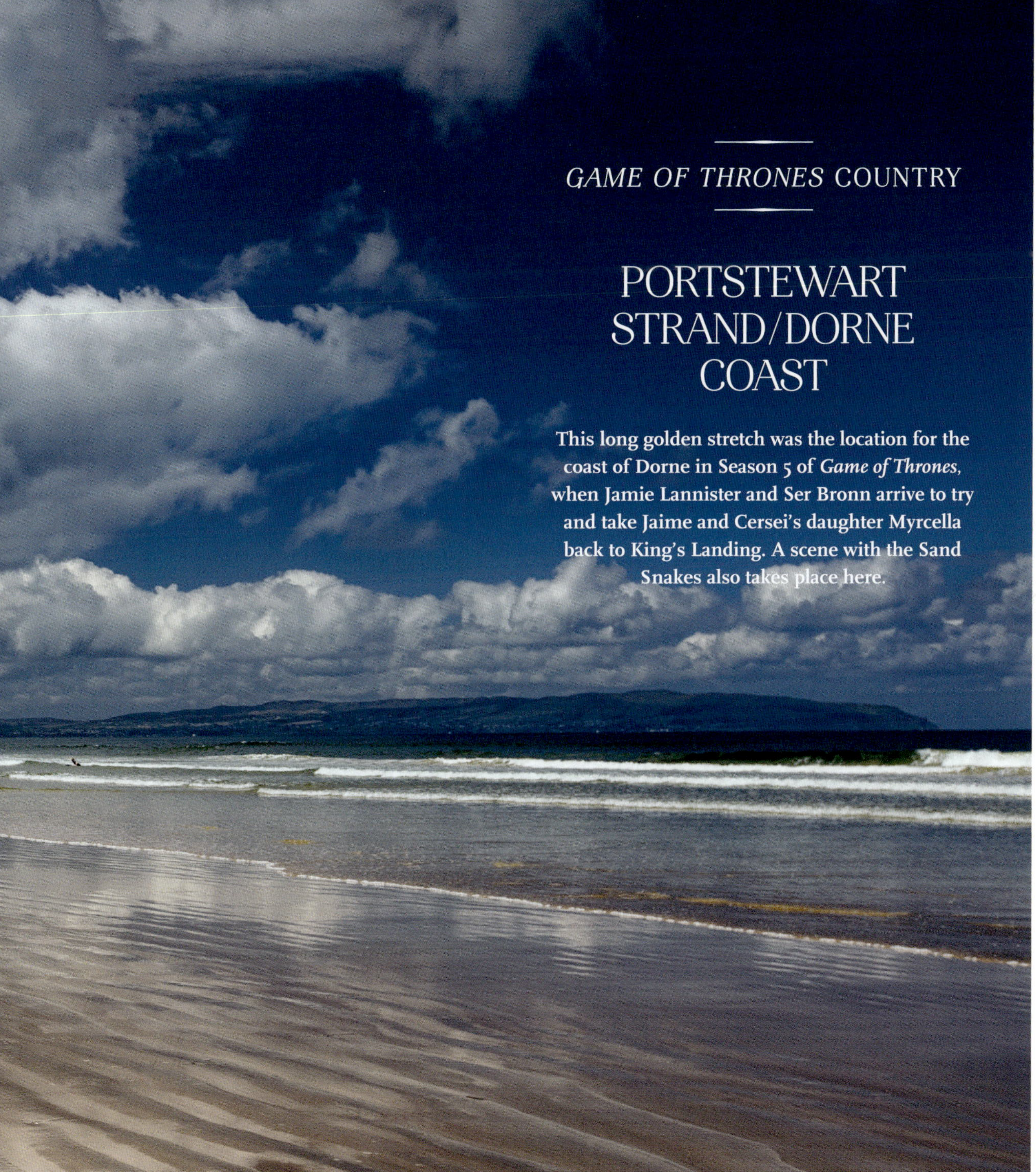

The family grew and became part of the local community, and the business expanded, but Morelli's – now run by Nino's son Damian – has remained at the heart of local life and its origins in San Andrea have never been forgotten.

The spacious restaurant that has recently replaced Peter Morelli's original Ice Palace might be bright and modern, but the traditional ice cream and range of delicious sundaes remain the taste of summer family holidays for today's generation of visitors as well as their nostalgic parents and grandparents.

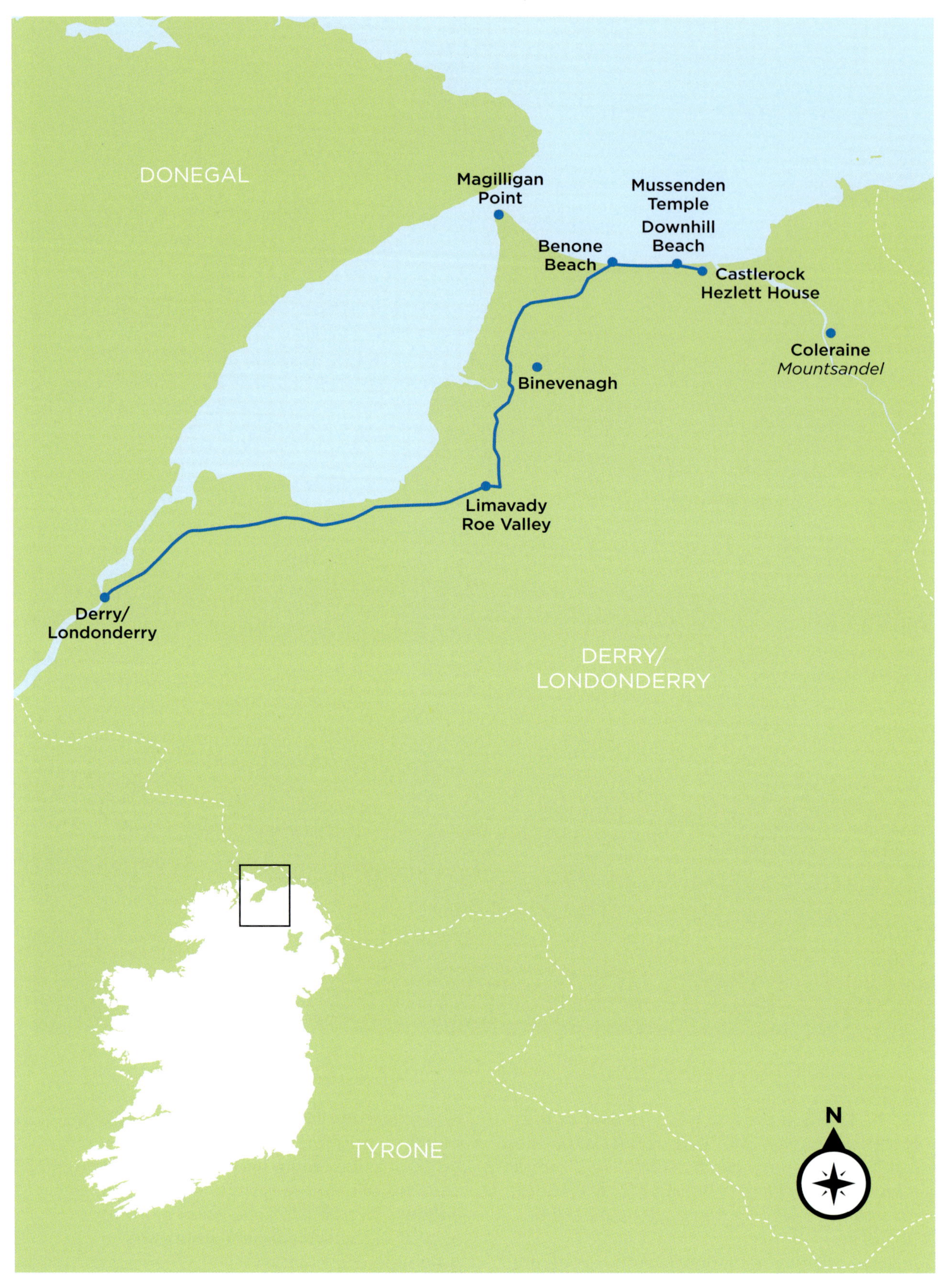

DONEGAL
Magilligan Point
Mussenden Temple
Downhill Beach
Benone Beach
Castlerock
Hezlett House
Coleraine
Mountsandel
Binevenagh
Limavady
Roe Valley
Derry/Londonderry
DERRY/LONDONDERRY
TYRONE
N

BINEVENAGH AND BEYOND

Now we weave between beautiful Binevenagh Mountain and the seemingly endless stretch of golden beach beside the coastal road. For sheer romance, Mussenden Temple, perched high above Downhill Beach (Dragonstone to *Game of Thrones* lovers) has few equals. Benone, one of Europe's finest beaches, attracts visitors for all kinds of water sports.

On to Magilligan Point, one of the largest sand-dune networks in the UK or Ireland, and its car ferry to beautiful Donegal across Lough Swilly. Now we're gearing up for a spectacular finish!

Through lovely Roe Valley Country Park, once the base of the O'Cahan clan who ruled a large part of the North, to Limavady, which has a strong connection with 'Danny Boy'. We end this epic journey in Derry City, home to some of Europe's most magnificent medieval walls, the symbolic Peace Bridge and a buzzing cultural life.

MOUNTSANDEL

From Portstewart the Causeway Coastal Route follows the River Bann to Coleraine, the first planted town in Ireland, before returning to the coast. When you reach Coleraine, you're within a couple of miles of the earliest known human settlement in Ireland, Mountsandel.

It was as recently as the 1970s that archaeologist Peter Woodman and his team discovered a Mesolithic settlement here dating back to at least 7600 BC. The presence of flint tools suggested that people were lured here by the salmon in the natural weir by the River Bann.

The earthen fort, located in lovely woodland, is far more recent, built by the Anglo-Normans following their 12th-century invasion of Ulster.

CASTLEROCK

By now the sight of endless golden Blue Flag beaches before rolling sand dunes with mountain views will be almost run-of-the-mill. Even so, Castlerock, just a mile or two before you reach Mussenden Temple, is not to be missed. Golfers can enjoy one of Ireland's finest links courses and the village retains something of its Victorian charm, not least in its Charles Lanyon-designed railway station.

The train journey from Coleraine to Derry along this stretch of line has been described by Monty Python star and travel broadcaster Michael Palin as 'one of the most beautiful rail journeys in the world'. Other Victorian delights include a famous row of houses above the beach known as the Twelve Apostles.

HEZLETT HOUSE

This beautifully preserved 17th-century thatched cottage is just off the A2, a mile from the Mussenden Temple and at the turn-off to Castlerock. The Hezlett family's long occupation of the house began with Isaac in 1766. His sons Samuel and Jack were on opposite sides during the United Irishmen Rebellion of 1798, when many northern Presbyterians joined the attempt to rid Ireland of British rule and usher in equality for all.

The repercussions of the rebellion's failure were terrible. Fortunately, Jack, a dedicated rebel, managed to escape to the US as his comrades were being hunted down by redcoats. Samuel, having backed the winning side, stayed on at the house. The farm and buildings were extended by successive generations of Hezletts before being taken over by the National Trust in 1976 and furnished in Victorian style.

MUSSENDEN TEMPLE

As you leave Hezlett House, Downhill Demesne is already in sight. Much like Dunluce Castle, it's the stunning location of the demesne that makes it such a popular visitor attraction. On the clifftop, high above beautiful Downhill Beach, its star attraction, Mussenden Temple, looks over the Atlantic.

Like the demesne itself, it is the creation of one of Ireland's most eccentric bishops, Frederick Hervey, a man King George III described as 'that wicked prelate' and another called 'that abominable wicked old fello'. While he indulged his personal wealth to the full, he was, it should be said, a generous man, and the city of Derry in particular benefited considerably from his largesse.

Frederick became the Earl of Bristol in 1779. A decade earlier the notorious ladies' man – among his mistresses, it was claimed, was Admiral Lord Nelson's great love, Emma Hamilton – had become Bishop of Derry, hence his subsequent title, the Earl Bishop. He was an unlikely choice in many ways, but for all his character flaws he did create something remarkably beautiful at Downhill.

The Bishop's Palace, the mansion he built, is now ruined, although it was still habitable as late as the 1940s, but you can wander around the woods he planted, not least the little arboretum known as the Black Glen. You can also visit the Mausoleum, built in memory of his brother, the dovecote and icehouse and a lovely little walled garden nearby.

Entrance is via two impressive gates: the Bishop's Gate if you want to visit the gardens and the Black Glen, and the Lion's Gate, which is topped by leopards. Why 'the Lion's Gate', then? Apparently, no one knew what a leopard looked like at the time, even though they were on the Hervey coat of arms.

But the visitors who flock here from around

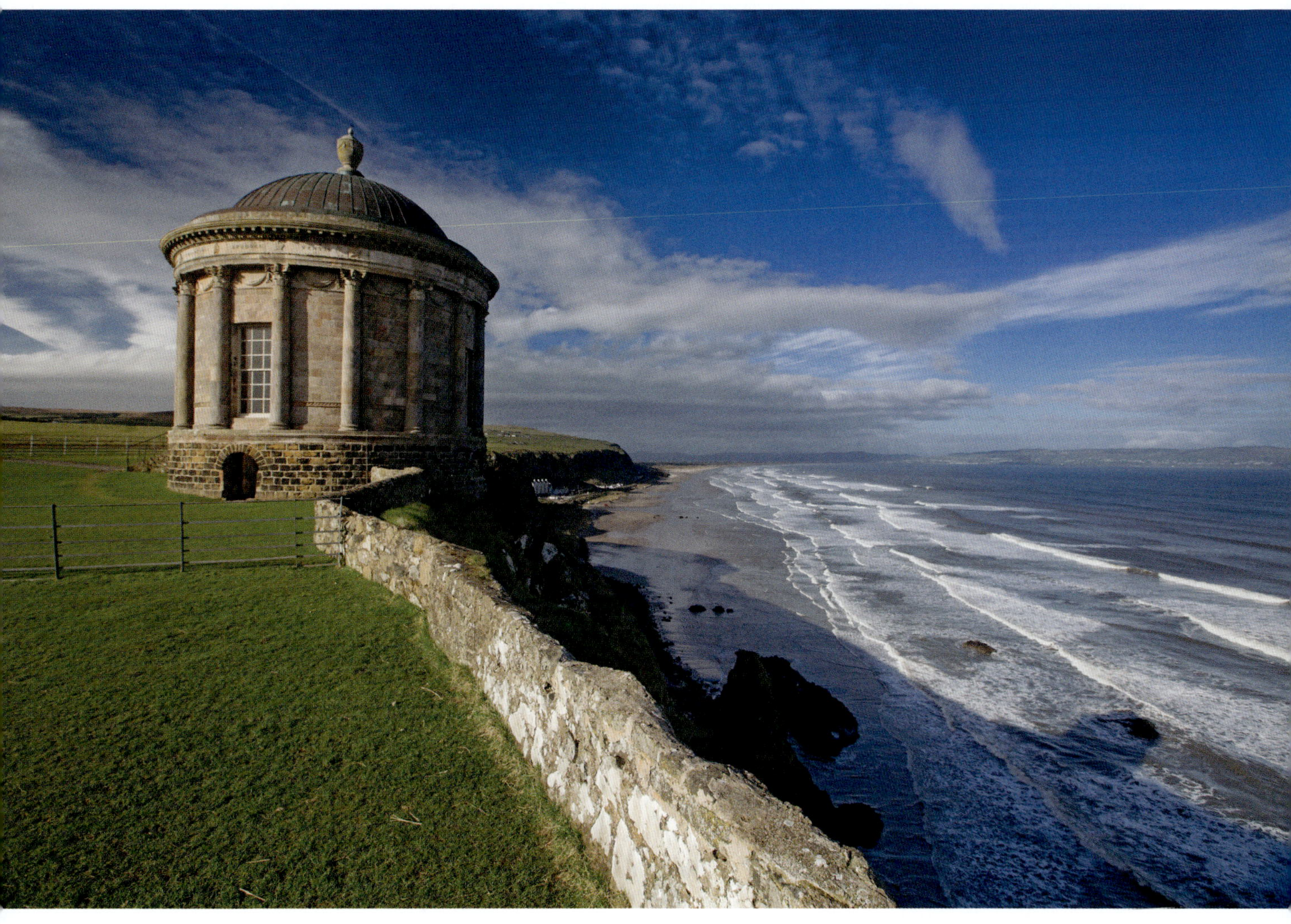

MUSSENDEN TEMPLE

the world have one destination above all on their minds. Situated so close to the cliff edge that one fears for its future, the Mussenden Temple has the most wonderful views. It once hosted the highly literate Earl Bishop's library and its true appeal is perfectly summed up in an inscription there: ''Tis pleasant, safely to behold, from shore, the rolling ship and hear the tempest roar.'

Needless to say, even this delightful folly is associated with scandal. The Earl Bishop built it for his niece, Frideswide Bruce, with whom he was accused of conducting an affair. Perhaps affected by the rumoured scandal, she died young and never got to use the temple built as her refuge.

The Earl Bishop finally expired in Italy in 1803 after an eventful life. It was fitting. Classically educated, he loved Italy and indeed based the design of the temple on the Temple of Vesta in the Roman Forum in the Eternal City. Following his deathbed request, the old boy was pickled in a barrel of sherry to be shipped back home.

It's hard to speak ill of him, unlikely bishop that he was, for his legacy remains for all to enjoy.

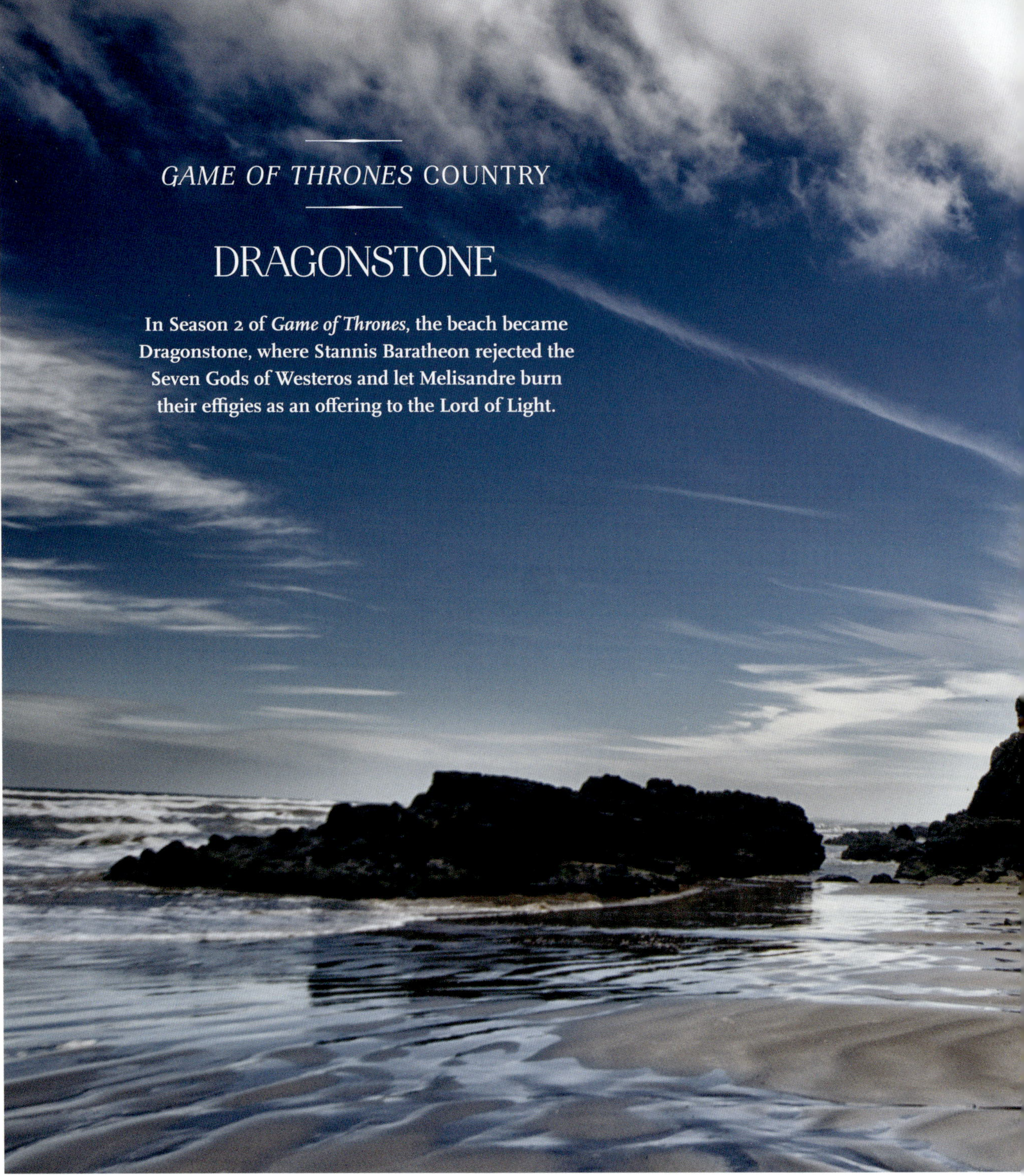

DOWNHILL BEACH

Sweeping down from the demesne, the road veers around tightly before opening up just as the railway line emerges from its tunnel beneath the cliffs to run alongside this beach, some of which lies directly beneath the Mussenden Temple. On the other side water cascades from sheer cliffs. It's a beautiful start to what is essentially a magnificent seven-mile stretch of beach that includes Benone and ends with the famous sand dunes of Magilligan Point.

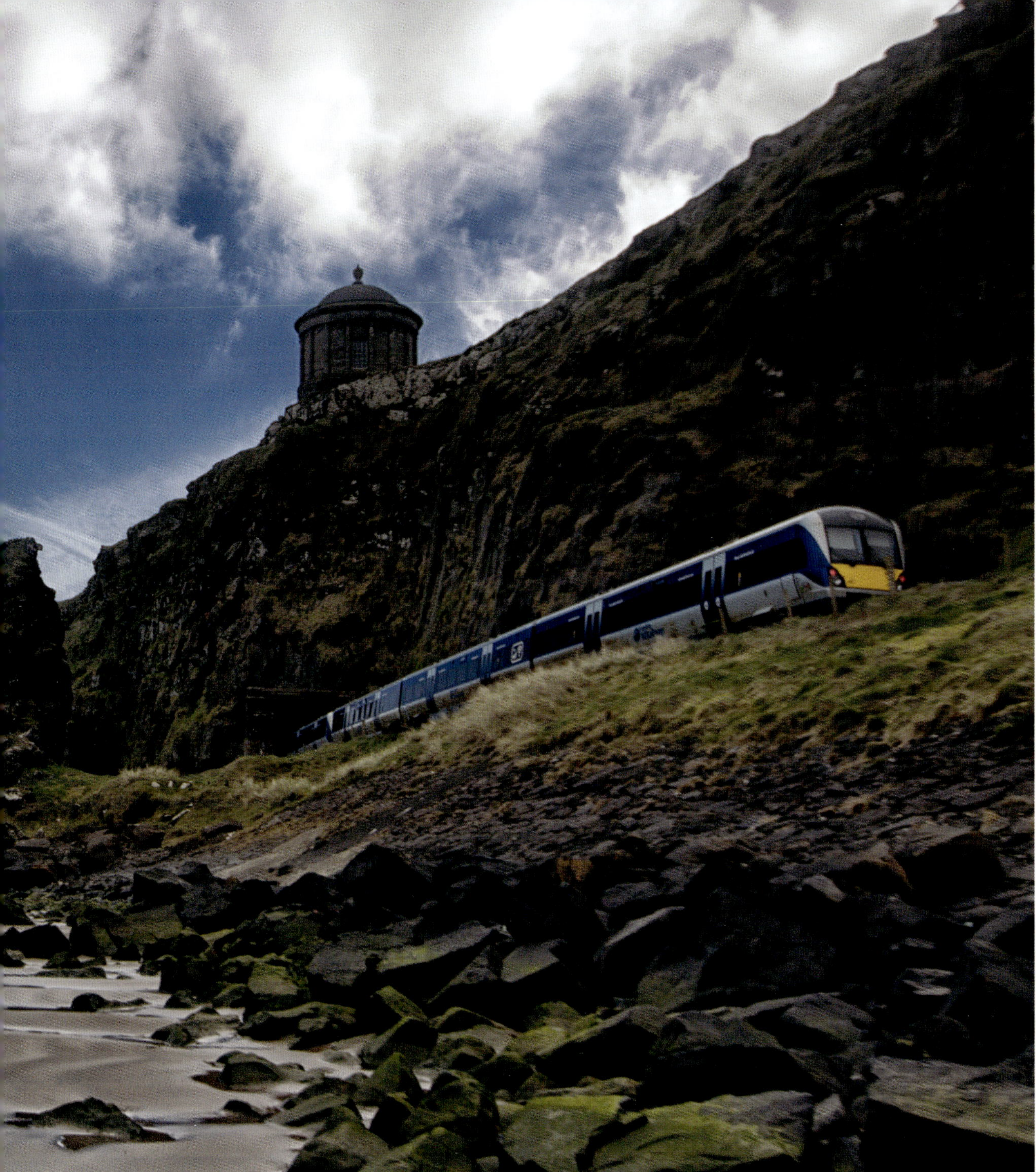

BENONE

A beach to rival any in Europe! Firm golden sands extend as far as the eye can see, with views of Benevenagh Mountain rising above the dunes and Donegal visible to the west. This Blue Flag beach attracts visitors for all kinds of water sports, including surfing, kite surfing, canoeing and jet-skiing, and you will often see people fishing from the beach. There are tennis courts, pools and indoor games at the Tourist Complex too, and a large caravan park nearby.

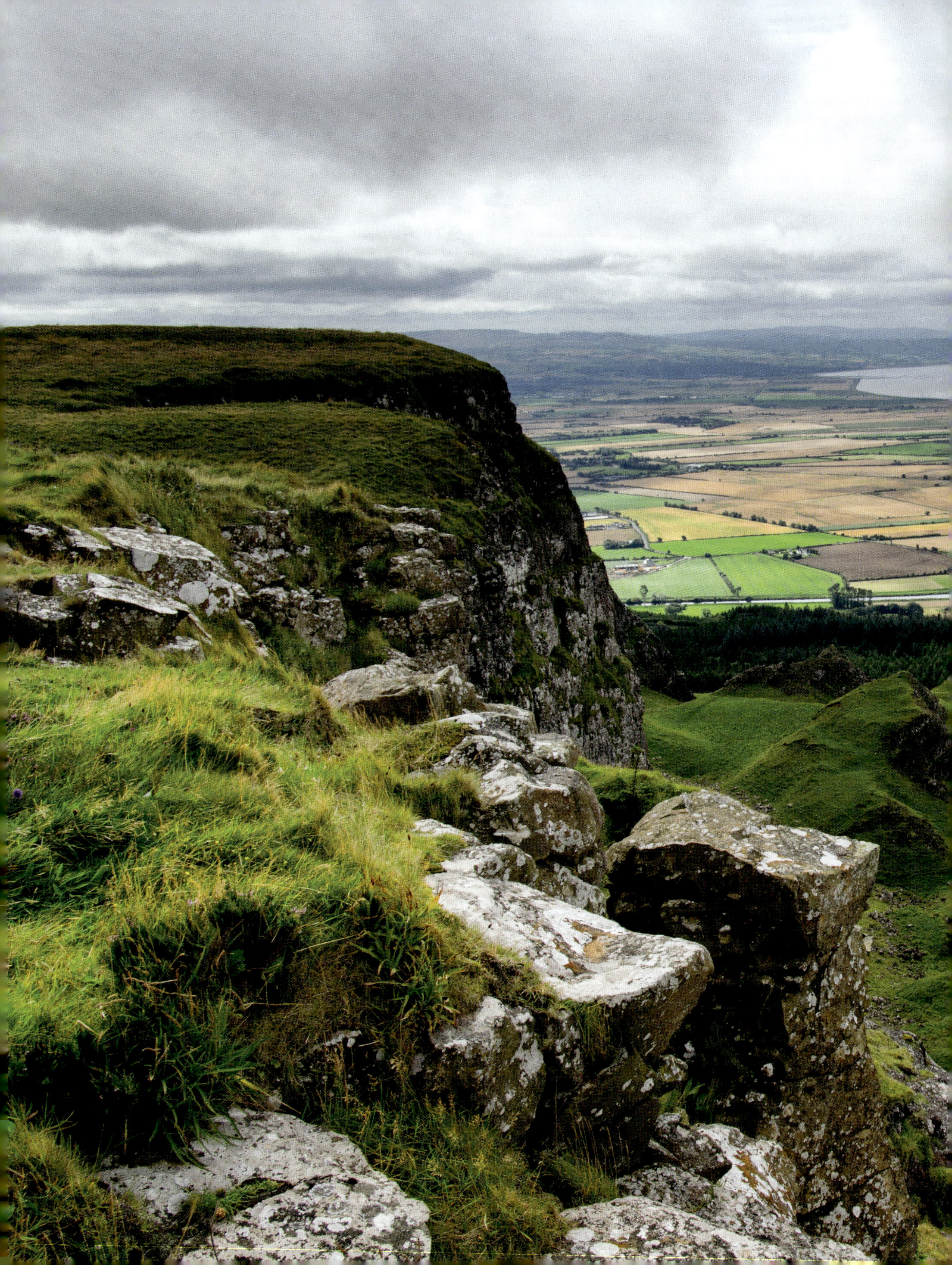

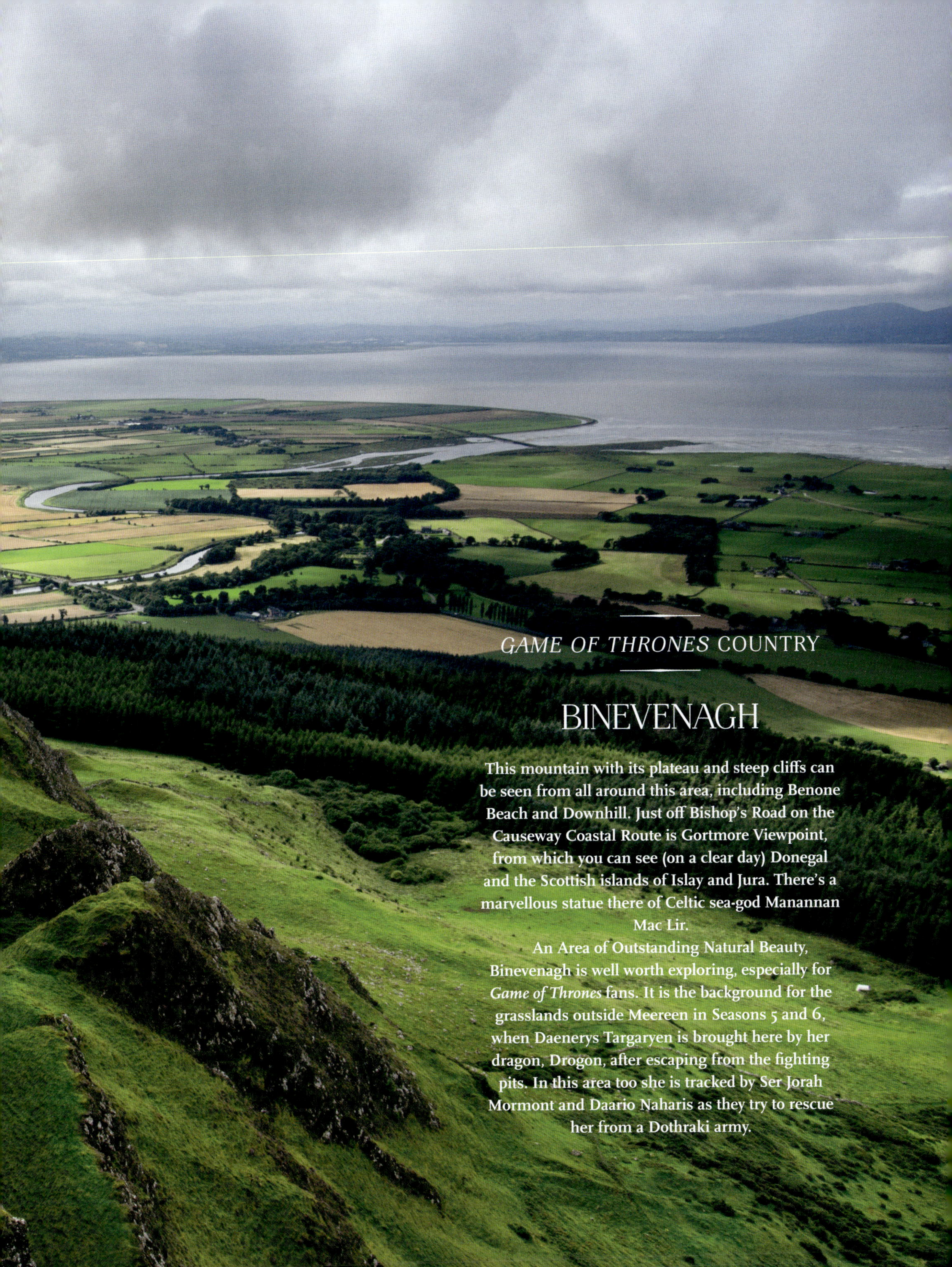

GAME OF THRONES COUNTRY

BINEVENAGH

This mountain with its plateau and steep cliffs can be seen from all around this area, including Benone Beach and Downhill. Just off Bishop's Road on the Causeway Coastal Route is Gortmore Viewpoint, from which you can see (on a clear day) Donegal and the Scottish islands of Islay and Jura. There's a marvellous statue there of Celtic sea-god Manannan Mac Lir.

An Area of Outstanding Natural Beauty, Binevenagh is well worth exploring, especially for *Game of Thrones* fans. It is the background for the grasslands outside Meereen in Seasons 5 and 6, when Daenerys Targaryen is brought here by her dragon, Drogon, after escaping from the fighting pits. In this area too she is tracked by Ser Jorah Mormont and Daario Naharis as they try to rescue her from a Dothraki army.

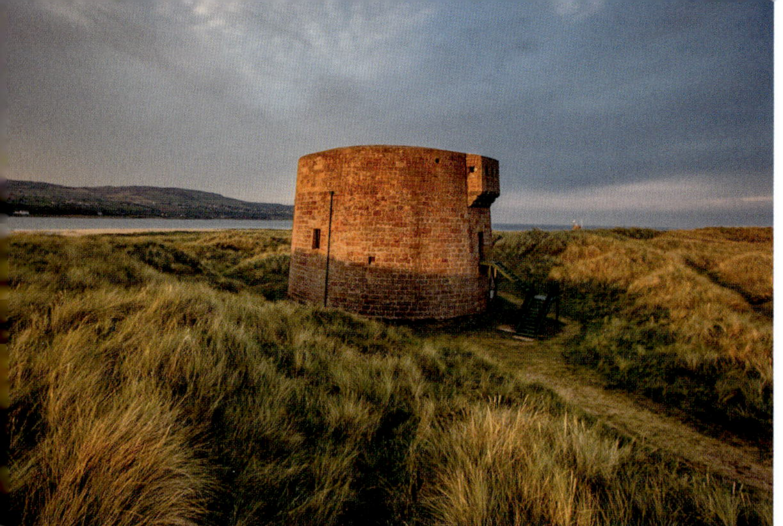

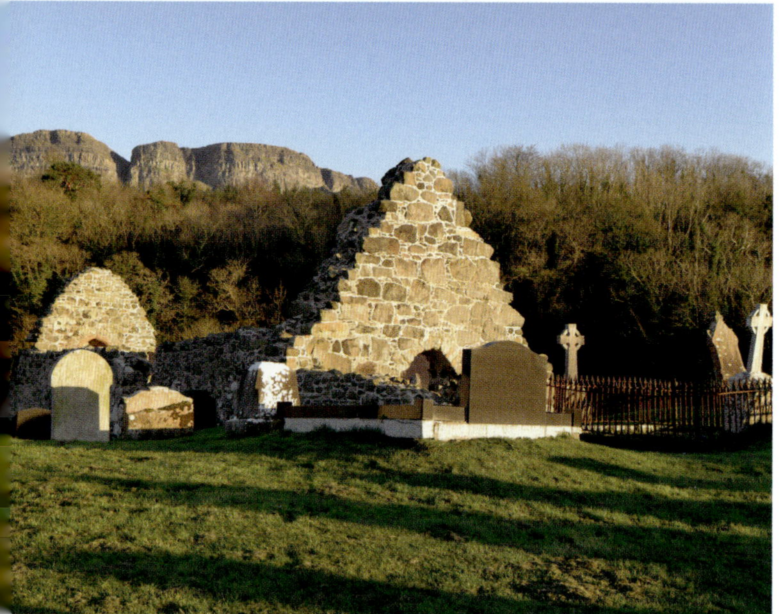

TOP: MARTELLO TOWER AT MAGILLIGAN POINT
ABOVE: ST AIDAN'S CHURCH

MAGILLIGAN POINT

The road around to Magilligan point is not as good as we have been used to, nor the scenery as spectacular, but our destination is worth the short journey. Enjoy a drink or meal by the fireside at the Hearth Bar as you decide whether to make the journey across Lough Swilly from the adjacent ferry terminal to Greencastle, in County Donegal in the Republic.

A few strides away you can view one of the Martello Towers that are dotted around the local coastline. They were built in the early 1800s, when Britain was preparing its coastal defences for an expected invasion by Napoleon. Such fears had been ignited locally back in 1798 when Theobald Wolfe Tone, leader of the United Irishmen, who had French backing, was arrested at Lough Swilly.

Tone's capture significantly contributed to the failure of the rebellion but alerted the British to the danger of a seaborne invasion from France, led by their detested enemy, 'Boney'. In the event it never materialised, although occasional forays by American privateers added to the tension. The round tower, which is not huge, had two 24-pounder guns. There is, however, no record of the garrison mounting fire.

If you have time, take a stroll around one of the largest sand dune systems in Britain or Ireland, where wild flowers like harebells and bird's-foot trefoil are resplendent in summer.

ST AIDAN'S CHURCH AND HOLY WELL

A short detour from Benone, this ruined medieval church is named for an early follower of St Patrick, St Cadan (later amended to Aidan), who is buried here. For centuries pilgrims made their way to the Holy Well here, whose waters are said to cure afflictions.

The current Catholic church is of a more recent vintage, built in 1826 following the relaxing of the Penal Laws that had so impacted on Catholic worship in Ireland. Donncha Ó hÁmhsaigh, a famous blind harper known as 'the last of the bards', who played at Mussenden Temple, is buried here. It is claimed that he was 112 years old when he passed away.

ROE VALLEY COUNTRY PARK

We have tended to focus on the House of MacDonnell as this journey has unwound. Now it's time to celebrate another powerful local clan: the MacDonnells' rivals, the O'Cahans. They lorded it over the area around Limavady for centuries and are even responsible for the town's name. On a stroll around lovely Roe Valley Country Park, you can see the rocky riverbank that was the site of their castle, from which they administered their extensive estate.

This is a lovely inland diversion from towering cliffs and endless beaches, a park

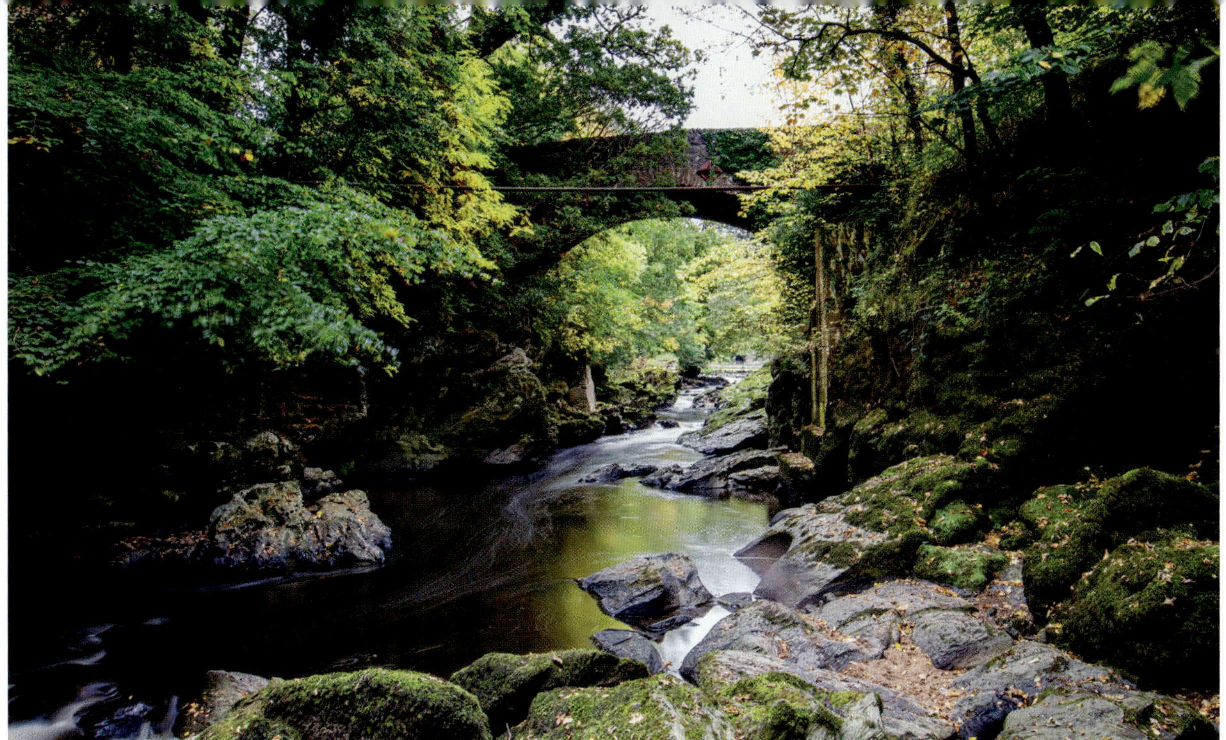

THE RIVER AT ROE VALLEY COUNTRY PARK

essentially arranged around the course of the tree-lined River Roe. Rocky gorges, thick forest, fields with grazing cattle: it's an idyllic way to spend an afternoon. And after heavy rainfall, when the water crashes through the rocks in a torrent of spray to the sea, it can be a spectacular sight.

There's an interesting museum here, focused on the linen industry that once occupied this land, where bright blue flax flowers spread over the fields in summer and linen was bleached beneath the sun.

You will also discover the source of the name 'Limavady'. It comes from a legendary tale of a wolfhound the O'Cahan clan had trained to warn them of approaching danger. On one occasion it came across a group of armed men moving toward the castle. Summoning all its power, it took a huge leap over the water to reach the castle and alert its owners to the imminent attack. *Léim an Mhadaidh*, Irish for 'leap of the dog', was anglicised as Limavady.

So powerful were the clan that a large part of modern-day Co. Londonderry was known as 'O'Cahan Country'. That came to an end following the defeat of the Gaelic chieftains in the Nine Years War and the subsequent Flight of the Earls in 1607, when most of the leading O'Cahans left Lough Swilly for Europe, forfeiting their lands in the eyes of the English Crown. The last great

O'Cahan chief, Donnell Ballagh O'Cahan, died in the Tower of London in the 1620s.

Their castle and estate were granted to a man we encountered back at Bushmills, Sir Thomas Phillips, who was granted the first lease for the now famous whiskey distillery. It was he that founded the new town of Limavady (the site of the original lies within the park).

'DANNY BOY' AND LIMAVADY

Limavady itself is a pleasant town best known for its connection with Ireland's most famous ballad, 'Danny Boy'. Local woman Jane Ross was the first to write down the haunting 'Londonderry Air' in the mid-1800s, having heard it played by a blind fiddler during the town's market day. She sent the music to a well-known collector of Irish music in Dublin.

Many years later the tune was sent to English lyricist Frederick Weatherly by his Irish sister-in-law. Weatherly had already written the lyrics of 'Danny Boy' to another melody, but now modified them to fit the Londonderry Air. First recorded in 1915, it soon became one of the most popular songs in the world. A statue of Jane Ross can be seen in Catherine Street.

Limavady is also home to Owen's Pub, where you will find *Game of Thrones* Door No. 5.

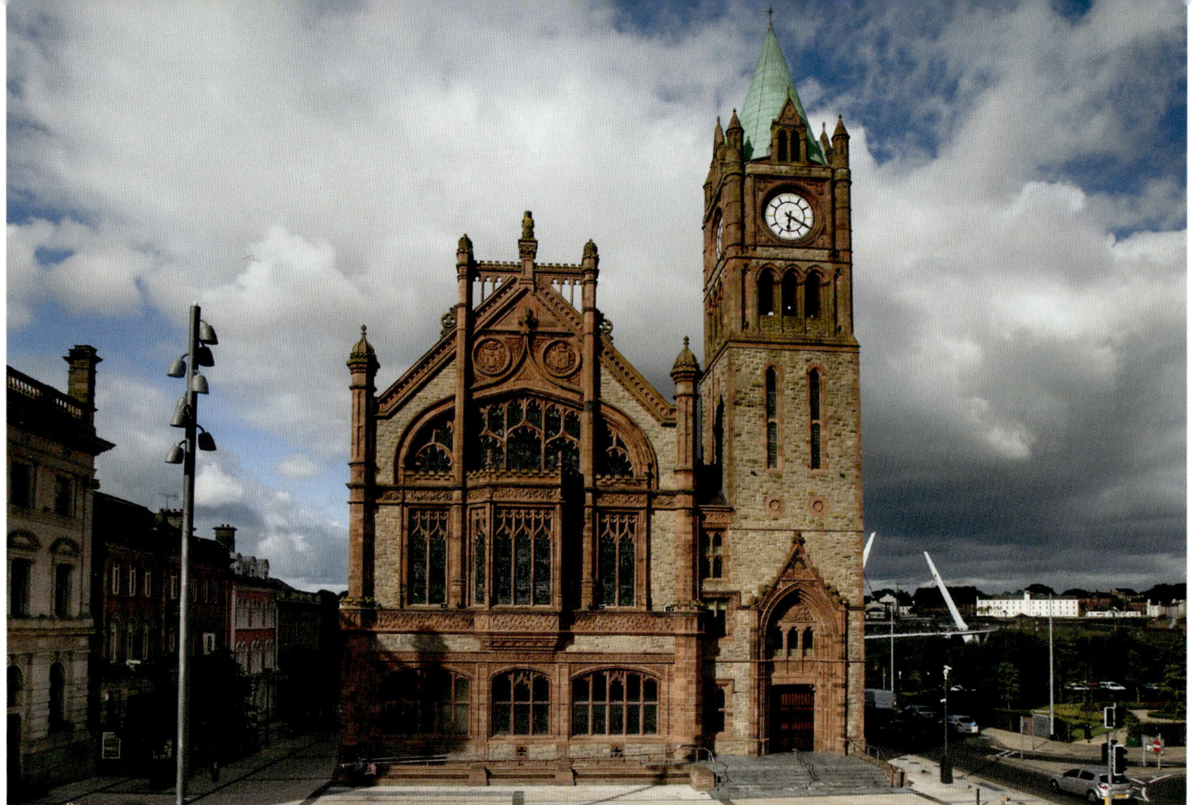

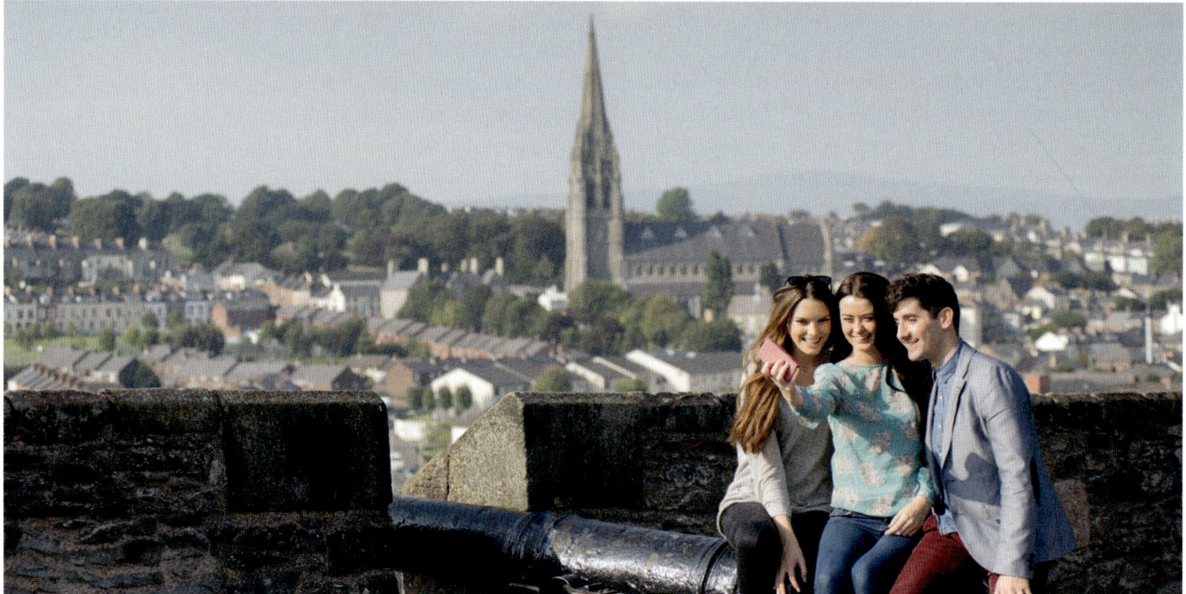

DERRY CITY

The walls of Derry are among the best preserved in Europe. The circular route around them reveals an extraordinary and still tangible history. Here, most famously, the city's largely Protestant population endured a desperate 105-day siege in 1688/9 to prevent the troops of King James II from entering.

Between 8,000 and 15,000 people died during the siege, as a result of the scarcity of food, terrible disease and the bombardment from the Jacobite troops. By the end, the survivors were reduced to eating dogs, cats, rats and mice (sold for sixpence each).

But they held out, and their ultimate success helped turn the tide of victory in favour of the army of William III, a triumph that ensured that the Protestant domination of Ireland continued for centuries. Ironically, William, later revered as King Billy by the Protestants of Ulster, was actually in an alliance with the Pope in an attempt to curb the ambitions of Louis XIV of France. Their heroism brought little benefit for the Presbyterians, who weren't treated much better than Catholics by the Church of Ireland establishment for some time to come.

Founded by St Colmcille (Columba), who brought Christianity to Scotland in the sixth century, Derry (from the Irish for 'Oak Wood', *doire*) was for several centuries largely a monastic settlement and even until Plantation, when it was renamed Londonderry, was a fairly small town.

In 1608 Sir Cahir Doherty, the Lord of Inishowen, responded to a slight from George Paulet, the Governor of Derry, by burning down the town. Doherty's rebellion against the Crown petered out, but the fact that such a rebellion could take place at all following the departure of the cream of Gaelic aristocracy in the Flight of the Earls caused James I to dramatically increase the scale of the plantation of Scots and English settlers, at the expense of the native Irish.

James ordered a full-scale rebuilding of Derry, and the City of London Guilds were chosen as 'the ablest body to undergo so brave and great a work'. So the 12 main London guilds were asked to pay for the new settlement and were also granted large parts of what is now Co. Londonderry. The design of the city became the template for towns in America like Charleston and Philadelphia.

For the Catholic population, the city has always been 'Derry'; for Protestants it is 'Londonderry'. A clumsy formulation, Derry–Londonderry, has been used for neutrality, but in truth most simply say 'Derry' for ease of use.

The old city, with its narrow cobblestoned streets leading off the great walls, is a delight to wander, and there's lots to see there. You can discover its eventful history right up to the present day at the award-winning Tower Museum. Not far away is Derry's most ancient building, St Columb's Cathedral, which was built in 1633 and was the first church built after the Reformation in Britain or Ireland. The beautiful but more modest St Augustine's, the 'Wee Church on the Walls', is on a site that some believe to be that of the original monastery founded by St Colmcille. The present Gothic-style Church of St Augustine was built in 1872.

The neo-Gothic Victorian Guildhall (named after the founding guilds), just outside the walls, has been refurbished and now has an excellent exhibition on the Plantation. The recently opened Siege Museum tells the story of the siege with various artefacts, video and interactive media.

But the DNA of Derry lies in its cultural life: in places like the Nerve Centre in Magazine Street, just inside the walls. The Playhouse Theatre, in Artillery Street, is the place for locally inspired drama.

Derry suffered disproportionately during the Troubles, not least during the Battle of the Bogside in 1968 and with the terrible events of Bloody Sunday in January 1972. You can get a real sense of the personal history of these times at the Museum of Free Derry, beginning with the story of the civil rights movement in the 1960s.

But today we are in different times and the forward-looking focus of the city and its people is reflected in a well-known phrase from Seamus Heaney's 'Cure at Troy', 'when hope and history rhyme'. The Nobel Laureate went to St Columb's College here, and loved the people and the vibrant cultural life that somehow endured during the worst of times.

Today that sense of hope is enhanced by the building of the magnificent Peace Bridge which leads over the River Foyle to the new centre of entertainment, the restored Ebrington Square, a former military barracks. Here you can get a unique taste of the city at the Walled Gate Brewery, where ex-Guinness brewer James McKillop now creates a portfolio of wonderful craft beers and also serves excellent food in the beautifully refurbished old military pay office.

WHY NOT DO IT ALL AGAIN?

We began our journey at the birthplace of *Titanic*, the world's most famous ship. Where better to end it than at the great Walls of Derry and the new 'Peace Bridge' that curves across the Foyle? In between we explored a landscape every bit as dramatic as the tumultuous history that enveloped it.

Where to now? We are on the doorstep of the Wild Atlantic Way, which traverses the coasts of western and southern Ireland. It's highly recommended, but, for a surprisingly contrasting perspective, why not retrace your footsteps? It's amazing how different the route will look as you head back towards Belfast. Do it in your own time, check out places you may have missed, and return to favourite spots. Happy travels!

First published 2020 by
The O'Brien Press
12 Terenure Road East, Rathgar,
Dublin 6, D06 HD27, Ireland.
Tel: +353 1 4923333
E-mail: books@obrien.ie. Website: obrien.ie
The O'Brien Press is a member of Publishing Ireland.
Reprinted 2025.

ISBN: 978-1-78849-096-2

Copyright for text © Seth Linder 2019
The moral rights of the author have been asserted.
Copyright for typesetting, editing, layout and design © The O'Brien Press Ltd

Photographs courtesy of Andy McInroy (Murlough Bay, p. 76; Fair Head, p. 78; Rathlin coast, p. 85; Rathlin caves, p. 86; East Lighthouse, Rathlin Island, p. 87; Dunseverick Castle, pp. 98–9; Giant's Causeway, pp. 100–1, 103, back cover; Lacada Point, p. 112); Patrick Lennon (St Aidan's Church, p. 124); Sean Paul McKillop (hurling match, p. 48); Chris Hill/Tourism Ireland (Giant's Causeway, these pages; SS Nomadic and Titanic Belfast, pp. 8–9; HMS Caroline, pp. 10–11; Glory of the Glens, pp. 44–5); Art Ward (the Aquarium, p. 27); the Morelli family (Morelli tea rooms, p. 113) and Carsten Krieger (Elephant Rock, p. 33 and Giant's Causeway, p. 102). Image of Whitehead Railway Museum (p. 24) courtesy of Mid and East Antrim Borough Council. Additional photographs courtesy of Tourism Northern Ireland and its commissioned photographers, in particular Brian Morrison Photography (brianmorrison.co.uk); and Tourism Ireland and its commissioned photographers, including Beth Ellis, Tony Pleavin and Stefan Schnebelt; and Shutterstock.

Cover design by Tanya M Ross www.elementinc.ie
Design and layout by Tanya M Ross www.elementinc.ie
Map design by Cathal Cudden www.brightidea.ie

All rights reserved. No part of this publication may be reproduced or utilised in any form or by any means, electronic or mechanical, including for text and data mining, training artificial intelligence systems, photocopying, recording or in any information storage and retrieval system, without permission in writing from the publisher.

8 7 6 5 4 3 2
28 27 26 25

Printed and bound in Drukarnia Skleniarz, Poland.

To the best of our knowledge, this book complies in full with the requirements of the General Product Safety Regulation (GPSR). For further information and help with any safety queries, please contact us at productsafety@obrien.ie.

Published in:

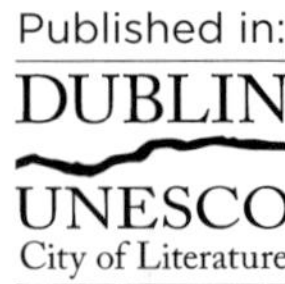

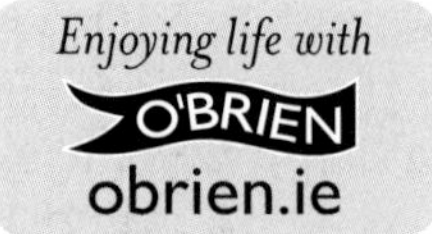